The Cult of Impotence

*Selling the Myth of
Powerlessness
in the Global Economy*

LINDA
McQUAIG

VIKING

VIKING

Published by the Penguin Group

Penguin Books Canada Ltd, 10 Alcorn Avenue, Toronto, Ontario, Canada M4V 3B2

Penguin Books Ltd, 27 Wrights Lane, London W8 5TZ, England

Viking Penguin, a division of Penguin Books USA Inc., 375 Hudson Street, New York, New York 10014, U.S.A.

Penguin Books Australia Ltd, Ringwood, Victoria, Australia

Penguin Books (NZ) Ltd, cnr Rosedale and Airborne Roads, Albany, Auckland 1310, New Zealand

Penguin Books Ltd, Registered Offices: Harmondsworth, Middlesex, England

First published 1998

10 9 8 7 6 5 4 3 2 1

Printed and bound in Canada on acid free paper ∞

CANADIAN CATALOGUING IN PUBLICATION DATA

McQuaig, Linda, 1951–
    The cult of impotence: selling the myth of powerlessness in the global economy

ISBN 0-670-87278-4

1. Fiscal policy – Canada. 2. International finance. 3. Democracy – Canada. I. Title.

HJ793.M36 1998   336.71   C98-930305-5

Visit Penguin Canada's web site at www.penguin.ca

To my wonderful daughter, Amy
Je t'adore!

CONTENTS

The Cult of
Impotence

Introduction to the Cult

❧

*One can only call the political impact of "globalization" the
pathology of over-diminished expectations.*
                                   —Paul Hirst and Grahame Thompson

❧

IT WAS JUST THE sort of irritating development that could ruin a
perfectly good day.

For months now, things had been gradually falling into place. That
is, things were looking more and more desperate. Not that anyone—
particularly someone as high up the policy-making food chain as
deputy finance minister David Dodge—liked to see the country in a
desperate situation. But Dodge, along with just about everyone else in
Ottawa's Finance department, knew that desperation, unfortunately,
was a prerequisite for the kind of sweeping government action they
had in mind.

So by late September 1994, it was hard for them not to be pleased
by the evidence that the nation's finances were careering out of control. The ever-accumulating national debt—a juicy $40 billion added
to its already grotesque size over the previous year!—surely made
everything pretty clear. By this point, it didn't matter what platform
the new Liberal government had been elected on. The numbers spoke
for themselves, screaming a message of unsustainability. The country,
bloated with debt, was tottering on a pair of too-high heels. A sudden
gust of wind and the whole unwieldy form might topple over, reducing our once-proud nation to nothing but a writhing failure sprawled

helplessly on the sidewalk for passers-by to gawk at and wonder: why was nothing done?

In his office, Paul Martin could be heard practising: "We are in hock up to our eyeballs . . . meet our target come hell or high water . . ." Gutsy stuff, to be delivered with bravado. Daniel in the lion's den. In only a few weeks, Martin was going to very publicly re-invent himself in two carefully planned televised broadcasts. No more deficit softie. Now, over the top, charge! Cape to the bull, shoulder to the wind. And the department could take at least some of the credit for helping him see the need for this full make-over.

Having seen it, Martin had become fanatical about doing it right, getting the message convincingly across to the public, which no one in Ottawa had yet succeeded in doing. So Martin's office was now constantly full of spin doctors showing him how to project his voice, move his hands, get the camera angle right. "Come hell or high water." Needs a little more edge in the voice. "Come *hell* or high water!" That's it. Forget your hands. Use your eyes. It was hard for David Dodge, peeking in from time to time, not to feel a little satisfaction. Here was the new, improved Finance minister, fresh from the department's intense deficit-immersion course, putting his own dramatic, earthy spin on the department's well-worn theme, managing through sheer performance to make it sound almost fresh. Everything was indeed falling into place.

And now this!

It goes without saying that the thirteen-page document that had just landed on David Dodge's desk was without merit. Anything that came to such ridiculous conclusions had to be. So it wasn't that the document risked shaking his faith, undermining the certainty felt by Dodge and those beneath him in the Finance department that they were on the right track, doing what had to be done. At this point, the fear wasn't even that Martin himself might experience doubts and retreat into the kind of confused thinking he used to display when he was in opposition. No. There was little chance of that now. Martin had gone too far, the philosophical make-over that the department had led him through over the past year had taken too deeply. His new zeal was real. *Come hell or high water* . . . After you say that enough you start to believe in it. No. The danger wasn't Martin's straying off course. The danger was the public, which was less predictable.

Dodge read the irritating document again. No doubt about it, there was some material in here that could easily confuse the public. Most troublesome was the suggestion that Canada's main problem was unemployment, not excessive government spending. The document noted that once full employment is achieved, "the budget gap of Canada vanishes." Not helpful. Indeed, this was the ultimate in dangerous, confused thinking. Such a view, if advocated by an editorial writer at a meeting of *The Globe and Mail* editorial board, would almost surely be enough to lead to a transfer to the Sports department. But the view was, nevertheless, infuriatingly popular with the public, who naïvely preferred to tackle the deficit by putting the country back to work rather than by substantially reducing the country's social programs. So with only five months to go before the department planned to bring down its crucial 1995 budget—in which social spending was to be cut to levels not seen in this country in fifty years—it was clearly not useful for the public to be exposed to this sort of thinking.

The biggest problem was the source. There were plenty of people out there saying this sort of thing. But they were mostly bleeding-heart softies, easily dismissed and ignored. This document, on the other hand, was from the head office of Goldman Sachs, one of the oldest and most respected Wall Street brokerage houses. The Opposition and the media would have a field day.

Draw up the bridge. Circle the wagons. Head them off at the pass. The department would have to be ready, and it would be. Extensive briefing notes had to be prepared for the minister to deal with questions about it in the House and in scrums with reporters outside.

After all the hard work of the past year, this could be just the kind of development that would get everything derailed. What was in the brains of those Goldman Sachs idiots anyway? Whose side were they on? Didn't they realize it was hard enough to orchestrate a sense of panic about the nation's excessive spending among the common people without Wall Street interfering, suggesting the nation's spending was *not* excessive? Sometimes it wasn't easy being deputy minister of Finance.

And, in truth, one couldn't entirely rule out the ultimate fear—that Martin himself could be derailed. God forbid. What if . . . *We're in hock up to our eyeballs . . . and the only solution is to put this country back to work!* You had to admit it sounded better, even if it was confused thinking.

The document had to be sent to the minister. But Dodge could weaken its impact by offering up his own harsh analysis of it. "Too sanguine a view," he wrote to Martin in a memo accompanying the Goldman Sachs report. "Could be used (misused) by those who object to the need for strong fiscal action."

～

CASE CLOSED.

David Dodge's fears never materialized. Evidently, people looking for ways to derail Ottawa's spending cuts don't subscribe to Goldman Sachs's economic reports.

If there had been any doubt that Paul Martin would be hailed the white knight of Canadian public finance, it quickly evaporated in the warm aftermath of his February 1995 budget. Business and the financial sector were awed by the deep, deep spending cuts that everyone on Bay Street had long pushed for, but few believed they'd ever live to see. The flimsy parliamentary opposition tried to find a few flaws to rail against in TV clips, but did little to challenge the essential spending-must-be-cut thrust of the budget. The media seemed satisfied and generally reflected the view that Martin had had no alternative.

But it wasn't until October 1996 that the matter could really be put to rest. With the publication of *Double Vision: The Inside Story of the Liberals in Power*, two prominent media figures in Ottawa delivered their judgment, pretty well wrapping things up. The two authors, Edward Greenspon, *The Globe and Mail*'s Ottawa bureau chief, and Anthony Wilson-Smith, Ottawa bureau chief for *Maclean's*, represented the two major national print media outlets in the country. And here they were teaming up to write the full story, as they saw it, not as their editors or publishers wanted it. Two independent, well-placed observers just telling it like it is.

At their book launch at the Ottawa press club, politicians mixed with journalists and bureaucrats, celebrating the publication of what appeared to be the definitive book on Ottawa in the 1990s. Like an account of some esteemed leader who rises to greatness after he sees the error of his ways, *Double Vision* is the story of Paul Martin's reckoning. Written with ample access to Martin and his closest advisers, the book is a kind of authorized biography of his conversion. It tells a tale of greatness in the making, of weakness overcome, of blindness that became vision. Paul Martin on the road to Damascus. Apocalypse Avoided.

That the country was to be fundamentally reworked, that hundreds of thousands of Canadians would lose their jobs in the wake of the cuts, that some of the poorest people would lose a major chunk of their income as a result of this conversion seemed outside the parameters of debate, as the party at the press club gathered steam. Indeed, with the publication of *Double Vision*, detailing the inside story of how Paul Martin found the courage to do what he had to do, it became clear that there was to be no debate.

Case closed.

WHAT A DIFFERENCE a year makes. The end of 1997, a year after the release of *Double Vision*, and Canada is a very different place. The deficit, which loomed so huge on the national political scene, crowding out virtually every other issue, is now virtually gone. No longer careering out of control, the deficit is quickly careering into oblivion.

Not since the Cold War evaporated almost overnight has there been such a sudden disappearance of a threatening enemy. Will pieces of the Fraser Institute's Deficit Clock soon become popular historical artefacts, like bits of barbed wire from the Berlin Wall?

By the time the Liberal government gets around to actually announcing the healthiness of the nation's finances in its Throne Speech in late September, the news has already trickled out. Indeed, for the previous six months, prominent Bay Street commentators have been openly marvelling at how quickly the deficit is shrinking. A new concept enters the political arena: fiscal surplus. All of a sudden, a major question has become: what do we do with the "fiscal surplus"? For the public, which for years has been trained only to think of getting by with less, the "fiscal surplus" doesn't immediately become a hot-button issue.

But it does with key opinion-makers, who are torn over the question. Whereas they had been pretty much of one mind in the past—government spending must be cut to reduce the deficit—they are now showing signs of disunity. Certainly, there is a strong consensus that previous levels of government spending must not be restored. But beyond this, there is much debate in government, business and media circles. The key questions being debated are: should the fiscal surplus go into debt reduction or tax reduction, and how quickly should the tax breaks be delivered?

One school of thought, represented by the Business Council on National Issues as well as the *Financial Post* editorial board, wants to see the crusade to reduce the annual deficit simply transferred to a crusade to reduce the nation's accumulated debt, with tax cuts to be delivered in the future. Other prominent participants in the debate, such as *The Globe and Mail* editorial board and CIBC Wood Gundy chief economist Jeff Rubin, argue that we should let the debt gradually decline on its own; they want tax cuts and they want them now.

Then there's Paul Martin, who talks of devoting 50 percent of future surpluses to restoring government spending (an idea frowned on by the financial élite), and splitting the rest between debt reduction and tax cuts. That certainly makes the Liberal government sound more socially progressive than those in élite circles. But it would be wrong to conclude from this that the government intends to restore spending. Indeed, Paul Martin's plan will do little to return government spending to anywhere near the levels it was at only a decade ago.

In the mid-1980s, spending on government programs amounted to more than 18 percent of our total national income. By 1999, when Paul Martin's cuts are fully phased in, spending on government programs will have dropped to less than 12 percent of our national income—a drop of roughly one-third. Even if the Liberal government follows through with its promise to devote 50 percent of future surpluses to spending, the level of government spending will remain minimal. Depending on the formula the government uses to calculate its surpluses, program spending, four years from now, will amount to either 12.2 percent of national income or 11.7 percent— roughly the same as the historically low level to be reached in 1999. In other words, the government fully intends to keep spending depressed to extremely low levels.

These calculations, by the way, are not the dreamchild of some social activist bent on exaggerating the size of the government's spending cuts. On the contrary, the calculations were done by John McCallum, chief economist at the Royal Bank of Canada, who wrote them up in a release that was widely distributed in the financial community in the fall of 1997. They fit with similar calculations done by experts at other leading financial institutions. And they also fit with calculations done by the Finance department. Paul Martin himself, in an interview, agreed they were "roughly" accurate.

But the numbers illustrate the extent to which the whole deficit-reduction process has changed the nature of how we divide up resources in this country. As Martin has noted, deficit reduction was achieved primarily through spending cuts; spending cuts have been seven times as large as tax increases. Asked about this, Martin explained in the interview that the government felt it had no alternative. He pointed to the example of Sweden, which dealt with its deficit primarily by raising taxes. "And they got killed," he said. "The international marketplace descended upon them with a hammer. Their interest rates skyrocketed, and they had to back off totally. . . . The only way in which one was going to be credible was in fact to deal with this essentially by reducing spending."

Yet even if Martin felt international financial markets left him no choice but to cut the deficit mostly through spending reductions, this doesn't explain why he is not now planning to restore more of that spending. Once the deficit is gone, and we are no longer supposedly under the thumb of financial markets, why shouldn't a bigger portion of the fiscal surplus be directed back to spending—the area that took the biggest hit in the deficit-reduction crusade? But this is not what the Liberals are planning, which reveals that their interest in cutting government programs now goes beyond deficit reduction. They are presiding over a long-term redirection of our national income away from government programs. They are taking us much closer to the U.S. model, with lower taxes and smaller government.

There's little evidence that this is what Canadians want. Donna Dasko, vice-president of Environics Research Ltd., says that Canadians continue to support strong social programs. An Environics poll in early 1997 found that when asked about what should be done with the fiscal surplus, 70 percent of Canadians said that their top priority was government programs—for job creation, health care and fighting child poverty. Surprisingly, only 18 percent of those polled favoured putting the extra money into debt reduction, and only 9 percent wanted to see it channelled into tax cuts—suggesting that ordinary Canadians have a very different set of priorities than do members of the financial élite. Indeed, Dasko says that polling done by Environics in the fall of 1997 shows that high unemployment far outranks all other issues as the biggest problem facing the country in the minds of most Canadians.

The massive government spending cuts of recent years were sold to a reluctant Canadian public on the basis that there really was no alternative. But now, presumably, there is an alternative. That's what we were told the whole deficit-reduction exercise was about—regaining control over our destiny. And politicians even tell us that we've now achieved that. "Today, we're in a position where we can make our own decisions," a very pleased Paul Martin said on "Pamela Wallin" on CBC-TV's Newsworld in late October 1997. Yet, even as we reach the promised land of deficit-free nirvana—the place where, we are told, the world will once again be our oyster and even the Finance minister claims we can make our own decisions—there are certain things we apparently still can't have, like jobs and social programs.

Case still closed.

~

FROM THE OUTDOOR café overlooking the shimmering water of Hamilton Harbour in Bermuda, the sun shines too brightly in the eyes of David Jones, making him squint.

Or is he squinting because the subject has turned to something so distasteful that his face has become contorted?

"If you inhibit cash flows, the alternative is war," says Jones, an affable, balding currency trader sipping a dark beer.

He is reacting to the notion of a tax on international currency transactions, that is, a tax on the $1.2 trillion a day that is traded on foreign currency markets around the world. The proposed tax, known as the Tobin tax, after Nobel Prize–winning economist James Tobin, would be set at a very low level—much less than 1 percent of the amount traded. But since the volume involved is so large, the tax could collect hundreds of billions of dollars in revenue each year. Some of the debate over the tax has focused on whether the money should be used exclusively to fund Third World development or whether some of it should be redirected back to the financially strapped treasuries of western nations, thereby creating a rare opportunity for society's high rollers to make a contribution to deficit reduction.

Before we start worrying about how to divide up the billions, there are a few problems. One is David Jones and the people whose money he trades. To them, the tax amounts to a restriction on the free movement of money. One of the reasons the $1.2 trillion floats around the world so effortlessly each day is that there are currently few restrictions on the movement of money. The major holders of capital in the world—chiefly the world's big commercial banks, large corporations and wealthy individuals, assisted by brokers like David Jones—can move money anywhere, anytime for no other purpose than to park it for a few days, hours—or minutes—where it can earn a slightly higher rate of interest. That slightly higher rate may be less than a cent on the dollar. But if you're moving $25 million, even for a few minutes, it adds up.

Clearly it's a lucrative business. In fact, this sort of trading is one of the reasons the Canadian banks—which are increasingly trading in this market—are reporting ever-rising profits. And traders like David Jones, who has brokered trading deals for CIBC and the TD Bank, have done nicely as well. In a good month, he can earn half a million dollars in brokerage fees. Perhaps it's not surprising he's not keen on a tax—even a little tax—on these capital flows. Perhaps he really does think that the only alternative is war.

But for the rest of us, such a tax might not be so bad. In fact, its real purpose isn't even to raise all those billions for world development. That's a secondary purpose. The real purpose is to slow down the flow of dollars around the world, to build a tiny little dike against the gushing torrent of free-flowing dollars, to, in Tobin's phrase, "throw sand in the wheels" of our incredibly fluid capital markets.

The reason we might want to do this is because all this free-flowing capital is intimately connected to Paul Martin's conversion on the road to Damascus. As long as capital can whisk effortlessly around the world, shopping for the best terms, it can wreak havoc on national currencies, as we saw in Southeast Asia in the fall of 1997. It can intimidate governments into thinking they must do whatever it wants. This can leave a guy like Paul Martin feeling fearful, afraid that the economy he presides over will be "killed" when international markets descend "with a hammer." Indeed, this can leave a guy like Paul Martin willing to do pretty much what these markets say.

Over lunch at Toronto's Canoe restaurant at the top of the TD Bank Tower, amid much fashionable chrome and pewter and striking views of the city's harbour, another personable currency trader is explaining the ins and outs of currency markets. We talk market talk—of puts and calls and straddles, of covered shorts and naked shorts. He's personable—that is, until dessert arrives, and he's confronted with a question about the Tobin tax.

Yes, he's heard something about it, he explains, before launching into a mini-tirade about the utter stupidity of the tax. He doesn't argue that the only alternative is war, but otherwise seems just as furiously opposed to it as was the trader in Bermuda.

It's getting harder and harder to resist the feeling that there must be something to this tax.

AN EXPERT IS HOLDING forth earnestly on CBC Radio's "Sunday Morning." It's pretty familiar fare, really. Dr. Ian Angell, professor of information systems at the London School of Economics, is explaining how most of the working population will soon be redundant.

"Isn't there an economic cost to writing off the world's workers?" asks host Ian Brown.

The question suggests that Brown has bought the basic parameters of the debate: that we discuss only *economic* cost. Brown is asking: How does the unemployment of most of the world's population fit society's basic business plan? No one mentions *human* cost.

Still, the question doesn't suit Dr. Angell. Impatience is detectable in his voice.

"This requires a total rethinking of the institutions of the industrial age. You must throw them away," says Dr. Angell, trying to make things nice and simple for Brown to grasp. "All your thinking has to be different."

As the interview progresses, Brown becomes increasingly sceptical of what he's hearing. His questions reveal that he's struggling to see how all this unemployment helps ordinary people. Answer: it doesn't.

But that's not the issue. The issue is that it's the future. Globalization, technology, governments can no longer coddle their people, they must focus instead on getting their financial houses in order, lowering their deficits and their taxes, etc., etc.

An emboldened Ian Brown asks something about how people are to survive. Dr. Angell is getting a touch irritated with these repetitive questions about human needs. Brown just doesn't seem to get it. The point is that we're in a brand-new age, the information age. Technology and globalization have made all these questions about human needs irrelevant. That's part of yesterday's menu. Today we simply watch as the technological juggernaut rolls on, squashing our needs.

"Is this a world you look forward to?" asks Brown, trying to make some sense of it all.

"That's neither here nor there," responds Dr. Angell.

"Is there some way we can stop this?" Brown asks anxiously. "Is there nothing we can do to avoid this dark future?"

That's when Dr. Angell snaps. "That question reflects the thinking of the machine age," he says curtly.

Hold it. Let's play that again slowly.

This line is more subversive than it first appears. It is perhaps as subversive a thought as it is possible to have. Dr. Angell is saying it's not just that we can't change things, *but we can't even think about the possibility of changing things;* to do so is to engage in old-style thinking.

So, it's not just that we're powerless to stop being pushed over the edge of the cliff in the new global world order. But to even try to prevent ourselves from being pushed over the cliff is a sign of regressive thinking.

The new way of thinking, as outlined by Dr. Angell, requires an acceptance of powerlessness, resignation to a world without solutions—a world of inaction and helplessness. That democratic impulse to assert one's rights must be contained, thwarted, rendered mute and inoperative.

Never mind the *democratic* impulse. It's actually the *human* impulse that's at stake here. The human impulse to act, to build, to create, to improve, to shape our lives, to use our brains to do better. It's called being alive.

It's just got to go.

"IMAGINE."

The word is half whispered. On the screen, we see a native girl of indeterminate age on a swing. Wistful. Dreamy. Free as the wind that blows in her face.

She is presumably imagining the possibilities, imagining a better world. Could she be thinking of change, improvement? Could she be thinking the *old way*? Perhaps a few weeks in a Dr. Angell re-education camp is needed.

But wait. This is a TV commercial for a bank. It's the Bank of Montreal, saying it is possible. Of course, it's never clear from the ad exactly what is possible. It seems to be suggesting that anything is possible. Surely that's the reason for choosing a young native girl for the part. We'd normally see the face of such a girl in the media only as part of a story about glue sniffing or teen suicide or young-runaway-turns-teen-stripper-and-ends-up-murdered-in-a-stairwell. But here, in the airbrushed world of the Bank of Montreal—or its hipper version, mbanx—this girl seems to be an inspired person, someone with limitless possibilities in front of her.

Surely if even someone like this—not an upwardly mobile white male in a suit, but a native female in a long skirt and cowboy boots—can have a dream, the possibilities out there for regular people must be truly endless.

And they are—when it comes to banking.

"At mbanx, we don't believe in limits," says the breathless prose in a print ad picking up the theme from the TV ad. "Your $13 monthly fee covers all your everyday banking needs and more. So go ahead and use any ABM on the Interac or Cirrus shared networks as often as you want. We won't charge you. Use your debit card. No charge. Call us any time. No charge. Do your banking on-line at mbanx.com. Our Internet service isn't just 'free for a limited time.' There's no activation charge. You just do it. No charge."

No wonder the native girl seems so blissed out. Imagine the possibilities. Why would anyone bother to sniff glue or commit suicide or get killed in a stairwell when there's a whole new wide world out there of . . . debit cards, on-line shared networks, activation charges . . . of, well, banking.

A black woman, pictured in the print ad, poses a question to those who are confused enough to still use other banks: "Do your remote banking services make you feel that way?"

M̲banx has an answer for that too. "At m̲banx, we see technology as something that links, not isolates. So, even though you may never see us, we're always here for you. In some ways, we're closer than any branch could be. And we guarantee you'll be satisfied with our service. Every time you call, you can speak with a portfolio manager whose job it is to know you, respect you, and make what you want happen. . . ."

Is this banking or telephone sex? Is there a difference?

The ad continues: "Is there still stuff your bank won't let you do over the phone? Whether it's 3 in the morning or Sunday afternoon, you'll get simple point and click access to your day to day banking. . . ."

Don't stop now. . . .

As we delve deeper into the m̲banx philosophy, we see that there is nothing here Dr. Angell would have trouble with. As long as the native girl confines herself to imagining the banking possibilities that lie ahead, she is simply marvelling at the high-tech corporate world engulfing her. She is not trying to assert herself or work towards a better world.

But what if her mind were to stray from contemplating the wonders of modern banking to, say, contemplating the scope of Canada's unemployment problem? The unemployment story is just as dramatic, in its own way. Perhaps it doesn't have the immediate drama of moving money from a savings to a chequing account in the middle of the night or paying hydro bills through the Internet. Mostly, it seems to be about people feeling depressed and hopeless because they can't find work. Huge numbers of people. Virtually an army of people. This world is worth exploring for a minute, because, with its sense of hopelessness, it is the flipside of the ever-expanding dreamy world of the mbanx commercial.

Sitting alone in their individual homes, depressed and angry and isolated, the army of the unemployed is difficult to visualize or relate to. Fortunately, however, Lars Osberg, an economist at Dalhousie University in Halifax, has come up with a graphic way to illustrate the size of this army and the enormous waste of its idleness.

First, let's get a sense of the numbers involved. What we really want to measure is the number of *needlessly* unemployed people in Canada. In other words, there will always be people in between jobs, or people choosing not to work for now. If we include these people in our army, we will artificially inflate its size. In the interests of understating the size of our army, let's assume a fairly high level of transitional unemployment. In fact, let's just take the level of actual unemployment that existed in Canada in 1989, before the onset of the most recent recession. Back then, Canada's unemployment rate was 7.5 percent. If we simply consider the unemployment we've experienced *above this level* since then, we find that the additional number of unemployed people amounts to an average of roughly 450,000 a year.

One way to illustrate the size of this army and the waste of its idleness is to figure out what this army could have built, had it been working. Let's suppose that our army was put to work building something highly labour-intensive—something like, say, the great pyramids of ancient Egypt. It would be hard to imagine anything much more back-breaking and laborious than the construction of these massive tombs. Built more than twenty centuries before the birth of Christ, these colossal structures consist of enormous stone slabs installed on top of one another in symmetrical form. What makes the story so striking is the lack of technology or even basic tools involved. The massive stone slabs were cut from solid rock, dragged out of the quarry and hauled a considerable distance on wooden sleds—without even the use of a wheel, which hadn't yet been invented. In an advance that no doubt seemed terribly sophisticated at the time, water was poured over the paths to lubricate the route and reduce the friction.

A recent analysis by Stuart Wier of the Denver Museum of Natural History calculated the sheer human energy involved in building the Great Pyramid in Giza in the twenty-sixth century B.C. under the reign of King Khufu. Writing in the *Cambridge Archaeological Journal*, Wier breaks it down fairly specifically. For instance, when the pyramid was just getting going, it would take about 2,840 men per day to work in the quarry, and some 5,540 to work in transport (that is, pulling the stones). As the pyramid got taller (it eventually reached the equivalent of a forty-eight-storey building today), it took fewer quarry workers and more haulers—eventually some 6,870 a day. When the pyramid was sixty metres high, 2,380 men were needed for lifting. Wier calculates that it would have taken some ten thousand men—about 1 per cent of the population of ancient Egypt—about twenty-three years to complete Khufu's resting place.

How would the army of needlessly unemployed Canadians have fared in pyramid construction? With the use of tractors and cranes, the modern equivalent of pyramids could be built relatively quickly. But for the sake of illustration, let's assume that the army of needlessly unemployed Canadians was busy building pyramids with the same technology that was available back in the twenty-sixth century B.C. No motors, no pulleys, no wheels. Just wood sleds, a little water and a great deal of lifting. Let's even assume that the Canadian pyramid workers get to work a comfortable Canadian schedule—a five-day work week, statutory holidays, a month's vacation—which would presumably slow things down from the Egyptian pace. Still, Osberg calculates that the army of needlessly unemployed Canadians could have built no fewer than seven pyramids since 1990 and be well on their way to completing their eighth.

Of course, the more significant question to consider is what could have been accomplished had they instead used modern technology and built something more useful than a tomb for a dead king. What if they'd built housing or highways, cleaned up the Great Lakes or operated day-care centres, or worked in the Canadian aerospace industry?

Imagine.

THIS BOOK IS ABOUT possibilities. It is about exploring the real limits of what is possible and what isn't in this age of the global economy. Is full employment possible? How about well-funded public health and education systems or a clean environment? Or is only all-night banking possible?

The dominant school of thought has become that of the naysayers, those who argue, essentially, that the market ultimately determines what is possible. It's an odd sort of situation we find ourselves in. The market offers us a giddy world of choice when it comes to consumer items: banking, cars, appliances, seat covers, bathroom fixtures, beer. Enter into any one of these consumer worlds, and one is confronted with a breathless array of possibilities. We can choose from hundreds of different car models, with thousands of options. Do we want a sedan or a hatch-back, leather or plush seats, cruise control, anti-lock brakes, air conditioning, wrap-around stereo, coffee holders that flip out or pull down? What about telephone sets—do we want them to be cordless or plug-in, to beep with incoming calls or simply record them on an answering machine, to look like a fire engine or like the Star Trek spaceship? Or dental floss: do we want it waxed or unwaxed, mint or plain, thick or fine, floss or tape. . . . One could get dizzy if it wasn't so exciting.

But when it comes to things that many people might consider more important—like whether we will have jobs, live in communities where water is drinkable, air breathable and no one will be left hungry or homeless—these things are apparently beyond our control. If we put in place policies that create the kind of society we apparently want, the market will move money out of the country, we are told. Thus, there are limits to what we can do in these areas. We have to stay within the dictates of the market. We have become captives of the marketplace.

It's interesting to note just how far we've moved outside the normal range of historical human experience. In his brilliant overview of world economic history, *The Great Transformation*, economic historian Karl Polanyi notes that the Industrial Revolution marked the first time in history that the notion of the private market was elevated to the central organizing principle of society. In earlier times, the market was only one of the forces around which society organized itself. Religion, family, custom, law, tradition were all considered more important. Now, if Dr. Angell and his ilk are to be believed, we've come to the point where not only has the market become the dominant force in our society, but its dominance is above reproach, above question. To suggest that we have a choice about what role the market will play in our lives is to fail to see that we've evolved to a supposedly higher plane—a plane where we now no longer have any choice about the market's power over our lives in areas that really matter, a plane where we are essentially impotent.

Thank God we've at least got all-night banking.

NOBODY HAS MADE A more compelling case for our collective impotence than the authors of *Double Vision*. This very readable book, with its rich detail of inside information, provides a bird's-eye view of the story of Paul Martin's odyssey from a slightly confused believer in a jobs-and-growth strategy to a reluctant adherent of the ultimately-we-are-impotent school of thought. Its importance goes beyond its readability. Its impeccable sources give it an authoritative voice. And it ultimately, and enthusiastically, endorses the government's position—indeed, it suggests there was no alternative, that the harsh medicine was unavoidable. In a sense, it can be seen as the definitive statement of the position of the government—almost an official, authorized biography of the Liberal government. But, unlike the usual press releases that the government puts out extolling its positions, *Double Vision* fills the government's story with life and character and struggle.

Like all good stories, *Double Vision* presents a tale of moral dimensions, of right and wrong, of wise and foolish. It ultimately presents Paul Martin's conversion as a contest between, on the one hand, clear-thinking pragmatists who, ahead of their time, understand and accept the new powerlessness and, on the other, a team of woolly-headed, well-meaning but ultimately foolish bleeding hearts who keep naïvely clinging to the notion that governments can do a lot to improve the lives of their citizens. At the centre of this clash is Paul Martin himself, an affable but essentially empty vessel who gains greatness only by coming to accept the wisdom of the impotence-advocating pragmatists.

The woolly-headed bleeding hearts, led by the woeful Lloyd Axworthy but also including cabinet ministers Sheila Copps and Sergio Marchi, come across as an enormously pitiful bunch. Axworthy, then minister of Human Resources, is continually depicted as pale, besieged, confused, ineffective, stumbling, a "Liberal on his knees" as the chapter about him is titled. Trudging on in his weak and incomprehensible attempt to reform the social safety net, Axworthy is seen as a well-meaning failure, one who subscribes to that fuzzy, warm-hearted belief that "having fought the good fight was as important as the outcome." As he shuffles ineffectually with his good intentions, he utterly fails to deliver, swept aside by the dynamic Paul Martin. "Martin, a powerful minister of finance with a head of steam and will of iron, ate the human resources minister for breakfast."

Arrayed against Axworthy and his motley crew of inept do-gooders are the pragmatists, the largely unsung advocates of impotence. Chief among them are David Dodge, deputy minister of Finance, and his senior staff, the "rationalists at Finance" who, to a man (and they all do seem to be men), are steeped in deficit obsession and seem to have been unable to sleep properly for years for all their worrying over Canada's credit rating.

Perhaps the most important of these pragmatists is Peter Nicholson, a former top adviser to Bank of Nova Scotia chairman Cedric Ritchie, who is brought into the department on special secondment and who becomes "an important figure in the Paul Martin story." Nicholson is bright, self-assured and talkative, with a Ph.D. in operations research. All summer long, through the hot days of July and August 1994, Nicholson conducts what amounts to an ongoing economics tutorial for Martin. In fact, Nicholson is not really an economist. But he makes up for that with his skill at numbers.

And what is the deficit besides a lot of big numbers? Nicholson is able to mesmerize Martin with the deficit's arithmetic of compound interest. It isn't that Nicholson is cold or callous. Indeed, he is a likeable, engaging man, a man not unlike the Finance minister himself. But Nicholson purports to know the limits of what the markets will allow; he knows "how unforgiving capital markets can be when they turn against you," as he said in a recent interview. He understands the true nature of impotence.

Double Vision essentially presents the notion that the government took the hard choices that were pragmatic and, ultimately, foresighted. We are reminded that Martin was a "humane and reluctant budget cutter" and that his goal in trashing social programs was ultimately to save them. The only alternative that is presented is the inept and clouded vision of Axworthy et al., who seem to be all heart and no brain. In *Double Vision*, anyone with brains sees the wisdom of the impotence school of thought. For instance, Judith Maxwell, a prominent economist and Martin adviser, doesn't let her well-known concern for social justice interfere with her conviction that everything must take a back seat to deficit reduction. Sure, she's socially concerned, but first comes the deficit.

The clear message is that there was no real debate within the Chrétien government. The confused utterings of the handful of socially

minded Liberals were soon revealed for the sophomoric impractical-
ity that they were and were shunted aside. More important, the message is that there was no real alternative, that it was either modern
pragmatism, grounded in economic and fiscal reality and a firm
understanding of the arithmetic of deficits, or bleeding-heart confusion, which wouldn't be able to distinguish arithmetic from ball-
room dancing.

Yet, curiously, there was one man in the upper ranks of the Liberal
government—a member of the Chrétien cabinet—who fit in neither
of these two camps. Like Nicholson, he was a whiz at numbers. But
unlike Nicholson, he was trained in economics—even the economics
of high finance, having obtained a Ph.D. in finance from the University of Pennsylvania. Moreover, he understood financial markets,
having spent twenty-six years of his life in one of the top jobs on Bay
Street, as chief economist and later senior vice-president of one of the
Big Six banks. If anyone in the top circle of government ministers and
advisers understood numbers, economics and the way markets actually operated, and how they reacted to government policies, it was
this man.

Yet, despite his Bay Street pedigree, he didn't side with the "pragmatists," and he didn't subscribe to the impotence school of thought.
Indeed, he argued constantly with the "rationalists at Finance," dis-
puting their assumptions and challenging their conclusions. At the
cabinet table, he pushed for a less obsessive approach to deficit reduction, for placing a higher priority on bringing down unemployment.
And he fought for these things not out of some mushy sentimentality
but with strongly grounded economic arguments. His very presence
was a challenge to the notion that the only choice was between economic pragmatism and bleeding-heart foolishness. Rather, he made a
compelling case for the deeply subversive view that there was a realistic alternative—an economically viable alternative.

Oddly, he never appears in *Double Vision*.

∿

IF A GROUP OF LEFT-WING activists were trying to devise a convincing scenario for a corporate conspiracy, it would have been hard to come up with something better than the little gathering at the Ontario Club.

As news of the Multilateral Agreement on Investment (MAI) gradually trickled out of the Ottawa bureaucracy throughout 1997, anyone who had been involved in the earlier free trade and NAFTA debates was highly suspicious. All across the country, small groups organized meetings to discuss this little-known treaty, which was being negotiated in Paris by representatives of the twenty-nine nations that make up the Organization of Economic Co-operation and Development (OECD). One solution would have been for the Ottawa bureaucrats to release endless drafts of the proposed treaty in the hopes of boring the public into indifference. Instead, however, those handling the MAI—assistant deputy minister of Industry Andrei Sulzenko and chief negotiator Bill Dymond—adopted the bizarre strategy of releasing very little information and assuring Canadians they had nothing to worry about, that the matter was in good hands.

To provide added assurance to the public, Sulzenko and Dymond even took their show on the road. They tried to set up a joint meeting with the University of Toronto's Centre for International Studies. Louis Pauly, the centre's director, was amenable, as long as the event was open to the public. The Ottawa team agreed, and pushed for a downtown location, easily accessible to the business community. Thus, the event, which attracted an eclectic mix of professors, protesters in Uncle Sam costumes, business executives and currency traders, took place in the unlikely setting of the Ontario Club, one of Bay Street's toniest haunts.

In their session, the Ottawa officials assured the audience that the MAI wasn't all that new; it simply built on terms that had already been established in earlier free trade treaties. This was exactly what many in the room most feared. Indeed, the combination of the secretiveness of the presenters and the Bay Street location was enough to feed the conspiracy fantasies of all but the currency traders, who alone are likely free of conspiracy fantasies. (They *know* that the world operates in their interest; that's not a conspiracy, that's just the way things should be.) From a public relations viewpoint, however, the Ottawa team's event at the Ontario Club was easily a disaster.

Whatever form the final treaty takes, certain broad themes have emerged. As in earlier free trade treaties, the MAI is an attempt to provide private international capital-holders and corporations with certain rights. *Toronto Star* columnist Richard Gwyn suggested it was like a "charter of rights for absentee landlords"—with no responsibilities or obligations to accompany these rights. In other words, the MAI is a one-way street in which capital-holders are given the power to challenge the laws of democratically elected governments and governments are given no reciprocal powers over them. This raises some interesting questions. For instance, will investors be able to challenge Canada's medicare system on the grounds that the government's monopoly in providing health care deprives them of their right to invest in the lucrative health-care field? The answer will be in the fine print of the MAI. But it does make one wonder why Canada is so gung-ho to get on board this train. As Gwyn puts it, "How necessary and productive and creative is it to be applying our talents and political energies to making the world safe for absentee landlords?"

One area of concern (among many) is whether the treaty will try to establish in international law the principle that capital must remain fully mobile, that governments cannot impose any restraints on this mobility. In reality, western governments currently impose very few restraints on capital mobility. But presumably enshrining this principle in international law could give it even more force. If so, ideas like the Tobin tax could be declared out of the question. Instead of simply languishing on the back burner, they could be removed entirely from possible consideration.

∼

ARE WE REALLY POWERLESS in the global marketplace? Have governments truly lost their sovereignty in the face of globally wandering capital and wickedly clever currency traders? There are many who would have us believe this. Typical of this school of thought is Walter Wriston, former chairman of Citicorp, who writes, "The new world financial market is not a geographical location to be found on a map but, rather, more than two hundred thousand electronic monitors in trading rooms all over the world that are linked together. With the new technology no one is in control." Wriston attributes this to the unstoppable forces of technological advancement: "[T]his new system was not built by politicians, economists, central bankers or finance ministers. No high-level international conference produced a master plan. The new system was built by technology." Or as new-age guru Jeremy Rifkin puts it: "The Information Age has arrived. In the years ahead, new, more sophisticated software technologies are going to bring civilization ever closer to a near-workerless world. . . . The wholesale substitution of machines for workers is going to force every nation to rethink the role of human beings in the social process." (What in the world does Rifkin mean when he talks of the need to "rethink the role of human beings in the social process"? Is Rifkin thinking we could perhaps remove human beings from the social process or assign them a more marginal role? What is the "social process" other than human society?)

While it sounds as if we're entering a brand-new, globalized techno-world, how much has really changed? Are we really in uncharted waters or just paddling through familiar waters in a fancy new boat, decked out with lots of new gadgets? In fact, the globalization of international finance is not a new phenomenon. It is rather a throwback to an earlier time. This is acknowledged by even enthusiastic advocates of the power of global markets, such as the well-known British magazine *The Economist*. In an article titled "Back to the Future," *The Economist* notes, "Capital is certainly more mobile now than it was two or three decades ago, but by some measures it was just as mobile before the first world war. In relation to the size of

economies, net capital flows across borders then were much bigg
than they are now. . . . The international bond market, too, was just as
active at the start of this century as it is now. . . . Today's free-flowing
capital fits with the long-term pattern."

Let's follow a little further what *The Economist* has to say on this,
because it is very revealing: "The anomaly is not, as many believe, the
current power of global finance, but the period from 1930 to 1970 when,
to various degrees, capital controls and tight regulation insulated
domestic financial markets and *gave governments more control over their
domestic economies* [italics added]." Indeed, it was in response to the
devastating Depression, starting with the 1929 stock market crash, that
governments around the world began to assert their power to bring
footloose capital under some degree of democratic control. Immediately after the Second World War, they established a new international
financial system that gave governments, for the first time, considerable
power over financial markets. With governments, rather than markets,
flexing their muscles, the result was an agenda more geared to popular
wishes, such as full employment and social programs.

That early post-war period was, in many ways, the Golden Age. But
now it is gone; full employment seems out of the question, no matter
how much the public might like it, and social programs just keep
shrinking, no matter how much the public seems to want them. The
question is why. What has happened? Can this change really be attributed to the "globalization of financial markets" when, as it turns out,
financial markets were just as global at the turn of the century?

It's true that the technology is dramatically different now—although perhaps not as different as we sometimes assume. At the turn
of the century, there were no computers, but international transactions could be made almost simultaneously after the completion of
the first transatlantic cable in the 1860s. This wasn't as fast or comprehensive as computer technology, but it did make virtually instant
international financial transactions possible. Computer technology
has now made it possible to move money even more quickly. But does
it follow that the faster movement makes it impossible to control

money? On the contrary, there's a flipside to this computer wizardry that is almost always omitted from discussions about the new techno-world of global finance: *the very technology that makes it possible to move money more quickly than ever before also makes it possible to trace that movement more easily than ever before.* This is crucial to the issue of regulation. If the movement of money can be traced, it can be monitored and regulated. Eric Helleiner, a Canadian political scientist who specializes in global finance, says the case can be made that "[i]nformation technology strengthens rather than weakens state regulatory capacity in the financial sector."

In other words, there is no reason—from a technological point of view—that international capital markets can't be regulated, as they were in the early post-war years. Indeed, if anything, it would probably be easier to regulate them now, because computers have made comprehensive tracking possible. The real problem, according to Helleiner and others, is not the technology but the unwillingness of governments to apply it to the task. Helleiner notes, "States have made little effort to use information technologies to control finance in the contemporary age." Interestingly, in the few instances where they have used it—such as in attempts to track money laundering by organized crime—the results have been impressive.

Which brings us to the key point of this book: the obstacles preventing us from gaining control over our economic lives have little to do with globalization and technology. The real obstacle is political. Governments have backed off from taking action to fight unemployment and provide well-funded social programs not because they lack the means but because they've chosen to render themselves impotent, powerless in the face of capital markets. The technological imperative turns out to be mostly a failure of will on the part of governments.

All these themes will be developed later in the book. But before we proceed, it might be useful to also draw attention quickly to one more important notion: namely, that the fundamental clash in economic policy debates today is much the same as it always has been. For all the changes in technology and the growing complexity of the language in our economic dialogue, the truth is that economic debate—and what is at stake—has changed surprisingly little. The essence of what's being debated remains fundamentally the same.

Here, then, is a shorthand version of the debate, to act as an easy guide in the coming chapters. There are basically two key items being continually fought over—whether money will be tight or loose, and how much government will redistribute resources, through social spending and taxation.

The first item, commonly referred to as "monetary policy," centres on how much a government will act to protect a nation's currency from inflation. Monetary policy is generally carried out by a nation's central bank, primarily through its power to influence interest rates in the country. If the central bank is primarily concerned with keeping inflation low, it will raise interest rates whenever it fears inflation. This will kill the inflation, but will also generally slow down the economy, throwing people out of work. Thus, a "tight" or "sound" monetary policy is generally favoured by those keen to protect the value of their financial assets from being eroded by inflation. (This is usually something of concern mostly to people with lots of financial assets—that is, rich people.) A "looser" money policy gives a higher priority to jobs, and therefore to keeping interest rates low. (This is usually favoured by people who are more concerned about having a job than about protecting the value of their financial assets—that is, most ordinary people.)

The second item, which comes under "fiscal policy," refers to how much the government will provide in social programs and who will bear the tax burden of paying for these programs. Since many social programs offer the largest benefits to those with the least resources and are financed by taxes paid by all, it is easy to see why high social spending is generally opposed by the well-to-do and favoured by the less well-to-do. Indeed, it is easy to see how society divides into opposing camps on these two issues. The rich generally benefit from tight money and low social spending. The non-rich—or the rest of society—generally benefit from looser money and higher social spending. The position favoured by the first camp has sometimes been identified as "right-wing," the second as "left-wing," although we could just as easily call them the "market" position and the "popular" position.

It has become fashionable to dismiss the very notion of such a debate. We are told the right/left split is no longer valid or relevant in the age of the global economy. While I have no attachment to labels like "right" and "left," I think the attempt to dismiss the labels is often also an attempt to reject the ideas behind them. It amounts to a denial of a real difference between the two positions, a denial that one position favours the rich while the other favours the non-rich. This attitude goes so far as to deny that there is any validity to the "left" or "popular" position; it even denies that looser money and higher social spending would actually benefit ordinary members of society. Such policies are being discarded, so the position states, not because the rich have managed to get their way, but because these policies are no longer relevant in the global marketplace, and they don't benefit ordinary people anyway.

Thus, in the global economy, there is only one valid position, and it is the position traditionally known as "right-wing." But now it's been stripped of that "right-wing" label, since there is no "left wing" any more to distinguish it from. This position is now simply called "pragmatic," "realistic," in line with the "realities" of the global marketplace. What used to be seen as "right wing" is now simply the reality. Policies that used to be clearly understood to favour the rich—policies that the rich have been pushing aggressively since time immemorial—are now presented as pragmatic and in everyone's interests.

The success of this position is reflected in the fact that a significant chunk of the public—including many who are far from rich—now believe that their interests lie in supporting the market agenda. In recent years, even social democratic parties, which purport to represent the common person, have keenly adopted the market agenda once they've attained power. Indeed, the spectrum of political debate has narrowed to the point that virtually any party in power these days seems to adopt it—despite the fact that the market agenda has delivered few concrete gains for ordinary people. While banks and stockholders have reaped handsome rewards, the economic well-being of the average Canadian has actually deteriorated over the past ten years, and most Canadians feel highly vulnerable about their future economic prospects.

The willingness of the public to tolerate these deteriorating conditions has a great deal to do with the cult of impotence. It's not that people are glad to see themselves squeezed financially and their children unable to find jobs. It's not that they feel a quiver of pride at the thought of Canadian banks earning billions of dollars and being able to compete in the big leagues of international banking. It's rather that they feel powerless to do anything about this reordering of political power and wealth in the country.

This has some startling implications for democracy. A crucial difference between the current century and the last one has been the rise of mass democracy, creating the possibility that governments would act on behalf of the interests of the majority, not simply, as in the past, on behalf of the interests of the rich. This exciting democratic breakthrough explains much of what happened in the early post-war years. But now this possibility is being shut down. Policies from the "popular" agenda, such as full employment and generous social programs, are dismissed as out of date, impractical, no longer possible. Governments are seen as impotent to deliver them. Governments are apparently only able to deliver policies from the other agenda, the pragmatic one.

This has involved a massive selling job, convincing people that although governments technically may have the power to implement the "popular" agenda, they can't actually do so. Ultimately, the case for this democratic impotence rests on the awesome power of financial capital and its ability to flee from a country implementing these sorts of "popular" policies. It is essentially a threat, the promise of a final mechanism to force countries to do as financial markets want. But there is also a softer line of attack, a theoretical argument, which tries to make the same case by persuasion. The case—that governments are powerless to impose "popular" policies—thus rests on both the threat and the theory. Let's start with the theory, which in some ways is the more insidious of the two.

CHAPTER TWO

Milton Friedman and the Pursuit of Powerlessness

~

If we continue to tie our hands with financial shibboleths . . . we are no better than the feckless castaway whose contribution to the solution of dealing with cases of canned goods was "let's just assume we have a can-opener."
                                                    —William Vickrey

Neither God nor nature decreed that involuntary unemployment need always be with us.
                                                    —Robert Eisner

Charles II once invited the members of the Royal Society to explain to him why a dead fish weighs more than the same fish alive; a number of subtle explanations were offered to him. He then pointed out that it does not.
                                                    —Alasdair MacIntyre

~

IT WAS JUST BEFORE six-thirty on an October morning in 1996 when the phone rang in the New York–area home of William and Cecile Vickrey, waking them both up. With a touch of trepidation, Vickrey, eighty-two, shifted his large body to the edge of the bed to pick up the phone. An early morning call had a worrisome sense of urgency; it was hard not to consider the possibility that this was news of a death or injury. Vickrey braced himself for what turned out to be one of the most important calls of his life. "Hello," he said, his voice still heavy with sleep. Within seconds, he realized no one was dead or even sick. The call was from the Royal Swedish Academy of Sciences, informing him that he had just been awarded the highest honour in economics—the Nobel Prize.

No economist would be anything but elated to hear such news. The Nobel Prize is probably the most widely recognized honour bestowed in any field, catapulting the winner instantly to international fame, including front-page coverage in major newspapers around the world. It signifies that the recipient has made a unique contribution, judged to be of lasting importance. Vickrey's Nobel, which he shared with British economist James Mirrlees, also carried with it a prize of more than $1.2 million. But as he sat in his pyjamas, listening to the news, he experienced a particularly delicious joy that went far beyond money or the sense of professional accomplishment.

Vickrey's prize was being awarded for work he had done decades earlier, applying abstract theories to come up with ingenious yet simple solutions for basic problems of daily living. In the 1950s, for instance, he had come up with practical solutions for solving congestion problems in public transit and energy utilities. He devised a model that essentially proposed different prices for different times of the day—a solution that ended up having a wide number of uses. He also came up with a new system of auction bidding that increased the chances that the goods being auctioned would receive their true value. Instead of potential buyers bidding against one another until the highest price emerged, Vickrey proposed that all participants submit one sealed bid. The highest bidder would win. But, in a new twist, the winner would not pay the price he or she had bid, but rather the price offered by the second highest bidder. If participants didn't bid what they thought the object was worth, they faced a greater prospect of losing the contest.

Vickrey's innovations were in some ways the beginning of "game theory," the study of how individuals can anticipate the behaviour of others in planning their own economic actions. Game theory became an increasingly important part of academic economics in the 1980s and 1990s, and Vickrey's highly creative contribution led to his wide recognition in the field. In 1993, he was elected by his peers to the prestigious post of president of the American Economic Association.

But while Vickrey was pleased by the intricate little solutions he'd devised for all sorts of problems, they were far from what had occupied his mind for the past couple of decades. Increasingly, he had become concerned with the broader issue of what he felt had gone wrong with the thinking in the economics profession, and the disastrous impact this thinking was having on economic policy. Particularly, he was incensed by what he considered his profession's "callous tolerance of unemployment," and its inordinate obsession with reducing budget deficits rather than tackling unemployment. He came to view his fellow economists as "apostles of austerity, most of whom would not share in the sacrifices they recommend for others."

Central to his critique was an attack on the widely accepted notion in economics that there is a "natural rate of unemployment," and that it is harmful to try to push the unemployment rate below this "natural" level. Vickrey dismissed the notion of this so-called natural rate of unemployment as "one of the most vicious euphemisms ever coined." To Vickrey, there was no fundamental reason unemployment couldn't be reduced to between 1 and 2 per cent of the workforce—a level that he noted hadn't been achieved in peacetime in the United States since 1926. "Practically, the desirable situation ought to be one in which any reasonably responsible person willing to accept available employment can find a job paying a living wage within forty-eight hours."

It was this sort of thinking that had led the economics profession to regard Vickrey, for all his obvious brilliance, as an eccentric. The hundreds of economists who had heard his presidential address to the American Economic Association meeting in Anaheim, California, in 1993 were taken aback by his focus on the need to make full employment the top national priority. "Is he cuckoo?" economist David Colander recalls someone near him in the audience whispering loudly.

Now retired after almost six decades of teaching economics at

Columbia University, Vickrey stayed on as professor emeritus, coming every day to the tiny, cluttered office at the university where he concentrated his efforts on exposing the fallacies in current economic thinking. With his large, exuberant spirit, restless intellect and slightly dishevelled appearance, he was increasingly known as a bit of an oddity. Despite his advanced years, he would think nothing of climbing into his car and driving hundreds of miles to a conference on a subject that interested him, attending every session. One professor who vaguely remembered seeing him at these sorts of conferences described him as looking like someone you felt you should buy a sandwich for.

On the Columbia campus, Vickrey was known for wandering into lectures on just about any subject. He would settle into the front row and often appear to be dozing off during the lecture. Then, all of a sudden, he would stir, rise up and electrify the room with some stinging question or critique that cut to shreds the essence of the lecturer's thesis. It was perhaps poetic justice that when Vickrey was delivering his address to the American Economic Association in 1993, the official managing the overhead slides for the presentation fell asleep, leaving Vickrey unable to proceed until the man was woken up.

That event in some ways summed up the response of the profession to Vickrey's increasingly strongly held views on the urgency of tackling unemployment. Economists who were intrigued by his abstract theories for reducing traffic congestion or improving public auctions seemed to lose all interest when he applied his immensely creative mind to a problem that seemed, to Vickrey at least, far more important. It wasn't that he approached the unemployment issue in a simplistic way; he applied the same kind of rigorous thinking that he had used in developing his solutions to more mundane problems. The difference seemed to lie in the fact that tackling the problems of traffic or public auctions was well within the mainstream, whereas his views on unemployment attacked the very foundations of what economics had become in the past three decades. It was not a message that the profession warmed to. Rather than letting him become their conscience, his fellow economists preferred to dismiss him as irrelevant.

It was this disdain among his colleagues that added the particularly delicious joy to the news from Stockholm. While the money was nice, Vickrey didn't really care about it. Constantly absorbed in his thinking, he was notoriously uninterested in his own material comfort. He and his wife already lived a comfortable life, and he certainly had no desire for a fancier car or a more elaborate home or an endless vacation. What deeply thrilled him about the Nobel Prize was the prospect of having a podium to reach the public with his message that economic policy had got terribly off track, that the single-minded obsession with deficit reduction should be replaced with a concerted national campaign for full employment and a fairer distribution of the nation's resources, and that all this—contrary to the dogma spread by his profession—was not just socially desirable but also economically sound. Although Vickrey had been saying this for years, as had some others, it was his enormous prestige and celebrity status as a Nobel winner that promised to give his pronouncements sudden prominence and credibility. No more lost soul looking like he needed a sandwich.

From the time Vickrey put down the phone after the call from Stockholm, his life was instantly transformed. He barely had a chance to give the details of the call to his wife, who had been listening with astonishment, before the phone started ringing constantly. The announcement had been released in Stockholm and picked up immediately on the news wires. There was an almost ceaseless barrage of calls from reporters, friends, colleagues. A press conference was quickly set for eleven that morning at Columbia, and an ecstatic Vickrey, sporting a colourful Paisley tie with a rumpled suit, arrived to be mobbed by reporters. After the press conference, he spent hours in individual interviews with reporters, then went straight to a champagne reception hastily organized by the economics department in his honour. Then there were more interviews, photos and TV appearances.

The reporters kept asking him about his ideas on traffic congestion and game theory. Vickrey answered these questions energetically, but kept turning the subject to what he considered more important issues. He kept telling them that what was desperately needed was not smaller budget deficits but larger ones, so that massive resources could be directed towards tackling the real problem of unemployment. The reporters listened, a bit confused; this wasn't something they'd heard before—at least not from a renowned economist. If these ideas had been coming from anyone other than the just-announced winner of the Nobel Prize in Economics, the reporters would have probably shut off their microphones, convinced they were talking to someone who understood nothing about economics.

Certainly, the media had shown little interest in Vickrey's thoughts before the Nobel Prize announcement. He had recently sent a powerful, twenty-two-page (single-spaced) critique identifying the main fallacies of current economic thought to the editors of the *New York Times Magazine*, but they had declined to publish any of it. Now Vickrey planned instead to use the critique as the basis for his acceptance speech at the gala Nobel ceremony in Stockholm, after he was presented with the award by the king of Sweden in front of a distinguished crowd of dignitaries and academics, and the international media. It was almost too delicious to contemplate.

The awards ceremony was two months away, and for now Vickrey was still overwhelmed with all the attention. Two days after that first phone call from Stockholm, he was in his office all afternoon and into the evening, fielding yet more calls and interview requests, the stack of phone messages on his desk continuing to build. He felt exhausted but exhilarated by the endless opportunities to publicize views he had spent a big part of his life thinking about. About eleven o'clock that night, he set off for the four-hour drive to Cambridge, Massachusetts, to attend a conference the next morning.

About forty-five minutes later, the police responded to a call about a car stopped in the right-hand lane and discovered Vickrey slumped over the wheel of his car, dead. An autopsy indicated he had died of a heart attack, likely brought on by the stress of the most exciting three days of his life. After he had finally reached the world podium at the age of eighty-two, Vickrey's long-held dream of launching an international campaign for full employment and common decency in economic policy died with him there on the northbound lane of the Hutchinson River Parkway. The chance of the public ever hearing about how the "most vicious euphemism ever coined" had guided economic policy for almost three decades seemed suddenly as remote as it had been three days earlier.

IF VICKREY'S PRESIDENTIAL address to the American Economic Association prompted scornful rebukes that he was "cuckoo," Milton Friedman's 1967 address to the same body prompted exactly the opposite response. A professor of economics at the University of Chicago and an important contributor to the U.S. National Bureau of Economic Research, Friedman held the audience of high-powered economists almost spellbound as he set out the argument that was to transform how governments around the world dealt with the problem of unemployment. There was another point of contrast between the two lectures. While the theme of Vickrey's address was the need to move unemployment to the top of the nation's priority list, the practical effect of Friedman's address was to move unemployment right off the list of priorities and shunt it into a no man's land where it was considered largely beyond human control.

To understand the revolution Friedman launched, it is necessary to see the prevailing views that he overturned. In the late 1960s, the thinking on unemployment was captured in something called the Phillips curve, named after the New Zealand economist A.W. Phillips, who had become a distinguished professor at the London School of Economics in the 1950s. The essential idea behind the Phillips curve was that there was a trade-off between inflation and unemployment. Phillips had reached this conclusion after carrying out an exhaustive study of data on wages and unemployment over more than a century of British history. In a highly influential academic article published in 1958, Phillips had provided evidence to show that the lower the level of unemployment, the higher would be the rate of inflation. This relationship, which formed a curve on a graph, was particularly true when unemployment was very low—the result was very high inflation.

In many ways this was a graphic illustration of the point made a century earlier by the German philosopher Karl Marx. Marx had argued that in order for capitalism to function well, there had to be a "reserve army of the unemployed," that is, a large pool of unemployed workers anxiously competing for scarce jobs. With this line-up of hungry job applicants at the factory gate, workers inside would have little clout in demanding higher wages. This wage restraint was crucial in allowing owners to turn a profit. Essentially, the Phillips curve illustrated Marx's finding. It showed that when members of the reserve army of the unemployed were able to find work, wages rose (and prices soon followed); on the other hand, when the ranks of the reserve army swelled, wages (and prices) dropped.

Although Karl Marx is not often cited in business circles today, his notion of the reserve army of the unemployed is implicitly accepted there. A recent headline in *Business Week*, "Can the Economy Stand a Million More Jobs?," could almost have been a chapter title from Marx's *Das Kapital*. Note that the *Business Week* commentary wasn't about whether a million more jobs could be created, or how to create them. Rather, it was about whether it was *desirable* to create them. Does business *want* a million more jobs to be created? The answer was apparently no. Low unemployment—that is, too many people working—"can be a dangerous thing," the article noted. "That's because federal officials—and most private economists—believe that when the jobless rate dips too low, employers are forced to bid up wages to attract the best workers." In other words, when too many people are working, employers are forced to pay higher wages. The *Business Week* article could have just as well been headlined "Why We Need a Reserve Army of the Unemployed."

The Phillips curve had some dramatic implications. It suggested that controlling inflation and maintaining low unemployment may not be compatible goals, that they may even work at cross-purposes. This put governments in a difficult situation, since both goals were seen as important to a successful economy, and government actions greatly influenced which goal would more likely be attained. Through their control over monetary and fiscal policy, governments could give precedence either to the goal of inflation control or to the goal of low unemployment. If they followed the "market" approach—tight money and low social spending—they would tip the balance towards controlling inflation. If they followed the "popular" approach, they would tip the balance towards low unemployment. The question "Which direction should the Phillips curve be tipped in?" became a fairly central issue in governing. When one added to the equation the fact that the wealthy tend to benefit more from inflation control while the rest of the population tends to benefit more from employment creation, it is easy to see how the Phillips curve—largely unknown outside the economics profession—is invisibly at the centre of much political as well as economic debate.

This is where things stood in 1967.

Enter Milton Friedman, a brilliant free-market zealot. The son of an immigrant dry goods merchant and a seamstress, Friedman grew up in modest circumstances in Rahway, New Jersey. With the help of scholarships, he completed his Ph.D. at Columbia and became an articulate advocate of the classical school of "laissez-faire" economics at the University of Chicago. In our shorthand system, laissez-faire economics can be easily placed in the "market" camp, favouring tight money and low social spending. Friedman was also a master marketeer of ideas. Although Edmund Phelps, an economist at Columbia University, had developed a similar theory, it was Friedman who had the intellectual and political savvy to sell it within the economics profession. Friedman took the essential concept in the Phillips curve but added a twist that entirely changed its meaning and its practical use. He introduced the concept that there was what he called a "natural rate of unemployment." The natural rate, in his view, was the level of unemployment that was necessary to prevent an increase in the rate of inflation. In other words, the relationship between inflation and unemployment wasn't simply a trade-off that could be adjusted in either direction. The trade-off worked in only one direction: unemployment could be adjusted to serve the goal of controlling inflation.

Friedman argued that there was a "natural rate" of unemployment for every economy, based on a number of factors, and that this natural rate was possible to measure. If an economy could achieve precisely this amount of unemployment, inflation would be held at a stable level. In other words, if the reserve army of the unemployed were exactly the right size, there would be no danger of inflation taking off.

However, it didn't work the other way around, according to Friedman. If a government decided that it was more concerned about fighting unemployment, it couldn't simply decide to allow a little more inflation. This might seem to work; lower interest rates and more government spending might indeed reduce unemployment. But, Friedman warned, *this would last for only a short while.* Ultimately, these policies would generate an ever-accelerating rate of inflation that would eventually become intolerable. The government would be forced to back down and push unemployment back up to its "natural" level. In the long run, the "natural" rate of unemployment would prevail no matter what governments did. It was simply natural law. Given this reality, governments might as well concentrate on the one thing they could achieve—controlling inflation.

Friedman's theory was based on an interesting interpretation of human behaviour. It started with the assumption that unemployment was largely a voluntary condition; if unemployment was high, it was because workers were choosing not to work at the low wages being offered in the marketplace. (This is a huge, unproven assumption, to which we will return later.) So when government stimulated the economy—by either lowering interest rates or increasing government spending—workers would see the rising wages and decide it was worth their while to accept a job after all. Thus, unemployment would drop as workers were attracted to the higher wages.

But it wasn't going to stay that way, Friedman argued. The problem was that along with rising wages, prices would rise also. If wages rose 10 percent, that would seem good only until prices caught up, also rising 10 percent. When this happened, workers would be no better off than if they had accepted jobs that they had apparently declined because of the low pay. It is at this point that Friedman's theory takes a truly curious turn. He argues that once the workers see that they are no better off than they would have been before, had they chosen to work at lower wages, *they will simply quit their jobs*, becoming once again unemployed. Unemployment will return to its previous high level, and inflation will now also be high. Friedman goes on to argue that in order to bring down unemployment again, inflation would have to be allowed to rise a notch higher and then, the next time, a notch higher still, etc. Hence, inflation will be ever-accelerating.

What is striking about this is the central premise: that workers simply decide not to work if inflation turns out to be higher than they expected. In order for this to happen as Friedman suggests, these workers would have to be highly attuned and attentive to the impact of inflation on their wages (even low levels of inflation). Such sensitivity to inflation might well characterize human behaviour in certain situations, such as in the case of a well-to-do investor trying to decide between placing some additional funds in stocks or bonds or holding the money liquid in a bank account. But surely a different set of factors is at play in the case of a low-paid worker trying to decide whether to be employed. Can Friedman really say with any certainty how the average worker will behave when confronted with the fact that inflation has caught up with his or her wages? Is Friedman some kind of expert in human psychology? Has he studied the behaviour of workers who face the prospect of inflation eroding their wage gains?

This is the kind of theory that was clearly developed by a well-paid economist sitting at a desk, working out a calculation to compare the "marginal disutility" of work with the "utility" of the wage. But does this bear any resemblance to real human behaviour when it comes to something as important in people's lives as their work? Don't people often accept jobs at low wages, in the interest of gaining job experience, in the hopes of getting their foot in the door of a desired career, out of a simple need for money, or because they feel better and happier in their lives when they're working? Do workers calculate only how much extra pain (marginal disutility) they will experience in having to work, and then measure that pain against the benefit (utility) of the wages they will receive—all the while taking into consideration how much buying power those wages will give them at the existing rate of inflation? The late British economist Joan Robinson dismissed this sort of argument as nonsense, insisting that the real choice workers faced was between working and starving.

The choice is no longer so stark in most western countries, where modern welfare systems have taken some of the sting out of unemployment. But the Friedman theory assumes there is no sting at all to unemployment any more, that, for most people, deciding whether or not to work is similar to deciding, on a lovely summer afternoon, whether to paint the garage or go for a picnic. (Painting the garage would presumably be less enjoyable, causing some form of marginal disutility, but it would save the cost of hiring someone to do it, thereby creating a utility.) It seems far-fetched, to say the least, to imply that the same sort of straightforward calculation applies to a decision about whether one will have enough money to adequately provide for oneself and one's family, and whether one will feel like a functioning member of society.

Friedman's assumption that workers will simply quit when they see their inflation predictions were wrong might be plausible in certain limited situations. For instance, a housewife in a comfortable middle-class situation might decide to return to work, partly for the extra income, and be discouraged when she discovered the extra cash she earns didn't go as far as she'd expected. Indeed, anyone with sufficient resources to fall back on—such as the independently wealthy—might make this sort of calculation, although it requires a bit of a stretch to imagine that this sort of person makes the decision to work simply for the extra cash.

But it requires more than a stretch to imagine that someone with no independent means of support beyond the meagre income of unemployment insurance, or the even more meagre and stigmatized income of a welfare cheque, can calmly make this sort of calculation. Perhaps a normal working person might do so in trying to decide whether to support a strike vote at his or her place of work. That would be a realistic dilemma: does it make sense to forgo income now, in the hope of winning a raise that would permanently increase one's income? This is a complex and difficult question many workers face, and it involves careful assessment, including determining how one's income is keeping pace with inflation. But it is not realistic to assume that workers faced with the choice of working with higher-than-expected inflation or not working will simply quit.

Friedman's whole concept ultimately rests on a basic premise of human behaviour that is unproven and, frankly, implausible. It rests on the idea that the behaviour of workers in low-paid jobs is driven almost exclusively by their sensitivity to inflation and its impact on their wages. Thus, according to his theory, unemployed workers will accept work, believing they are getting an adequate wage. But when inflation catches up with that wage, they will see they have been fooled and—having endless options and not a care in the world—they will simply quit their jobs. It's interesting to note that in this scenario, these workers will not be quitting their jobs in order to seek other jobs, since, presumably, inflation will erode the wages of those jobs too. Rather, it seems, they will quit and remain idle, considering this preferable to working in the face of inflation.

Essentially, Friedman is assuming that workers will behave in a way that is downright irrational, quite contrary to their own self-interest. If they were rationally assessing the situation and acting in their own interest, they would conclude the opposite: that they were *not* better off quitting their jobs, since even with a generous unemployment insurance system, they would in fact be worse off. (Under current Canadian regulations, unemployed workers qualify for benefits equivalent to only 55 percent of their former salary and must often wait more than a month before receiving benefits at all.) When one considers their additional losses—forgone contributions to their pension plans, loss of seniority, difficulty in finding future employment—the financial losses they face are potentially enormous. In assuming that these workers will quit their jobs in the event of inflation, Friedman is assuming that they will systematically behave in an irrational fashion. Why wouldn't he assume that they might instead behave rationally—by staying on the job and perhaps forming a union to press for higher wages?

The more one thinks about it, the more implausible Friedman's theory of worker behaviour becomes. Even if some workers in low-paid jobs did follow Friedman's intricate logic and behave in the irrational way he suggests, is it reasonable to assume that this would be the *general* behaviour, that all or even most workers in this situation would necessarily respond this way? We are clearly not dealing here with some basic instinctual human behaviour, such as that a hungry person will seek food or a tired person will seek sleep. The suggestion here is almost the opposite, that hungry people will give up food if it doesn't turn out to be as tasty as they had expected it to be.

Friedman's entire system is built on his unproven, somewhat bizarre interpretation of how workers in marginal jobs will respond to inflation. If his assumptions turn out to be wrong, if he can't predict with any certainty the workers' behaviour in the situation he describes, then his theory seems to rest on no real foundation. Friedman has built a brilliant theoretical model to superimpose on it, backed up by sophisticated mathematical equations, but ultimately his theory may rest on nothing more than the shifting sands of an unproven theory of human behaviour.

What if Friedman's theory of human behaviour is wrong? What if workers don't necessarily quit whenever inflation erodes their wage gains? What if they instead keep working even if it means lower "real" wages—perhaps because they feel they don't really have much choice? If that's true, then government could perhaps stimulate the economy—with lower interest rates or increased government spending—without the disastrous inflationary results Friedman predicts. The key result of such stimulation might be to increase the spending power of workers, thereby fuelling healthy growth in the economy.

And what if Friedman has misunderstood an even more basic aspect of the problem? What if the reason workers are unemployed in the first place is not, as he suggests, because they refuse to work at the going wage, but because there are not enough jobs available? Friedman has simply assumed that all unemployment is voluntary—an enormous assumption. What if it isn't? Then perhaps we have gone off on a wild-goose chase, searching for some imaginary perfect level of unemployment that will allegedly keep inflation in check, when the real problem is simply that the economy is depressed and could be revived with a little stimulation? James Galbraith, an economist at the University of Texas (and son of renowned Canadian-born economist John Kenneth Galbraith), raises the possibility that "we have been running from the phantom of accelerating inflation for more than two decades. The result: a self-inflicted wound, a socio-psychological disability, of colossal proportions."

FRIEDMAN'S THEORY QUICKLY swept the economics field and appeared to be validated by events in the 1970s, when attempts to push unemployment down seemed to lead only to more inflation. But events in the 1980s and 1990s have provided evidence that appears to contradict Friedman's theory, raising fresh doubts, to which we will return later.

It is clear, however, that Friedman succeeded masterfully in changing the prevailing view on how to deal with unemployment. Despite the challenges, his theory continues to dominate economic thinking today. The impact has been enormous. Essentially, Friedman managed to destroy the case for government stimulation of the economy for the purpose of reducing unemployment. According to him, such government intervention was useless in the long run, and even harmful, since it created a situation where inflation would accelerate. Thus, when it came to using the key levers of monetary and fiscal policy to help create employment, the Friedman theory held that governments were impotent and should remain that way.

It is interesting to note that this ban on government intervention in the economy did not extend to controlling inflation. The Friedman theory specifically required that government intervene, through monetary and fiscal policy, to achieve the goal of stable inflation. This fit with the thinking of classical economics—namely, that the government's role in the economy was chiefly to maintain a tight money policy, which would protect the value of the currency by controlling inflation. Beyond this, government was supposed to mostly stay out of the picture and let "natural" market forces take over. Friedman's theory, then, was an abrupt turn back to the laissez-faire, market-oriented world of classical economics, where governments, apart from protecting the value of the currency, are supposed to leave markets to work things out on their own. What Friedman had really done was to construct a theory of how modern economies work, based on the classical, laissez-faire school of thought.

A key aspect of the classical school was that unemployment would be solved automatically, if governments would just stay out of the picture and let the market work its magic. According to this school, high unemployment was simply the product of overly high wages, which prevented employers from making a profit. If employers declined to hire workers at those high wages, the workers, desperate and hungry, would be forced to drop their wage expectations to the point that the employers found it profitable to hire them. The adjustment mechanism was the desperation of the worker. Without it, the "natural" laws of supply and demand wouldn't work.

But the desperation of the worker wasn't what it used to be in the old days when the classical theory was devised. The growth of the welfare state in the post-war years was badly distorting the proper working of the "natural" laws of supply and demand. Basically, government supports were preventing workers from feeling desperate enough to behave as spelled out in classical theory. In essence, what Friedman's "natural rate of unemployment" theory did was to come up with a way to measure the extent to which government intervention had interfered with the desperation level of the worker. If government intervened too much—with unemployment insurance schemes and welfare programs, for instance—workers would not feel sufficiently desperate, and this would push up the "natural" rate of unemployment. And, as we've seen, in Friedman's view, the natural rate was the one that would ultimately prevail. Thus, the more the worker's desperation level was reduced through government intervention, the higher the ultimate rate of unemployment would be.

It followed, then, that if governments wanted to reduce unemployment, the way to do so was to remove social supports. By making the worker feel more desperate, the government could bring down the natural rate of unemployment, which was believed to be the way to bring down the actual rate of unemployment. Thus, even though governments were powerless to bring down unemployment by using the key levers of monetary and fiscal policy, they *were* able to reduce it by taking away crucial social support systems, thereby making the worker feel more desperate and willing to work. In essence, Friedman was suggesting that if workers wanted jobs, they should not press government for lower interest rates or more government spending; rather, they should press government to cut social programs and anything else that protected them from the harsh realities of the market.

Friedman had dressed up the old harsh medicine of classical economics with a spiffy new gloss. By establishing the notion of a quantifiable way to measure the desperation level of the worker (not a term used by Friedman), he had put a more scientific-sounding spin on the old solution of solving unemployment by driving down wages. It was no longer necessary for economists to argue that the only way to deal with unemployment was to let market forces push wages lower. Such assertions could have the unfortunate effect of sounding callous and mean-spirited, as well as moralistic.

Now, with Friedman's natural rate theory to back up the classical school, economists could argue instead that the only way to drive down unemployment was to reduce something that came to be called the *Non-Accelerating Inflation Rate of Unemployment*, or NAIRU. The NAIRU was just a fancier name for Friedman's concept of the natural rate of unemployment, which was just a derivation of classical economics. But the term "NAIRU" sounded highly quantifiable and therefore scientific. Indeed, economists would devote huge amounts of time to discovering the exact level of the NAIRU for any given economy—was it 8.4 percent or 8.9 percent or 7.3 percent? It sounded awesome in its specificity, certainly not something that could be challenged on the grounds of being unfair. It wasn't a question of fairness or unfairness. What was involved here was science.

But what did it all mean? In practical terms, it meant quite a lot. Friedman had subtly adjusted the concept of the Phillips curve so that it was no longer about seeking a balance between unemployment and inflation. Instead, controlling inflation was clearly to take precedence. In Friedman's natural rate theory, the goal was to achieve a state in which the inflation rate would not rise. The key to establishing this situation was to find the right or "natural" level of unemployment. Thus, unemployment was not only assigned a lower priority than inflation, it was actually to become a tool, a vehicle, a lever for achieving inflation control. Therefore, the level of unemployment—and remember we're talking about people's lives here—was to be nothing more than a mechanism to be adjusted in the interests of attaining the true goal: inflation control.

In a sense, Friedman had created a brilliant theoretical justification for imposing the rules of classical economics. Workers could press as much as they liked for government interventions to reduce their vulnerability and minimize their desperation level in the open marketplace, in the interest of improving their lives and increasing their bargaining power with employers. But in the end, they would be no further ahead, because whatever interventions they managed to win would simply drive up the so-called natural rate of unemployment or

NAIRU, and this would ultimately mean they would face higher unemployment.

Imagine the following simplified scenario. A country has an unemployment rate of 8.7 percent. Popular pressure forces the government to make its unemployment insurance system more generous. With the worker desperation level reduced due to the more generous unemployment insurance system, economists now recalculate the country's NAIRU and decide that it has risen from 7.5 percent to 8.2 percent. But this is getting dangerously close to the actual unemployment rate of 8.7 percent. Officials in the government's Finance department as well as its central bank believe that if the actual rate of unemployment drops below the natural rate, all hell will break loose, or at least inflation will take off. So, they are getting very nervous. Then there is a slight upturn in the economy, causing actual unemployment to drop to 8.6 percent. This meagre improvement in the unemployment situation is greeted with mild enthusiasm by the public. The next month, unemployment drops again to 8.5 percent; a feeling of optimism can be detected in department stores, which seem almost "bustling." Inside government and the central bank, however, there is panic.

If the authorities want to head off a rise in inflation before it gets started, they figure they have to act in advance. With the magic NAIRU number at 8.2 percent—rather than at its earlier level of 7.5 percent—officials consider things are now too close for comfort. They decide that it's time to jack up interest rates, thereby choking off growth and driving up unemployment. (If the NAIRU were still at the 7.5 percent level, unemployment would probably be allowed to drop lower, before authorities felt it necessary to jack up the interest rates.) In this scenario, government and central bank officials have done what is expected of them under NAIRU theory: they have raised interest rates because unemployment was considered to have dropped too close to the NAIRU. Sometimes, in real life, they even make pre-emptive strikes, raising interest rates on the basis of nothing more than the possibility that unemployment *might* drop too close to the NAIRU—as happened in Canada in October 1997.

The point in this example is that the NAIRU concept has effectively undermined the popular choice of a more generous unemployment insurance system. If citizens want a more generous system, they can have one. But this will have the effect of pushing up the country's NAIRU, which will mean the government will be more likely to raise interest rates, creating more unemployment. The citizens are thus in a no-win situation. The more concessions they win through the democratic process to improve their lives, the more they will be punished with higher levels of unemployment. The NAIRU concept confines them to a deep hole; if they succeed in climbing partway up the walls, they will automatically be knocked back down. The only alternative is to accept what the market gives them, to accept their own impotence.

～

IT WAS ALMOST AS if the group of dissident Canadian economists was trying to signal that they wanted to be left alone. Or at least that they weren't prepared to compromise, either in their economic theory or in their discomfort. It was a weekend in March 1993, and there was no thought of meeting on the balmy British Columbia coast or in the big-city excitement of Montreal or Toronto. That would be too easy, too mainstream. The meeting was about unemployment—not how high it should be in order to control inflation, but how to bring it down. And dealing with unemployment in that way was as far from the thoughts of the mainstream economics profession as the Sudbury location was from the thoughts of the typical southward-yearning Canadian in March. Certainly no one coming to the conference at Laurentian University thought of this as a junket. Among the hardy stock of economists arriving in Sudbury for the event was an old man who looked as if he might be just looking for a place to get out of the cold, and maybe cop a sandwich or two.

It was William Vickrey, who, despite his dishevelled appearance, was well known to those attending the Sudbury meeting. Although

Vickrey had not yet won his Nobel Prize, he was serving that year as president of the American Economic Association. His appearance in Sudbury certainly came as a surprise; such a high-profile figure in the U.S. economics world generally doesn't find time to attend small gatherings in remote Canadian locations. Besides, Vickrey's name had not even appeared on the program.

In fact, he was a last-minute invitee. Conference organizer Brian MacLean, an economist at Laurentian, had invited him to speak after the two men met at a conference earlier that month at Columbia University. MacLean thought it unlikely that Vickrey would agree to come to such a small event at such late notice. But the subject of the conference delighted Vickrey; it was so rare and refreshing to see a group of economists focusing on unemployment. And if unemployment seemed high in the United States, at around 7.5 percent that year, it was that much more outrageous in Canada, hovering just above 11 percent. Vickrey accepted the invitation, and even offered to make the two-day drive from New York City by car in order to save the conference the cost of his airfare. MacLean insisted that Vickrey fly. In the end, Vickrey did fly, although he never submitted any expenses for reimbursement from the conference. Because there hadn't been time to get Vickrey's name on the program, MacLean ran around campus posting a quickly produced flyer that read: "The president of the American Economic Association will be here; will you?"

Vickrey lived up to his reputation. He dozed off in sessions from time to time, only to rise up at the end and ask penetrating questions. And to many at the conference who had followed his writings on the unemployment issue from afar, he did not disappoint. "It was like watching an aging rock star that they'd worshipped for a long time," commented MacLean. Rejecting the notion that the United States was already operating at full employment, as NAIRU advocates insisted, Vickrey gave an address about the need for what he termed "chock-full employment"—that is, unemployment in the 1 to 2 percent range.

The functional modern buildings of Laurentian University, perched on top of a hill rising gently above Lake Ramsey, seemed like the

perfect setting for such offbeat ideas: empty, remote, peaceful, a beau-
tiful setting for a walk at another time of year. Inside the sprawling
buildings, the economists filled the overhead slide projectors with
graphs, drew mathematical equations on blackboards and generally
communicated with one another in as much technical jargon as any
group of mainstream economists would. It was only their conclusions
that were different.

And their conclusions *were* different. Vickrey was the most unorthodox in his views. But there was a general agreement about the
failings of mainstream economics to deal with the unemployment
issue, and a general cynicism about the NAIRU. Lars Osberg, from Dalhousie University, had just published a paper in the prestigious academic journal *European Economic Review*, mounting a detailed, highly
technical critique of the NAIRU. The paper concluded that the NAIRU
was very unreliable as a tool for economic policy. Shelley Phipps,
another Dalhousie economist, attacked one of the foundations of
NAIRU theory: that government programs that reduce the desperation
of the worker drive up unemployment. Phipps cited evidence showing that a high proportion of those working and not working wanted
more paid work, not less, that the real problem was insufficient work
offered by employers. Both Phipps and Osberg challenged the way
economists generally assume workers regard unemployment as equivalent to a paid holiday.

But perhaps the most intriguing critique of the NAIRU at the Sudbury event came from Pierre Fortin, a wiry, highly energetic economist from the Université du Québec à Montréal. Fortin had built a
solid reputation in mainstream economics, churning out an impressive series of articles in international academic publications and serving as president of the Canadian Economics Association. His wife was
the high-powered Michèle Fortin, head of Radio-Canada television,
and the Fortins together had five children. If anything, Pierre was considered fairly conservative by the standards of the Sudbury gathering,
being a keen supporter of free trade and fiscal restraint.

Indeed, Fortin considered himself a conservative. But he had come to Sudbury because he believed Canada's high unemployment rate was unnecessary, ultimately an inefficient use of the country's resources. The more he looked into it, the more he came to question the basic assumptions of Friedman's natural rate theory. As he told the Sudbury conference, the evidence increasingly didn't seem to fit with the theory. According to the theory, raising unemployment above its natural rate for a relatively short period of time should have the effect of permanently pushing down inflation. In other words, if the reserve army of the unemployed was swollen temporarily to an even greater size, the effect would be not only to keep inflation from rising, but to actually drive inflation down and keep it at this lower level. Canadian studies on the NAIRU, based on the formula developed by Friedman, had defined this more specifically for the Canadian situation. They had argued that maintaining unemployment two percentage points above its natural level for a one-year period would have the effect of driving down inflation by one percentage point permanently. Although this would involve a decline in the economy's overall output (GDP) that year, it was deemed to be worth it. The pain of higher unemployment would be short-lived, and the gain resulting from lower inflation would be large and lasting.

Fortin noted that in fact this didn't seem to be true. In the four years following the recession of the early 1980s, unemployment in Canada had averaged about 10 percent—roughly two percentage points higher than the natural rate, as estimated by the Bank of Canada. According to the NAIRU theory, this should have driven down the inflation rate by about one percentage point per year, for a cumulative total of 4 percentage points over the 1984–87 period. Instead, inflation declined by only 1.3 percent (from 5.7 percent to 4.4 percent). As Fortin noted, the Canadian situation was similar to what was happening in France, Italy, Belgium and the United Kingdom, where unemployment levels well above their natural rates were failing to bring down inflation. Indeed, it seemed that an ever-larger reserve army of the unemployed was necessary just to keep European inflation from rising. "The North American and European experiences of the 1980s call the Friedman view into serious question," Fortin told the Sudbury gathering in his precise and careful manner.

In Europe this phenomenon had become quite pronounced, leading some economists to begin questioning whether unemployment could be pushed up briefly in the interests of inflation control, and then brought back down. What seemed to be happening instead was that unemployment, once raised, got stuck at the higher level. If it was brought back down, it would set off a new round of inflation. This phenomenon, which was dubbed "hysteresis" by two distinguished U.S. economists, Olivier Blanchard of the Massachusetts Institute of Technology (MIT) and Lawrence Summers of Harvard, was the exact inverse of what Friedman had described. Rather than attempts to reduce unemployment pushing inflation ever higher, as Friedman claimed, this new phenomenon suggested that attempts to reduce inflation require permanently higher unemployment. This raised the alarming possibility that while a permanent reduction in inflation could be achieved, it would not be through some "short-term pain" of high unemployment, *but only through the long-term pain of permanently higher levels of unemployment.*

Friedman had perhaps failed to see this because he assumed that unemployment levels were simply an economic factor that governments could tinker with. He overlooked the fact that pushing up unemployment involved seriously damaging people's lives, and people don't always behave well when their lives are severely damaged, when they feel humiliated and powerless, even worthless. As Martin Luther King once noted, "In our society, it is murder, psychologically, to deprive a man of a job. . . . You are in substance saying to that man that he has no right to exist." It's true—faced with this most devastating of insults, people often behave very badly, drinking excessively and even becoming violent. Or, more commonly, they simply lose their positive outlook on the world, their work skills and their employability; they lose their capacity to compete effectively for jobs. Yet it is this large pool of labour competing for jobs—this reserve army of the unemployed—that maintains a downward pressure on wages and therefore keeps inflation in check. If recessions cause large numbers of workers to lose their skills and their employability, they will no longer be able to provide a very effective reserve army—an army that is able to compete intensely for the few available jobs. Therefore, new recruits of freshly unemployed, still skilled, warm bodies will be necessary to swell the ranks of the reserve army, maintaining that crucial downward pressure on wages.

What Blanchard, Summers and Fortin were raising amounted to a major challenge to Friedman's theory. Friedman had argued that the temporary pain (of high unemployment) would produce long-term gain. There was a certain puritanical appeal in this: deny yourself pleasure now and reap bigger satisfaction down the road. But if the denial turned out to be long-term, involving ever-greater levels of denial, the prize down the road would come to seem less and less satisfying. If so, the promise of short-term pain for long-term gain was bogus. Instead, what was being offered was long-term pain for no clear gain. In other words, Friedman had nothing to offer. We were back to the simple Phillips curve, where the trade-off between inflation and unemployment had to be carefully managed. There was no simple "permanent" solution.

There were other aspects of the NAIRU theory that didn't jibe with the evidence in Canada. One apparent contradiction of the theory was provided by the unemployment insurance system—a crucial element in almost all calculations of the "natural" rate of unemployment. Since the early 1970s, Ottawa has repeatedly altered the unemployment insurance system, providing a feast for economists intent on calculating the Canadian NAIRU on an up-to-the-minute basis. Yet the changes have not produced results consistent with the theory. Watch what happens.

In 1971, the Liberal government of Pierre Trudeau revamped the existing unemployment insurance system to make it considerably more generous, providing higher pay, wider coverage and greater accessibility. Stories quickly emerged in the media and elsewhere about people abusing the system, about young people spending the winter skiing in Mont Tremblant or sailing on the west coast, with their UI cheques being forwarded to them from an address back home in Peace River or Moncton. Economists, stunned by the significant reduction in the desperation level of the Canadian worker, had little trouble agreeing that the Canadian NAIRU had shot up significantly. But, to the consternation of the economists, the actual Canadian unemployment rate stubbornly failed to follow. This was perplexing because, according to NAIRU theory, the more generous unemployment insurance system should have made workers more inclined to opt for the pleasant life of being unemployed. But they didn't for almost a decade—a fact noted by the Organization for Economic Co-operation and Development. In one of its surveys of Canada, the OECD expressed surprise over "why it took so long for this [more generous] legislation to be reflected in a higher rate of unemployment." (One possibility was that apart from a small number of freeloaders, the vast majority of Canadian workers actually preferred to work, regardless of the generosity of the UI system.)

Even more inexplicable is the evidence of what has happened since Ottawa began making the system less generous, starting in the mid-1970s. In theory, the reductions should have allowed for a lower NAIRU, allowing unemployment to drop substantially without triggering inflation. And yet unemployment has risen instead. By 1997, Ottawa had severely gutted the unemployment insurance system, reducing it to pre-1971 levels. Yet unemployment remained above 9 percent, and the Bank of Canada justified interest rate hikes in the summer and fall of 1997 on the grounds that it had to do so to head off inflation.

None of this is meant to suggest that Friedman—winner of the Nobel Prize for economics in 1976—is anything other than a brilliant theorist. Furthermore, the concept underlying the natural rate of unemployment has some undeniable truth. The notion that increasing the desperation level of workers will increase their inclination to work is clearly true in some basic sense. In Third World countries, where social support systems are few or non-existent, the desperation level is great and workers can be enticed to do very hard and unpleasant jobs for very low pay—jobs that they might well decline if an adequate social support system were in place.

But there are many questionable aspects to the way Friedman has developed his theory around this obvious truth. Apart from his bizarre assumptions about human behaviour, which we have already explored, there is the more technical problem of measurement. Many factors influence the desperation level of workers and how secure they will feel turning down jobs that don't appeal to them. How can a reliable method of calculation be constructed?

In fact, there is no standard method of calculating the NAIRU. Every economist simply comes up with his or her own way of doing it. The popular factors to measure include the unemployment insurance system, the welfare system, minimum wages, the payroll tax, the degree of unionization. But each study uses different combinations of these factors and assigns a different weight to each factor. Mix and match.

The generosity of the unemployment insurance system is an obvious factor in most calculations, but it is not at all clear how to measure it: should one look at the level of benefits, the duration of benefits, how easy it is to qualify for benefits, or some other aspect of the system? Canada, for instance, introduced a system of varying regional benefits, whereby the benefit levels are influenced by the local unemployment rate. What impact does this have on the overall generosity of the unemployment insurance system, and how much weight should this change be given in adjusting the NAIRU?

Another item that is sometimes factored into NAIRU calculations is the degree of unionization. This one's more nebulous, but workers perhaps do feel less vulnerable in a more unionized society. Or do they feel more vulnerable if they are not themselves union members, fearing the unions will close ranks around their own members? And how should unionization be measured? By the number of workers unionized, by the militancy of the unions, or by the society's attitude towards unionization and strikes? Furthermore, in making comparisons among the desperation levels in different countries, should one look, for instance, at the level of unionization or the trend in the level: is unionization on the rise or on the decline? It is easy to see how vastly different estimates of a country's NAIRU can exist.

Consider two recent Canadian studies—one prepared by officials in the federal Finance department, and the other by officials in the Bank of Canada. Both studies, done in 1996, came to sharply different conclusions about exactly where the Canadian NAIRU had been in 1994. The Finance study concluded that the NAIRU had been 7.4 percent; the Bank of Canada weighed in with a calculation of 9.5 percent. Between the two key parts of our government that shape policies directly affecting unemployment, we got two very different estimates of what the unemployment level should have been, and therefore at what point interest rates should have been raised to head off inflation. (The difference between unemployment of 7.4 percent and 9.5 percent amounts to roughly 300,000 workers.)

The NAIRU has also proved elusive in the United States. Economists there have been surprised in recent years to see unemployment continue to drop below their NAIRU estimates without setting off inflation. In the early 1990s, many economists calculated the U.S. NAIRU at around 6 percent, only to find actual unemployment drop to 5.5 percent, then 5.1 percent and then 4.7 percent, without an upturn in inflation. James Galbraith argues that this should have led to more scepticism about the whole concept of the NAIRU and its usefulness. "It is often necessary to revise a parameter once or twice in light of new information," he argues. "But to hold to a concept in the face of twenty years of unexplained variation and failure is quite another matter."

None of this seems to have dampened the quest for ever-deeper probing in search of the true NAIRU. Some economists have gone off in search of more "time-sensitive" explanations—trying to factor in the amount of time it takes for changes in the workers' desperation level to show up in the unemployment rate. Oddly enough, few seem to consider another possibility: that the NAIRU, in addition to being, in Vickrey's words, "the most vicious euphemism ever coined," is also almost useless as a guide to anything.

A number of other prominent economists have raised some powerful critiques of the NAIRU. Robert Eisner, who also served as president of the American Economic Association, has questioned the reality of the labour market Friedman described—whether workers really do simply quit their jobs when they find inflation catching up with their wages, whether employers are always eager to cut wages, even if it means losing some of their best workers, and whether unemployment happens only because workers won't accept lower wages, rather than because employers can't find a market for their products. U.S. economist Franco Modigliani has also attacked Friedman's theory for its implication that unemployment is necessarily a voluntary condition. Modigliani, another Nobel laureate in economics, has mockingly suggested that Friedman assumes major recessions or even depressions are simply the product of "epidemics of contagious laziness." Furthermore, in recent years, there have been a number of high-powered academic attacks on Friedman's theory from mathematical economic theorists challenging the notion that there is a specific rate of "natural" unemployment.

Given the impressive credentials of some of the critics of the NAIRU, it is surprising that the theory has enjoyed such wide acceptance. James Galbraith notes that when Albert Einstein wrote to Franklin Roosevelt in 1939 about the horrendous possibilities of the atomic bomb, he had the full support of his scientific colleagues. There was no disagreement among scientists about the technical details of the bomb. Yet economists can't agree on what the NAIRU is in any given situation, what the process is for determining it or even whether the concept is valid at all. Galbraith argues that it would be inconceivable that an economist could win the backing of the profession for an Einstein-like letter to the chairman of the central bank, warning of imminent inflation, based on a particular estimate of the NAIRU. "If you cannot imagine such a thing," Galbraith told a group of economists at Washington's Georgetown University in September 1996, "then we as a scientific profession have not advanced this concept to the point where it is suitable for practical use."

⟿

IT IS HARD TO IMAGINE an economic theory of recent years that has had a bigger impact on the lives of ordinary people than Milton Friedman's concept of the natural rate of unemployment. By arguing that government efforts to stimulate the economy were ultimately useless in reducing unemployment in the long run—and harmful because they would set off inflation—Friedman succeeded in giving a theoretical base to the view that governments could and should do nothing about unemployment (other than remove social supports). This was manna from heaven for conservatives who have always disliked the notion of governments intervening in the economy in order to create jobs or to increase the level of social support available to workers.

The traditional conflict between the goals of controlling inflation and reducing unemployment—with the rich championing inflation control and ordinary people championing unemployment reduction—had been transformed beyond recognition. Under Friedman's theory, there was no more conflict. Controlling inflation became the top priority, and all efforts of monetary and fiscal policy were to be directed to this end. The goal of reducing unemployment was simply abandoned, on the grounds that it was impossible to achieve (other than by increasing the desperation level of the worker, which was advocated). Indeed, unemployment was to become a tool in the arsenal of the war on inflation.

And Friedman had carried out this fundamental revolution in economic thought without appearing to take sides between the rich and the rest of society. In Friedman's formulation, government was impotent to do anything but control inflation, which, it so happened, was exactly what the rich wanted. And it was all done in the name of science.

⟿

THE AGING MEMBERS OF the international relations committee of the League of Women Voters of Bronxville, New York, could hardly believe their luck. Professor C. Lowell Harriss, an economist from Columbia University, had agreed to address them.

Harriss had just been selected to go to Stockholm to be fêted at the royal palace by the king and queen of Sweden and accept the Nobel Prize on behalf of his late colleague, William Vickrey. As luck would have it, Harriss had decided to prepare for the Stockholm ceremony by giving a talk on Vickrey's ideas to a local group. The international relations committee of Bronxville's League of Women Voters was keen to have him. Its members were thrilled when he accepted their invitation. Although it wasn't as good as being invited to the Swedish palace themselves, for the small group of fairly frail league members who were able to make it out on a cold November night in 1996 to hear Harriss speak before he set off for Stockholm, it felt like a near-brush with royalty.

Harriss, eighty-four, who first met Vickrey in graduate school at Columbia in 1935, had spent almost fifty years as his colleague in the economics department. The two men had even worked together in the U.S. Treasury department during the Second World War, and their wives had been good friends over the years. So it was perhaps fitting that Columbia should select Harriss to accept the honour on behalf of his long-time colleague.

But in another way it wasn't appropriate at all. Harriss had always respected Vickrey, but, by his own admission, he hadn't realized how important Vickrey's contribution to economics was until Vickrey was chosen for the Nobel Prize. Harriss quickly reread some of Vickrey's earlier work and found himself now fully able to appreciate its brilliance. But Harriss's sudden interest in Vickrey's theories included only work he had done decades ago—the same work recognized by the Nobel committee. Being a mainstream economist, Harriss had little or no interest in Vickrey's wild ideas about full employment and the deficit.

So when Harriss spoke to the League of Women Voters, he focused heavily on Vickrey's ideas for relieving traffic congestion. It was a big hit with the league. "His talk kept the audience spellbound," recalled Elsie Hall, the chairwoman of the league's international committee. "His presentation of Vickrey's economics opened up a new world for us. . . . Lowell put his listeners in everyday situations of frustration: behind the wheel of their cars, sitting in a traffic jam. All through Lowell's talk we were astonished by how adventuresome and exciting economics could be."

Similarly, when Columbia University sponsored a colloquium to honour Vickrey in April 1997, it focused exclusively on his ideas for improving traffic congestion. Called "Pricing Transportation Right: William Vickrey's Legacy," the colloquium featured presentations with titles such as "Review of Road Pricing in America" and "The Potential for Highway Incentive Pricing in the Tri-State Region."

What the colloquium guests, the women at the league—and the audience in Stockholm—did not hear was anything about the ideas that had consumed Vickrey with a passion for the past two decades, the ideas that he had wanted to present on the world stage in Stockholm. They didn't hear his arguments, for instance, about how the official method of measuring joblessness masked the true scope of the problem of mass unemployment and its contribution to poverty. Solutions such as job training, Vickrey had argued, mostly had the effect of "moving selected individuals to the head of the queue," rather than solving the basic problem of lack of jobs. Vickrey had insisted that a true solution, initially at least, would have to involve more government spending, including long-term investment in badly needed infrastructure. Also vital, he had argued, was a redirection of monetary policy away from the inflation obsession, which in the past two decades had driven up real interest rates, redistributing wealth to the rich and depressing overall economic growth. And Vickrey had, above all, wanted to expose the fallacy of Friedman's concept of the natural rate of unemployment, which had provided the comfortable justification for tolerance of mass unemployment.

Lowell Harriss returned from his encounter with royalty thrilled by the whole experience, showing off to the press the gilt-edged invitations, ornate menus, posters and books from the unforgettable week of gala events in Stockholm. Harriss told *The New York Times* that he was determined to act as a missionary to keep alive Vickrey's ideas and ideals. With this in mind, he even accepted an invitation to address another meeting organized by the international relations committee of the League of Women Voters, to be held at the Reformed Church in Bronxville. This time members of the public were also to be invited so that they too could hear about the exciting possibilities economics offers for solving the problems of traffic congestion.

IT'S INTERESTING TO imagine what the League of Women Voters— or the wider public—would have thought of Vickrey's views on the horrifying reality that economics has created by encouraging the notion that the unemployment problem is insoluble.

The NAIRU, by providing a justification for government inaction on the job front, has been a key element in the cult of impotence. Far more than just an influential theory, it has been the cornerstone of economic policy for most western governments over the past three decades, including, as we'll see in the next chapter, the Chrétien government in Ottawa.

CHAPTER THREE

The Suit Goes to Ottawa

~

Unemployed people pay less tax. That is one of the most certain laws of all in economics. It should be inscribed on plaques and hung in the offices of prime ministers and premiers across the country.
—Douglas Peters, senior vice-president of the Toronto-Dominion Bank, explaining the growth of the Canadian deficit

~

THE PHILLIPS CURVE AND Friedman's redesign of it go a long way towards explaining the defeat of the Conservative government in the 1993 federal election. To the extent that that defeat could be blamed on leader Kim Campbell—rather than on her enormously unpopular predecessor, Brian Mulroney—it seemed to have something to do with her apparent indifference to the issue of unemployment, which had hovered well above 10 percent for the previous three years. Campbell suggested that there was little government could do to fight unemployment and seemed to calmly accept the notion that there would be no significant drop in the jobless rate until the next century. This nonchalant attitude towards unemployment went down poorly with the electorate, leaving the field clear for the Liberals' final burst to the finish line. All Liberal leader Jean Chrétien had to do was suggest that he favoured the traditional Phillips curve approach over the Friedmanesque one espoused by Campbell; in other words, he would use the power of government to bring down unemployment faster. He said that repeatedly (although without mentioning the Phillips curve), and won handily.

Many commentators have suggested in retrospect that Campbell was simply being more honest. This suggestion was made, for instance, by former Conservative politician Ron Atkey during a 1997 TV panel discussion on "Pamela Wallin Live" about "lying in politics." Atkey presented it as an integrity issue: Campbell had told the truth and been prepared to take the consequences, whereas Chrétien had been dishonest, dangling the prospect of jobs before the Canadian people, knowing he couldn't possibly deliver. Another possibility is that what Campbell told wasn't "the truth" at all, but rather reflected the perverse thinking of the prevailing economic orthodoxy, with its adherence to the notion that governments should use unemployment as a vehicle for controlling inflation.

Campbell had received strong backing from business and financial interests, and one of her few promises during the leadership race was something that pleased them a great deal: a strong commitment to the war on inflation. This war had been launched in earnest by the Bank of Canada in 1988, under then-governor John Crow, and Campbell was signalling that a Conservative government run by her would continue to support Crow's aggressive anti-inflation stance. Her casual attitude towards unemployment sprang from an understanding that if employment was to be sacrificed on the altar of inflation control, there would not likely be much good news on the job front in the foreseeable future. Fighting unemployment would not be her government's priority; controlling inflation, which her well-heeled backers considered more important, would take precedence. Campbell's "truthfulness," then, wasn't her willingness to admit the cold facts of economic reality, but her willingness to admit the unpleasant truth of what her government had in mind for the Canadian people.

Just what the Liberals were up to was less clear. To be sure, they displayed far more political savvy. They knew that a concept like the NAIRU, no matter how you dress it up, isn't a big seller with the public, which intensely dislikes unemployment. Indeed, if ordinary citizens were ever really to understand how our political leaders have allowed unemployment to be used as a tool for fine-tuning the inflation rate, they would undoubtedly throw the rascals out and demand a thorough purging of the ranks of government economists. Most politicians—except slightly naïve, inadequately tutored ones like Campbell—know this or at least sense it, and avoid the minefield.

Certainly Chrétien's Liberals took a different tack, both in opposition and in the 1993 election campaign. In opposition, the Liberals vigorously attacked the Tory government for allowing the Bank of Canada to raise interest rates relentlessly in its drive to reduce inflation after 1988. In the election campaign, NAIRU-type thinking was nowhere to be seen. The Liberals' Red Book of election promises, of which Paul Martin was one of the key authors, accused the Tories of having "systematically weakened the social support network . . . [and] taken billions of dollars from programs that support children, seniors and people who have lost their jobs." This is exactly the course of action advised by those subscribing to the NAIRU, as part of the need to increase the desperation level of the worker. Indeed, to NAIRU supporters, this is the way to create jobs! But the Liberals distanced themselves from this sort of thinking during the election campaign, boasting that unemployment insurance—the whipping boy of NAIRU-huggers—was part of "the Liberal legacy," along with other fine social interventions like public pensions.

Instead of solving unemployment by stripping Canadians of their social supports, the Red Book promised "a series of measures to put Canadians back to work and to foster economic growth." They specifically mentioned major government investments in a national infrastructure program, research and development, and a national child care program. All this was very un-NAIRU-like. Not even the deficit was supposed to stand in the way of job creation in the Liberal plan. Unlike Conservative and Reform Party promises to eliminate the deficit, the Liberals promised the more moderate goal of reducing it to 3 percent of GDP in three years, and to achieve this "in a manner that is compatible with putting Canadians back to work." The Tories, with support from many mainstream commentators, suggested that the Red Book promises were impractical, and that

Chrétien was promising pie-in-the-sky dreaming about jobs that couldn't be delivered.

So it was a small coup for the Liberals when they succeeded in enlisting Doug Peters to run as a Liberal candidate. A senior vice-president and chief economist of the Toronto-Dominion Bank, Peters was an articulate advocate of the notion that the country needed jobs before deficit reduction, and his stature in the financial community lent a note of credibility to a Liberal campaign built around these themes. Here was a major Bay Street figure saying that making jobs the top priority was not pie-in-the-sky dreaming. It could and should be done. Chrétien had personally pushed to get Peters on board early. And words from some of Peters's speeches had been lifted directly into the Red Book. But, as Peters would soon discover once the Liberals swept to power, a jobs-and-growth strategy, while happily mouthed by Liberal candidates and well received by a job-hungry public, provoked little more than scorn inside the government department that actually shaped the nation's economic policy.

AS A YOUNG BOY growing up in the lean 1930s in Brandon, Manitoba, Douglas Peters looked almost frail. His small stature and low body weight had led to his being singled out at school by public health authorities worried about possible cases of malnutrition, as unemployment tore through the Prairies. Along with twin girls at the school, eight-year-old Doug Peters had failed to meet the minimum size and weight standards on the chart, and therefore qualified for special government-supplied food supplements. As it turned out, the twins weren't underfed, just late bloomers, who not long after the public health test attained a robust and healthy girth. And Doug was also far from being malnourished; indeed, as the son of a doctor, he was probably one of the best-fed children in the Depression-ravaged city.

But Peters was in many ways different from what he seemed. His frail appearance and pleasant manner helped disguise a deep-seated feistiness, a willingness to go for the jugular at times, a kind of reck-lessness in dealing with authority. Perhaps it was the mild-mannered quality in Peters that made it possible for him to survive, years later, as an iconoclast on Bay Street—not a place notorious for its tolerance of dissidents from mainstream economics. His success may have been partly because Peters still looked and acted, in a way, like the smallish, apparently undernourished boy at the Brandon public school. There was no "in-your-face" quality about him. His subversiveness was not of style, but of the more profound sort—of content.

In his early years, Peters had not seemed headed for any of this. Although always very bright, he performed abysmally during his first year in the pre-meds course at the University of Manitoba, where he excelled only at basketball and bridge. When this resulted in a 40 per-cent average, the dean pointedly told his father that young Doug was "not university calibre." So Doug Peters headed off to the nearest unemployment office in Winnipeg. It was quickly determined that since he had no real training or university education, there was only one place for the young drop-out: a bank.

Peters was lucky to land a job in 1948 as a junior clerk in a down-town Winnipeg branch of the Dominion Bank; his main responsibil-ity there was changing the nibs on pens in the bank's inkwells. He was lucky again when Queen's University in Kingston, Ontario, decided to give him another chance at academic life. At twenty, he headed off to Queen's, where university officials soon came to the same conclusion as the dean at the University of Manitoba. After Peters failed two courses, Queen's threw him out. Once again, untrained and unedu-cated, Peters seemed destined for a banking career. This time he joined the Bank of Montreal, where he worked in various branches as a loans officer in Winnipeg and Swift Current, Saskatchewan, for the next ten years. He married and had two children. Things were looking more and more like a quiet career in mid-level prairie banking.

By 1960, a more mature Doug Peters was ready to try the academic world again, and Queen's gave him another chance. He entered the Bachelor of Commerce program there and, surprisingly, did extremely well. He particularly excelled in several courses in moral philosophy, which he took as electives. He graduated with the university's Medal in Commerce and was greeted with scholarship offers from Harvard, Columbia and the University of Chicago. He opted to study finance at the prestigious Ivy League University of Pennsylvania, and its affiliate, the Wharton School of Finance and Commerce. His days of poor academic performance were now behind him. He became a top-notch student, receiving extensive financial support from the Canada Council and the Ford Foundation.

But while Peters was starting to behave like someone headed for a career as a senior banker, he had in fact landed in a place embroiled in debate and controversy about the most fundamental economic issues—issues that would stir deep emotions on Wall Street and Bay Street for years to come. It was the mid-sixties and the economics profession was going through a major transformation, rapidly distancing itself from the theories of the great early-twentieth-century British economist John Maynard Keynes, whose ideas, although never applied exactly as Keynes had intended, had had enormous influence in western countries since the Second World War. Keynes was the godfather of the school of economic thought that, in our shorthand system, we can identify as "popular" as opposed to "market" in its orientation. This is of course a highly simplified description of Keynes's sophisticated economic theories, which we will explore in more detail in Chapter 6. But for now, the important point is that Keynes essentially supported the notion that government should play a key role in ensuring full employment and delivering strong social programs.

By the time Peters arrived at the University of Pennsylvania in 1964, the post-war boom was starting to lose some of its momentum and there were signs of economic trouble ahead. This put Keynes's ideas under increasing attack from market-oriented economists, led by Milton Friedman, who had long opposed the enormous growth in the role of government that had been the hallmark of the Keynesian experiment. Nowhere were Keynes's ideas more keenly debated—and defended—than at U of Pennsylvania. In addition to Keynes's being under attack from the academic right, there was a strong surge of activism from the left on major U.S. campuses, as the counter-culture movement gained momentum in its critique of the Vietnam war and in its broader critique of capitalist society.

Nothing in Peters's background had prepared him for the intense intellectual experience he was to have at U of Pennsylvania. By this point, he was already thirty-five years old with a wife, two teen-aged children and ten years' experience in local banking. He dressed in conservative suits, just as he had as a banker, and held beliefs that could only be described as conservative. Still, for all his conservatism, he was, during his years in Pennsylvania, profoundly moved and inspired by the intellectual challenge of Keynesianism.

Peters became close friends with two other Canadians studying economics at Penn—Arthur Donner, who later became a well-known Canadian economist, and Robert Rabinovitch, a Montrealer who went on to be a senior adviser to Pierre Trudeau and then a high-level executive in the Bronfman empire. Although the three Canadians formed a lasting connection based on their endless hours of conversation and debate, they could not have been more different in their Penn days. Rabinovitch, who was only twenty-one when he arrived, was intense about politics, having been active in Quebec as an undergraduate. Young and single, he was deeply involved in the U.S. anti-war movement and shared the counter-culture values of a 1960s activist. Knowing there would be a good job waiting for him when he graduated from Wharton, he was preoccupied at this stage in his life with improving the world.

Donner occupied the middle ground between the young, radical Rabinovitch and the stodgy, older Peters. At twenty-seven, Donner had already had some experience with the work world and was returning to graduate school as a mature student, with a wife in tow. To both Rabinovitch and Donner, Peters seemed almost like an old man, partly because of his age and partly because of his small-town conservatism. Although he was distinguishing himself as a brilliant student, Peters behaved more like a banker. He worked nine to five—an unusual schedule for someone buried under the workload of Wharton's graduate economics course—returning home each evening in time for dinner with his family. When Rabinovitch and Donner would see Peters arriving at the library at 9:00 A.M. sharp, they would joke to each other: "Here comes the Suit."

While Peters's studies focused on narrow banking interests, his life at U of Pennsylvania brought him into contact with some intellectual giants. Penn was the stamping ground of Lawrence Klein, a Nobel Prize–winning economist who had caught the attention of the U.S. Senate's McCarthy committee investigating so-called un-American activities in the early 1950s. Klein was no communist, but he had written an influential book, *The Keynesian Revolution*, which was sympathetic to the notion of a strong government role in the economy. Upon discovering that he was under investigation, Klein had left the country for a more relaxing academic post at Oxford. By the mid-sixties, he had returned to U of Pennsylvania and become a major figure in the debate over Keynesianism. Meanwhile at Yale University, James Tobin, another Nobel Prize winner and former adviser to President John Kennedy—and later advocate of the Tobin tax—was also an impressive Keynesian economist and key figure in the raging debate.

But perhaps the economist who cast the longest shadow over the economics department at Penn was Sidney Weintraub. A distinguished but unpleasant professor, Weintraub was spearheading the defence of the Keynesian fort and, for the most part, keeping the enemy at bay. Respected, hated, feared, Weintraub was a dominant figure. He was simply a powerhouse—a small, plump man with a dominating intellect and a caustic personality that could make students wither. The fact that Weintraub never won a Nobel Prize, despite his considerable academic contributions, may have partly explained his acerbic manner in dealing with the world. Weintraub had what could only be described as a cruel streak in him. He used the Socratic method of teaching, beginning a sentence and then turning to a student—any student at any time could be singled out—to complete it. A wrong or inadequate response would frequently provoke an insulting tirade from Weintraub—as an older student from India painfully discovered. On one occasion when the student gave a wrong answer, an exasperated Weintraub replied, "There are planes flying to India every day, Mr. Singh," with the clear implication that Mr. Singh might as well just climb right onto one of them.

Even an excellent student like Doug Peters could be picked on by Weintraub. During the oral defence of his Ph.D. dissertation (on U.S. banking laws), Peters made a reference to a statement by Keynes. When it was Weintraub's turn among the examining professors to question Peters, he asked which work of Keynes's the statement was drawn from. Peters cited the chapter and section where the statement appeared in Keynes's major work, *The General Theory*. Weintraub, whose knowledge of Keynes's massive volume of work was awesome, shot back, "No. You're wrong." Flustered, Peters cited another of Keynes's works, only to be told again he was wrong. This continued for an excruciating amount of time, with Peters desperately searching his mind for the correct citation, and each time Weintraub emphatically announcing that he was in error. The result was a disastrous performance for Peters, who came across looking confused and uncertain precisely at a time when he was supposed to appear so knowledgeable that he was unflappable. Peters was awarded his Ph.D. anyway, and only later realized that Weintraub was simply testing him: his original Keynes citation had been correct.

But while Weintraub could be cruel and insensitive, he had other traits—intellectual rigour, a deep commitment to social justice and a scrappy, fighting spirit—that made him something of a hero to many, including Peters. Weintraub was passionate in his commitment to Keynesian economics, and in some ways was a purer Keynesian than Keynes himself. Even in courses that ostensibly had little to do with the debate over Keynes, Weintraub managed to insert some Keynesian themes.

In one course Weintraub taught, he devoted the entire second half to the issue of income distribution. Although some considered this excessive, the subject of income distribution rightly belonged at the heart of the economics debate. Keynes saw the issue as central to the organization and operation of the economy. Yet increasingly, as the purely market approach to economics came back in vogue and economics was studied in a more theoretical and mathematical way, such questions were banished from the economics classroom, ending up in "softer" disciplines such as political science and sociology. As the economics discipline retreated to the pre-war belief in leaving decisions in the hands of the market, there was little place for the notion that inequality was something that governments could or should address.

Weintraub was also deeply committed to the Keynesian vision of full employment and had little patience with economists who were more concerned with fighting inflation. Weintraub accused Milton Friedman of blocking government action on joblessness by creating "an ideological canon of complacency" with his "fanciful" theories about the natural rate of unemployment. Weintraub had particular scorn for economists—"ensconced in comfortable jobs"—who advocated using unemployment to keep inflation in check. "[T]hose who find unemployment as a praiseworthy public policy should, in decency, resign and become inflation-fighters themselves, rather than force the hardships on less adaptable members of society."

Weintraub was not indifferent to inflation. Indeed, he agreed that the central bank had a role to play in controlling it, but he rejected giving inflation control precedence over fighting unemployment. To avoid this, Weintraub suggested that inflation be held in check partly through mechanisms that would have less impact on unemployment. For instance, he advocated special taxes on corporations that raised wages or salaries too quickly. "The intent is not to collect more tax revenue but to act as a posted speed limit," he wrote. A similar concept was later proposed by William Vickrey, who advocated imposing taxes on corporations that raised their *prices* unduly.

With emotion running high in the debate over Keynesian economics in the late 1960s, Friedman bravely accepted an invitation to come right into the heart of the enemy camp to give a lecture at the University of Pennsylvania. Friedman's lecture was a huge event in the intellectual life of the university, and all serious students of economics and finance, including Peters, Donner and Rabinovitch, were in attendance. Although the audience was generally hostile to Friedman's point of view, it listened respectfully as he spoke—all except for Weintraub, who, from a seat in the audience, increasingly turned the session into a two-person jousting match.

But this wasn't a Ph.D. dissertation, where the professors enjoy a kind of omnipotent power and can torment their student-victim at will. In this case, the object of Weintraub's derision controlled the microphone. And Friedman knew all the tricks of academic warfare, having spent a lifetime in its trenches. Furthermore, Friedman was naturally a brilliant debater, and Weintraub's arrogant and sarcastic jabs undermined his own effectiveness, making Friedman seem almost sympathetic. After the lecture, the talk in the hall was a grudging acknowledgment that Friedman had performed well.

It had the feel of an important lost battle, towards the end of a failing war effort. With even the U of Pennsylvania's economics department unable to defend the Keynesian fort, how could ordinary people be expected to rally to the defence of a system they knew little about? For the most part, in fact, they had no idea that this debate was even going on.

But if the winds were blowing in favour of a resurgent market-oriented economics, they had little impact on Doug Peters. Having come to Pennsylvania in search of a good grounding in banking, Peters certainly left with that. His excellent academic credentials led to a number of job offers—including an intriguing offer from the University of Manitoba to replace the retiring dean who had once called Peters "not university calibre."

But Peters also left Pennsylvania with his head and heart won over to Keynesianism. He had been enormously influenced by Klein and Weintraub, particularly Weintraub. In many ways, he was very much Weintraub's student—ruthlessly logical, focused on the broader issues, keen to influence the policy debate, but he had none of Weintraub's nastiness or mean-spiritedness. Still, beneath Peters's pleasant, easygoing exterior was a toughness of mind and a reckless willingness to challenge the powerful. "He's braver than he looks," says Donner.

That bravery was going to come in handy. Peters decided to accept an offer to join the senior ranks of one of Canada's most venerable financial institutions, as chief economist of the Toronto-Dominion Bank. So, fresh from his deeply inspiring encounter with Keynesianism, the Suit arrived on Bay Street just as the wind blowing against Keynesianism was about to turn into a gale.

LIKE ALL THE MAJOR banks, the Toronto-Dominion was a bastion of conservatism. But, in the case of the TD at least, it was a Red Tory kind of conservatism. Chairman Allan Lambert, although a full-fledged member of the Canadian establishment with a host of directorships and memberships in many exclusive Toronto clubs, was an old-fashioned conservative who never forgot his humble roots. Born in Regina, Lambert had joined the TD Bank at the age of sixteen and had worked all over the country, including his first stint at bank managing in Yellowknife. Lambert regarded his career in banking not unlike a career in the public service; in his view, banks performed what amounted to a public service, providing financial stability for the community. This was a far cry from the new strain of laissez-faire, anti-government conservatism that was stirring emotions on Bay Street. Lambert's breed of public-minded conservatism meshed comfortably with Doug Peters's Keynesianism, and Lambert became almost like a mentor to the young chief economist. Despite Peters's senior rank within the bank, he always called the chairman "Mr. Lambert."

But if Peters had found a sanctuary on Bay Street, it was a relatively dull one. He set to work advising the bank on government revisions to the Bank Act. But while the subject was technical and complex and one that he understood well, Peters missed debating the most fundamental issues of economic policy—the debate that had so fascinated him at U of Pennsylvania. By comparison, Bay Street was a dull and uninteresting place, consumed by the passionless pursuit of making money.

Whatever tolerance Keynesianism had enjoyed in financial circles in the early post-war years was quickly gone. The new conservatism, with its submissive acquiescence to markets and its hostility to big government, was far closer to the heart of most Bay Street types, and they keenly embraced it. But the transformation from a tacit acceptance of Keynesianism to an enthusiastic endorsement of the new conservative economics was all happening without the intellectual cut and thrust that Peters had found so captivating at graduate school. Where was the thrill of a Weintraub–Friedman encounter over the role of government in achieving full employment and an equitable distribution of the nation's resources? Instead, Bay Street offered a bunch of bond salesmen trying to convince their customers that long-term yields looked promising.

Peters partly relieved his boredom by helping Arthur Donner, his old friend from University of Pennsylvania, get a job across the street in the economics department of the Bank of Nova Scotia. At least that would give Peters someone to talk to. Donner, who had gone from the Wharton School to the staid Federal Reserve Bank in New York, was also finding himself missing the old days in Pennsylvania; even Sidney Weintraub was starting to look good from a distance.

Although they could never recreate the intellectual ferment of Pennsylvania, Peters and Donner pulled together a group of intellectuals from Bay Street and academia and formed a loose discussion group called the Econoclasts. The group, which even included some non-Keynesians, met in the evenings, renting a private room at a restaurant, where they could spend three or four hours seriously discussing and debating economic policy issues, without having to pay homage to the new gods of inflation control, smaller government and deficit reduction. Rabinovitch, their other friend from Pennsylvania, would even arrange specially to be in Toronto to attend the Econoclast meetings. The meetings never led to government policy changes, but there was something liberating and exciting about getting together such a powerhouse of economic talent and, free of the cant of the new powerlessness, realizing that there were alternatives.

Neither Peters nor Donner was content simply to discuss the big issues. As the new economics began to crop up in actual government policy, both men felt frustration. They were convinced that the change in direction was a mistake that would seriously damage the economy and have far-reaching negative impacts on the lives of Canadians. What particularly alarmed them was the dramatic policy changes that were taking place at the Bank of Canada, Ottawa's central bank.

The actions of central banks were crucial. Keynes had argued about the importance of maintaining demand in an economy, that is, maintaining sufficient money in the hands of consumers so that they could spend, and thereby create growth and employment. As a result, Keynes is popularly associated with policies such as government job-creation projects that pump money directly into the economy. While Keynes did endorse this sort of stimulus in certain circumstances, his preference was for maintaining demand through monetary policy—that is, through the central bank keeping interest rates low enough that people could afford to borrow money.

In the early post-war years, the Bank of Canada, along with central banks in most western nations, had generally followed the Keynesian prescription, maintaining low interest rates to promote job growth. This was continued through the 1960s and early 1970s, when the Bank of Canada was presided over by Louis Rasminsky, an economist with a long and distinguished record working in international financial organizations, including the League of Nations and the International Monetary Fund. Rasminsky knew Keynes personally, having worked closely with him during the long process of restructuring the global financial system culminating in the Bretton Woods conference in 1944. The two men had great respect for each other.

But with the appointment of Gerald Bouey as Bank of Canada governor in 1973, the central bank veered sharply away from Keynesianism. In the face of stubborn inflation, Bouey adopted a controversial new strategy, known as monetarism, championed by Milton

Friedman. Monetarism had gained respectability in international academic circles, but had yet to be tried by U.S. monetary authorities. Its central premise—the same premise that shaped Friedman's theories on the natural rate of unemployment—was the importance of curbing inflation, which was to be achieved by controlling the growth of the money supply.

As the Bank of Canada experimented with monetarism, Peters and Donner watched in horror. Not only was Canada's central bank embracing this dangerous new theory, but virtually the entire financial and academic establishments were supportive. In less than a decade, this unproven theory, along with Friedman's notion of the natural rate of unemployment, had become the new gospel in academic and policy circles. To argue against it was to put oneself well outside the loop of accepted opinion. But Peters and Donner hadn't studied at the feet of Sidney Weintraub only to sit by silently as Canada's central bank and its academic and financial élite succumbed to such folly.

Donner came up with the idea that he and Peters should write a book denouncing monetarism. By this point, Donner, unable to cope with the stifling atmosphere in the banking world, had left the Bank of Nova Scotia and ended up as an independent consultant. So, while he risked alienating potential clients by expressing unorthodox views, he was probably as free as anyone on Bay Street ever was to express a dissenting opinion. Peters, on the other hand, was still chief economist of the TD Bank, which, like the rest of the financial community, had been supportive of the central bank's new direction.

This is perhaps understating the situation. Banking was a small, clubby world, deeply integrated with the country's power structure. By holding much of the nation's capital, banks enjoyed enormous power over just about every aspect of the economy. But banks were also highly dependent on government; they needed federal licences to operate, were subject to federal regulation and relied on the central bank as the lender of last resort. So, despite their enormous power and profit-generating capacities, banks had to keep up good relations with government. And no part of government was more crucial to the banking community than the central bank.

Indeed, the private banks worked closely with the Bank of Canada. The central bank was constantly monitoring credit conditions in the country and relied on feedback from the private banks. The central bank also relied on the private banks to behave responsibly in currency markets, in order to prevent undue fluctuations in the value of the dollar. From time to time, the CEOs of the private banks were summoned for meetings with the central bank's governor. So it would be no trivial matter if the chief economist of a major bank were to publicly criticize the direction of the Bank of Canada. It had never happened before. Peters set to the task with enthusiasm. Finally here was a chance to breathe some life into the staid public debate over economics. It was strangely exhilarating, yet also a little scary. Donner, mindful of Peters's position at the bank, advised caution, from time to time suggesting they tone down some of the language in the book. But Peters wanted the language stronger.

In the end, Peters and Donner accused the central bank of choking economic growth with its rigid adherence to monetarism. Instead, they argued, the bank should consider adopting the Weintraub scheme for controlling inflation—taxing corporations that raised wages too quickly. This way, the bank could curb inflation "without retarding the growth of economic activity." Peters and Donner even wrote a grateful acknowledgment to Weintraub in the front of the book. It was like being at the University of Pennsylvania all over again.

The Monetarist Counter-Revolution, published in 1979, caused a minor sensation, almost entirely because of Peters's senior position at the TD Bank. Although Peters had not been identified as a banker in the book, the press quickly pointed this out. What would have otherwise been just another dull, semi-academic book about economics became a well-publicized political story about a senior banker attacking the Bank of Canada. Peters had made a bold step out of the economic closet. He soon received his reward—a letter from Weintraub fondly referring to his two former Canadian students as his "northern lights."

Peters got away with his little outburst. The reason had a great deal to do with Richard Thomson, who by this point had replaced Lambert as TD chairman at the tender age of forty-five. Thomson had much the same background as Peters; he was born in the early 1930s in Manitoba and spent his summers in the cottage area of Carlyle Park, Saskatchewan, where Peters's wife's family also vacationed. Partly because of their personal connection and partly because of Thomson's open-minded approach to banking, Peters went unpunished.

Emboldened, Peters pushed further, becoming the outspoken gadfly of government economic policy. Although other Bay Street economists sometimes shared his dissenting views, they were not inclined to speak out. At a meeting of chief economists from the major banks in the early 1990s, a number of the others expressed criticisms of government and central bank policy that were, if anything, even stronger than Peters's own views. "But they wouldn't go public," Peters recalls. He believes that Richard Thomson was simply more tolerant than the other bank CEOs. "He let me have a degree of freedom not available in the other banks."

Peters's attacks even became somewhat personal. In 1992, he took a public swipe at the austerity policies of former Finance minister Michael Wilson, suggesting that the "Bennett buggies" of the Depression years had been replaced with "Wilson wagons," which were pulled by "unemployed auto parts workers." *The Toronto Star* reprinted the remarks, attributed to the chief economist of the Toronto-Dominion Bank. Wilson was furious.

But Peters's real outrage over economic policy was focused on John Crow, who had replaced Bouey as governor of the Bank of Canada. Monetarism—the notion of controlling inflation through the growth in the money supply—had faded from the scene, having been widely considered a failure after its few years in fashion. But the fixation on controlling inflation remained and grew more intense under Crow, who pushed up interest rates sharply, starting in 1988.

Peters could barely believe the drama he was watching unfold in Ottawa. He knew John Crow personally and had not been impressed by Crow's grasp of economics or international finance. Crow, who was born in Britain, had worked at the International Monetary Fund in Washington before joining the Bank of Canada in the early 1970s. Shortly after Crow's appointment as Bank of Canada governor, he and Peters had both attended an annual meeting of the Federal Reserve Bank of Kansas. The meeting, at Jackson Hole, Wyoming, attracted an élite group of academics, as well as banking and government officials. Peters, who knew many at the prestigious international gathering, partly from his years at an Ivy League graduate school, played a bit of a father figure to the shy, slightly awkward Crow, introducing him to some of the heavy hitters at the event.

But whatever fatherly feelings Peters may have once felt for the new governor quickly evaporated as Crow began relentlessly pushing up interest rates. At one point, Canadian interest rates were five full points higher than U.S. interest rates, choking growth here and swelling the ranks of the unemployed. This wasn't just defying Keynes, it was turning Keynes upside down and shaking him violently.

Peters considered Crow's anti-inflation policy, which was much more extreme than that of the U.S. central bank, to be bordering on the incoherent. He requested and was granted permission to appear before the House of Commons Finance committee in the spring of 1989. Noting that his views were solely his own, Peters identified himself in front of the committee as the chief economist and senior vice-president of the Toronto-Dominion Bank. Then, without mentioning Crow by name, Peters launched into a scathing attack on the governor's policies.

Peters told the committee that Crow's policies had "raised interest rates to such a height that the probability of a recession has risen to at least 50 percent." Furthermore, he noted, the high interest rates had driven up the deficit by almost $5 billion in the past year—a foretaste of the even larger increases in the deficit that would follow in the early 1990s as Crow moved his assault on inflation into high gear. Peters told the committee that Crow's policies made "no sense whatsoever." Then, sounding very unlike an official of one of the major banks, he concluded unequivocally that Crow's policies "must be changed."

To Crow, Peters's attack was impudent. No longer the slightly awkward young man pleased to be introduced around by Doug Peters at Jackson Hole, Crow had been transformed into an imperious central bank governor. He phoned Richard Thomson and said he wanted to come to Toronto to explain how monetary policy worked. Crow said it would take one and three-quarter hours.

The request was unprecedented—the governor of the central bank offering to give a private tutorial on monetary policy to the chairman of one of the big private banks. Clearly Crow's intent wasn't really to give a tutorial, but rather to make the case that the TD Bank's chief economist knew nothing about monetary policy and should refrain from airing his views on the subject publicly. Thomson agreed to meet Crow, but requested that Peters be present. Crow said fine, he'd bring along deputy Bank of Canada governor Chuck Freedman.

The meeting took place in Thomson's spectacular 1,600-square-foot corner office on the eleventh floor of one of the TD towers in downtown Toronto. The walnut-panelled room featured large windows, sumptuous chesterfields and fine art, including an exquisite Lawren Harris original. But the centrepiece in the room was a large, Bauhaus-style, imposing wooden table, with chrome and leather trimmings, surrounded by ample leather chairs. In the middle of the table was a clock, which faced towards Thomson. Although tolerant and open-minded, Thomson did not allow others to waste his time—ten minutes of Thomson's time was not easily come by.

As soon as the visitors from the Bank of Canada were settled into their leather chairs, Crow began his remarks. It quickly became clear that he intended to give a lecture on the mechanics of monetary policy. He explained how overnight rates worked, how the reserve system operated. This was definitely introductory level stuff, which Thomson, after two decades as TD chairman, knew extremely well. Yet Crow continued. From time to time, Chuck Freedman would be called upon by Crow to present charts to illustrate various points he was making. Peters had been instructed by Thomson not to be caustic or challenging, so he remained largely silent. Only Thomson occasionally interrupted

Crow's monologue. While he supported low inflation, even Thomson couldn't resist noting the large number of Canadian companies that had gone bankrupt since the central bank had embarked on its high-interest-rate course. Crow responded that such developments were beyond the control of monetary policy. Then he returned to explaining how monetary policy worked. At the end of an hour and three-quarters, he finished.

Thomson and Peters walked their guests to the elevator. Once the elevator doors had shut, Thomson commented to Peters that he had never been so insulted in his life.

IN THE SPACIOUS boardroom inside the Finance department, Doug Peters sat at the right hand of Paul Martin. Before any important budget decision was presented to cabinet for approval, it was threshed out here. For endless days that blended into endless weeks before the newly elected Liberal government's first budget in February 1994, Paul Martin, now the Finance minister, and Doug Peters, now the minister of international financial institutions (more commonly known as the junior Finance minister), sat side by side, facing the senior officials of the Finance department. In many ways, it was here that the real decisions were made. By the time the budget plans moved out of this room to be presented to cabinet committee and then to cabinet itself, the direction was pretty well set and had the support of the Finance minister, with his enormous clout at the cabinet table. The best shot at shaping the ultimate direction of the budget was actually right here, in the boardroom of the Finance department.

But the department was not exactly the University of Pennsylvania. Peters's Keynesian views, particularly his constant emphasis on making unemployment a higher priority than the deficit, made him highly suspect within the department. Led by deputy minister David Dodge, associate deputy Scott Clark and assistant deputy Don

Drummond, the department was of one mind: only the deficit mattered. International investors would soon pull their money out of the country—or demand ever-higher risk premiums on government bonds—if the deficit wasn't wrestled to the ground. There could be no peace without deficit reduction.

So here was the situation: the Liberal government had been elected on a platform that had clearly stressed the importance of jobs and had attacked the unpopular Conservative government for its single-minded fixation on deficit reduction. Yet now, only months after that massive victory, the senior officials in the Finance department were basically saying that only deficit reduction mattered. Responding to that popular hunger for jobs was simply out of the question. Financial markets would not allow it.

For Peters, the obstinacy of the department was infuriating. He was facing a brick wall of small-minded economists who were behaving more like bean-counting accountants than architects of a healthy economy. As Peters constantly argued, the Canadian economy faced a number of crises, of which unemployment was the most important and the deficit was somewhere down the ladder. Ironically, Peters now found himself confronted by a group that seemed even more inflexible in its views than the crowd on Bay Street. Indeed, Bay Street was starting to look like a virtual commune of free thinkers compared with this deficit-fixated isolation cell in the nation's capital. While Bay Street had perhaps considered Peters a bit of a maverick for his outspokenness, few had questioned the intellectual merits of his positions. And no one there had even really tried to shut him up; the press had recorded his words and featured them prominently. But here, after actually being elected to government and being given a seat at the cabinet table, Peters found himself virtually ignored for the first time, his carefully thought out positions rudely dismissed.

In fact, both Peters and the department economists agreed that 11 percent unemployment was too high, but they disagreed on two fundamental issues: by *how much* was it too high, and *why* was it too high? Both issues had to do with the NAIRU. Relying on calculations done by the Bank of Canada, the department considered the NAIRU for the Canadian economy to be "at least 8 percent." That, of course, meant that the department considered unemployment could not drop too close to 8 percent without triggering inflation in Canada. If the unemployment rate dropped from 11 percent to 10 percent or below, officials in the department and in the Bank of Canada would have to worry about inflation starting up. So while the department economists felt that 11 percent unemployment was too high, they considered it only somewhat too high. In their minds, the Canadian economy was operating only slightly below what it was capable of operating at without setting off inflation. Another way of saying this was that Canada's "output gap" was small, that is, the economy was producing only slightly fewer goods and services than it would produce if unemployment dropped to its "natural" rate of at least 8 percent.

Peters, on the other hand, considered Canadian unemployment dramatically too high. He was not a great fan of the NAIRU to begin with, believing it to be a highly questionable tool for use in public policy. But if he had to come up with an estimate of what he thought the so-called natural level of unemployment would be for Canada, he would have put it closer to 6 percent—a long way from the Bank of Canada's estimate of at least 8 percent, a difference of about 300,000 jobs. Thus, in Peters's mind, the economy was operating drastically below capacity, it was suffering from a severe "output gap"—in the range of 10 to 12 percent. (Since the total size of the national economy amounted to about $700 billion a year, an output gap of 10 percent meant that the nation was failing to produce another $70 billion worth of goods and services each year, largely because so many Canadians were idle.) Peters was infuriated by department estimates putting the output gap at only 2 to 3 percent. "Get those goddamn charts out of here," the usually soft-spoken Peters screamed on one occasion after the department sent up its latest output gap charts to his office.

Peters and the department economists also disagreed on the reason for Canada's unemployment problem. Peters, using a Keynesian analysis, believed that the problem boiled down to a lack of demand in the economy, due to a lack of consumer spending power. If the private sector couldn't generate sufficient demand to maintain high levels of employment, then government should help out, either by lowering interest rates or by increasing government spending. Given the size of the federal deficit, lower interest rates were definitely the preferred route. But it was counter-productive for the government to embark on such large spending cuts at this point, since the cuts would only take more money out of consumers' pockets, thereby exacerbating the problem of insufficient demand.

The department economists saw things quite differently. They accepted the theory of the NAIRU; therefore, they concluded that unemployment was high because Canada's social support system was too generous. Indeed, being NAIRU adherents, they didn't focus directly on unemployment. They accepted that the government's top priority should be inflation control, which was largely handled by the Bank of Canada. The main contribution of the Finance department should be deficit reduction, getting the government's fiscal house in order. To the extent that they diverted their attention from the deficit to unemployment, it was to consider ways to reduce social supports, or what they called "labour market disincentives"—such as Canada's overly generous unemployment insurance and workers' compensation systems and labour protection laws. In their view, the only way to reduce unemployment was to increase the desperation level of the Canadian worker, along the lines advocated by Milton Friedman.

With such divergent viewpoints, Peters and the department officials were locked in an ongoing battle. Peters was constantly annoyed by the memos that came up from the department, explaining in great detail some aspect of the economic situation, but always, in his view, based on wrong assumptions. "This is the worst piece of economic analysis I've read since the Tories," Peters scribbled on one June 1994 memo that came up from the department, before he sent it on to Martin. For their part, the department economists considered Peters irrelevant, yesterday's man. Most of the time, they simply ignored him.

Of course, the real battle between Peters and the department officials was not about abstract economic policy, but about winning over Paul Martin. Martin has often been portrayed, including by himself, as a reluctant cutter of government programs. "There is a lot of cutting that hurts. I didn't like that at all," he said recently. It's certainly true that Martin is, by nature, attracted to the idea of building things, rather than tearing them down. The former CEO of Canada Steamship Lines and son of a popular former Pearson-era Liberal cabinet minister by the same name, Martin grew up in Windsor, Ontario, and spent most of his life expanding empires. He is a doer, the kind of person who prides himself on getting things done in a creative and constructive way. While the department was essentially pushing him to accept the impotence of government in crucial areas such as job creation and social policy, Martin instinctively believed the opposite: that government had enormous sweep and power to do good in the country. In his youth, he had watched his father play a significant role in the building of Canada's social welfare system, although he self-deprecatingly admits now that he was probably paying more attention at the time to the fate of the Detroit Tigers. Given a choice, then, between getting out of the deficit dilemma by allowing the economy to grow—something that appealed to Martin anyway—or by gutting many of the programs that his own father had constructed, every bone in his body leaned towards the growth scenario.

But Martin was also ambitious. He understood that there would be no future to his political aspirations if he didn't hold on to the support he had traditionally enjoyed in the business and financial communities. And their agenda was unequivocally deficit reduction—by spending cuts. This was certainly the advice he was getting from Peter Nicholson, the adviser he had brought in from the Bank of Nova Scotia. Nicholson was highly effective, dealing deftly both with department officials and with Martin, and meshing their positions into a coherent package. Like Martin, Nicholson was not an economist and some of his arguments ranged beyond the scope of economic theory. But he, like Martin, had the knack for presenting ideas in a way that made them appear to be part of a broad vision. It was Nicholson who convinced Martin that tackling the deficit—not creating jobs—was the truly heroic, visionary course of action for the 1990s. That this was also the course favoured by Bay Street certainly added to the strength of its appeal.

With his first budget, delivered on February 22, 1994, only months into the new government's mandate, Martin showed himself still in the midst of some sort of inner struggle. The budget was a confusing mish-mash of both wishful thinking about economic growth, as well as program gutting in the name of deficit reduction. The main program gutting was a $2.4-billion cut to the already pared-down unemployment insurance (UI) system, making eligibility rules tighter and reducing benefit levels. Of course, in the view of Finance department economists, this cut could also be seen as a job-creation program; in the twisted logic of the NAIRU, the way to create jobs was to increase worker desperation, which cutting back UI payments certainly did. Thus, although the unemployed may not have realized it, they had much to be thankful for in this first Martin budget.

The UI cut would also have the effect of transferring a major burden of deficit reduction to the unemployed, who were being forced onto a more Spartan diet so that money could be saved for Ottawa's deficit reduction program. Of course, this was not what the UI plan had originally been designed to do. Paid for jointly by employers and employees, the system had been designed to assist workers during periods of joblessness, not to generate surpluses to pay for the government's revenue shortfalls. On the contrary, it had been structured so that if the deficit in the UI plan became too big, the government would make contributions to the plan out of general tax revenues. This was a way of ensuring that if unemployment rose too high, the whole country would be making a contribution to helping out the unemployed. It was also hoped it would act as a prod for governments to take the unemployment problem seriously; if unemployment were allowed to rise too high, governments would have to make a significant contribution to the costs.

The cuts to the UI system, first by the Mulroney Conservatives and now by the Liberals, turned this logic upside down. Instead of the rest of the country helping out the unemployed in difficult times, the unemployed were being called upon to help pay off the debts of the whole country. Indeed, by 1997, the further-pared-down UI plan, now absurdly renamed Employment Insurance, was generating an annual surplus of $4.5 billion—money that went straight into general deficit reduction.

Most of the rest of the program gutting was postponed until the next budget. In the meantime, Martin was projecting that the deficit would fall somewhat, mostly because, with lower interest rates, the economy would improve and tax revenues would grow over the following year. This formula—low interest rates creating stronger growth—was exactly the formula for deficit reduction that economists like Pierre Fortin and Doug Peters had recommended.

But it was evidently not the kind of deficit reduction that *The Globe and Mail* had in mind. Martin addressed a meeting of the *Globe*'s editorial board only about a week after the budget, when the general reaction to it was still fairly positive. (That is, the general reaction of media and business commentators was still fairly positive. It's unlikely that the tens of thousands of low-income families suddenly faced with losing their UI benefits and being forced onto welfare felt that positively about the budget.) But, apart from the *Globe*, most of the rest of the mainstream media, as well as Bay Street and Wall Street, were initially fairly supportive of Martin's first budget. At the meeting in the *Globe*'s editorial boardroom, Martin was confronted by editor-in-chief William Thorsell, who accused the Liberals of trying to use a growth strategy to shrink the deficit. *Say it ain't so!* While many Canadians would undoubtedly find merit in such a strategy, the idea was clearly anathema to senior *Globe* editors and writers, who had their hearts set on deep spending cuts. Martin was extremely defensive, arguing that he certainly wasn't relying exclusively on growth to shrink the deficit.

What is striking about Martin's meeting with the *Globe* editorial board is how single-minded the *Globe* side was. When one listens to a tape of the cantankerous, two-hour encounter, one is struck by how all the *Globe* editors, reporters and columnists who spoke at the meeting shared a single point of view. They accused Martin of not cutting the deficit deeply enough and twisting the numbers to make his cuts look deeper than they were. Much of it sounded as if Martin was being grilled by a group of professional accountants who had summoned him to defend his accounting methods. No one from the *Globe* asked a single question about the impact of the unemployment insurance cuts on Canadians or about whether a growth strategy might in fact work. If anyone at the meeting had harboured any thoughts along these lines, he or she clearly felt it was wise not to express them.

The most emotionally charged confrontation at the session was between Martin and Andrew Coyne, the *Globe*'s neoconservative gadfly, who had written the editorials relentlessly attacking the budget. Coyne has the rapier wit of a good high school debater, and he used it to try to debunk just about any notion that deviated even slightly from pure market orthodoxy. Like Martin, he was the son of a prominent Canadian figure who had played a major role in an earlier political era. But unlike Paul Martin Sr., who is associated with championing social programs, James Coyne, a former governor of the Bank of Canada, is known for his extreme anti-inflation policies that finally led to his public showdown with former prime minister John Diefenbaker. Coyne lost the showdown and resigned in semi-disgrace. His views have been taken up and defended with vigour by son Andrew. It would be hard to get much more committed to anti-inflation extremism than Andrew Coyne is.

Coyne is enormously assertive and not easily diverted from his line of argument. This helps explain why, at certain points in the meeting, he seemed to virtually take control of the session, essentially accusing Martin of being dishonest and gutless. He clearly got under Martin's skin.

After the meeting, Coyne's editorials continued unabated. The authors of *Double Vision* argue that the fractious meeting and Coyne's editorials had a significant impact in converting Martin to a deficit hawk. Certainly, the *Globe* added to the pressure on Martin, partly because the *Globe* has an impact on other media and financial commentators. Although most commentators had been quite gentle on Martin in the early weeks after his first budget, they came around to the *Globe*'s view that he had been timid in his deficit reduction. It is intriguing to speculate on how much Martin's deficit conversion may have been influenced by *The Globe and Mail*, which, after all, speaks for no one but itself and its fabulously rich owner, Ken Thomson. Responsibility for Martin's conversion perhaps even lies heavily with one zealous young *Globe* columnist who, in a strange way, may have finally achieved James Coyne's revenge.

ANDREW COYNE'S OBSTREPEROUS behaviour could not have been more helpful to the department economists in their quest to firm up Martin's anti-deficit resolve. They had only partly succeeded in achieving their aim with Martin's first budget, which they regarded as an acceptable first try at deficit reduction. But the next budget, in the winter of 1995, would have to be much tougher. It helped that Peters had been marginalized by this point, simply outmanoeuvred by more politically savvy department officials, so there was no longer a voice— even a soft-spoken one—within the department offering up any resistance to the deficit mania. Still, Coyne's shrill attacks were an added bonus. In his precocious and provocative way, Coyne was saying what the dull accountant types in the department had long been saying— and he was saying it publicly in a way that embarrassed Martin in front of the audience he most cared about.

Martin's full embrace of economic orthodoxy was signalled in the fall of 1994, with the release of a Finance department paper called "Agenda: Jobs and Growth"—also known as the "Purple Book." The book, released amid considerable fanfare, was widely considered to be a key to understanding the thinking within the department. Martin recalls that he himself was deeply involved in the writing of the Purple

Book, along with his executive assistant, Terrie O'Leary, and Peter Nicholson. Like many government papers, the title of this one provides little indication what the document is actually about. In fact "Agenda: Jobs and Growth" actually makes the case for rejecting a jobs-and-growth strategy. Full of pop references about "the globally integrated economy," "round-the-clock capital markets," the "revolution in technology based on the microchip," and "knowledge and information at the cutting edge," the Purple Book lays out the case *against* government fiscal or monetary action on the job front. It argues that the rise in Canadian unemployment rates over the past couple of decades has been caused by an increase in the "core rate of unemployment"—that is, the "rate of unemployment which cannot be forced lower without causing inflation to accelerate." This is, of course, pure NAIRU theory. The Purple Book even embellishes Milton Friedman's concept a little, strengthening his argument about the futility of using government stimulus to reduce unemployment.

Friedman had argued that stimulative government action—such as lowering interest rates or increasing government spending—might work in the short run but, by setting off inflation, it would fail *in the long run*. The exact meaning of "in the long run" was never defined, but the phrase conjured up notions of a far-off time. Perhaps worried that many Canadians might be more concerned with making their lives manageable *in the short run*, even if it meant taking their chances *in the long run*, the Finance department apparently felt the need to exaggerate how truly fleeting the good times would be. Hence the Purple Book argues that government stimulus would produce no extra jobs "except very temporarily"—making it sound as if the most that could be expected might be nothing more than an afternoon of work.

The Purple Book follows through with NAIRU theory by suggesting that governments *can* reduce unemployment—if they're willing to cut back those "disincentives" that have apparently lured Canadians out of the work-force in droves. Realizing that they are straying close to sensitive territory here, the Finance minister and his co-authors of the Purple Book are careful to acknowledge that popular support exists in Canada for "[p]rograms of income security—including Unemployment Insurance (UI), Workers' Compensation and various forms of social assistance." But such programs, the Purple Book continues cautiously, "are now understood to harbour features that can discourage the active search for work." And that's only the beginning. "Added to these disincentives has been a growing body of labour market regulation (largely provincial) designed to increase employment security and augmented by a body of legal precedent which has strengthened safeguards against arbitrary dismissal." One begins to get a sense of the scope of the problem.

With so many generous support systems out there, it was hard to imagine why anyone bothered working any more. Certainly, it was almost unthinkable that unemployment could be brought down below 8 percent. After all, many of the unemployed were simply not in the mood to work—too lazy, listless and unwilling to give up afternoons by the pool.

A whiff of this sort of thinking can be seen in an internal 1994 memo, in which David Dodge estimated the costs of unemployment for the previous year at roughly $45 billion. Ironically, Dodge's point was to show that other estimates—such as the one produced by the federal Human Resources Development department ($77 billion) and another one produced by the Ottawa-based Canadian Centre for Policy Alternatives ($109 billion)—were way off-base. Dodge is suggesting that the true costs of unemployment to the Canadian economy in 1993 were *only* $45 billion. *What a relief!* In fact, Dodge's estimate amounts to an extraordinary admission (in an internal document released only as a result of requests filed under Access to Information legislation) of the enormous costs to the economy of high unemployment.

But it also contains some insights into how the unemployed are viewed by senior department officials. Dodge's lower estimate is based on the notion that the natural rate of unemployment for the Canadian economy is somewhere around 8 percent. Thus, any amount of unemployment *above* this level is not, in the department's view, made up of regular, unemployed people who are willing and able to work.

Rather, it is made up of people who are somehow defective, and therefore their unemployment is not really that much of a loss to Canada's overall productivity. "[T]he productivity of the unemployed worker is typically much less than the average worker," he wrote in the memo. When contacted by a reporter for Southam News, Dodge tried vainly to explain his meaning, which, while completely obvious to economists in the department, was probably fairly incomprehensible to the general public, as well as being fairly insulting to the unemployed: "It's not saying that at 8.5 percent [unemployment] every unemployed worker out there's stupid, lazy or doesn't have a leg or something. . . . It's a problem that as you push below that natural rate of unemployment, what you're starting to do is . . . use labour less efficiently."

Martin's acceptance of NAIRU theory, evident in the Purple Book, set off alarm bells within the labour movement. The Canadian Labour Congress prepared a report outlining how negatively the application of NAIRU theory affects workers. CLC president Robert White expressed his concerns in a letter to Martin and included a copy of the CLC report. In his reply, Martin sounded almost like Patty Hearst during her abduction. He set out basic NAIRU theory: "Experience has shown that allowing inflation to rise does not create lasting jobs, it will only create more inflation. As prices go up wages follow, pushing prices up further in a spiral which gathers momentum." A NAIRU by any other name would smell as sweet.

Martin's letter, no doubt drafted by a department official, went on to essentially deny the entire thrust of the arguments that Liberals, led by Jean Chrétien and finance critic Herb Gray, had made with such passion in opposition. Martin himself had criticized the Bank of Canada's high interest rates for strangling growth and contributing to the recession. Now, after the department had apparently clarified a few points to him as minister, Martin had a completely revised view of the events responsible for that terrible recession.

He still thought that the events of the late 1980s had been a disaster for Canada, and assured White that he was determined to make sure "that we never repeat the experience of the late 1980s." But his assessment of what had gone wrong was now firmly rooted in NAIRU theory: "At that time growth was strong and job creation was rapid. *But as the unemployment rate fell below 8 percent,* firms began to experience serious difficulties getting qualified staff and inflationary wage pressures started to emerge. This was at a time when over a million Canadians were still unemployed. Simply put, the economy was not doing a good job of matching available workers with available jobs, in part because many individuals simply did not have the right skills or *had no incentive to take the available jobs.* That is why structural reforms are needed [italics added]."

In this revised version of events, the Bank of Canada and its policy of pushing up interest rates was apparently off the hook for the recession. Indeed, the only reference to the bank's anti-inflation campaign, which Liberals used to revile with such gusto, was his now-supportive position that the government and the bank "should continue their efforts to keep inflation low." Now, it seemed, responsibility for the 1990–91 recession lay heavily with the many Canadian workers who simply "had no incentive to take the available jobs." In other words, Canadian workers were not sufficiently desperate. Hence the need for "structural reforms," such as the cutbacks to the unemployment insurance system, which Martin delivered in his first budget. Since the UI system had been too generous in the late 1980s, Martin now apparently believed that the Bank of Canada had had little choice but to put up interest rates "as unemployment fell below 8 percent"—the magic NAIRU number. The lesson for avoiding such a devastating recession in the future? Remove more social supports.

Asked recently about the NAIRU, Martin was anxious to distance himself from the concept. "I think the NAIRU is theoretically of interest," he said. "From a practical point of view, it's of little consequence." Indeed, in February 1997, Martin publicly floated the idea that Canada's unemployment rate could and should drop to around 5 percent. Alarmed at such talk, the department economists quickly took steps to bring the minister back to his senses. Within a few days of Martin's reckless comment, he received a memo from the department, signed by deputy David Dodge, suggesting that he had been mistaken. "Could Canada's natural rate fall that low?" the memo asked. "The answer is, likely not without further changes to the structure of Canada's markets." When the memo became public—again through a request filed under Access to Information legislation—there was a brief flurry of media speculation about a rift between the minister and the department over the appropriate unemployment rate. Martin's response was to chastise the department for putting such rebukes of his statements in writing.

On the other hand, in some ways it can be useful for Martin to appear to be at odds with the more orthodox members of his department over the sensitive issue of unemployment. After all, the public wouldn't respond well to the department's view that 9 percent is about as low as unemployment can go before interest rates must be raised to ward off future inflation. So Martin doesn't mind looking more moderate on the issue. Asked if there was a difference of opinion between himself and the department over the NAIRU, Martin readily conceded, "Absolutely." Indeed, the Finance minister seems to be increasingly shy about endorsing the NAIRU concept in public.

But the real question, of course, is: does Martin shy away from endorsing the NAIRU concept in policy decisions? It appears not. In the summer and fall of 1997, Bank of Canada governor Gordon Thiessen raised interest rates four times despite the fact that there was virtually no inflation in the economy. The rate hikes were prompted by the drop in Canada's unemployment rate to 9 percent, triggering fears that it was inching dangerously close to the NAIRU. Did Martin agree with those interest rate hikes? "Yes, I do," he responded. While the NAIRU may not make for good politics, it apparently still forms government policy.

As Martin began to get the hang of the full mantra of economic orthodoxy, Finance officials were keen to prevent him from becoming confused by contrary points of view. So there was more than a little concern among senior department officials when the Goldman Sachs report, mentioned in Chapter 1, arrived in the department in

September 1994, just as the anti-deficit juggernaut was reaching its full momentum.

Written by senior Goldman Sachs analyst William Dudley, the paper questioned the severity of the Canadian deficit situation. It noted that what mattered in assessing a country's fiscal situation was not the sheer size of its budget deficit but the *sustainability* of its budget policies; that is, did the policies encourage the debt to shrink, relative to the size of the economy? Goldman Sachs was simply restating an established principle in public finance: as long as a government's debt is getting smaller, relative to the overall size of the economy, it is becoming more affordable. This is similar to the kind of private financial situations we can all easily understand: if one is making payments on a car, and one's income rises, the payments on the car become more affordable.

This way of looking at the debt gives a more meaningful understanding of its true size than simply reciting a lot of large numbers. After all, the size of the national debt is really only relevant to the size of the country and the country's ability to carry the financing charges. Again, it can be helpful to imagine a private financial dilemma: is a $25,000 car too expensive? For a bank teller earning $12,000 a year, probably yes. For a bank chairman earning $2.5 million a year, clearly no.

The Goldman Sachs report thus looked at the "gap" between government budgets and what is needed for "sustainability." And it concluded that "for Canada, the gap is relatively modest, at about 2 percent of GDP." It went on to make some international comparisons and found that Canada didn't look too bad, compared with many other advanced nations. "The fact that the budget gaps are smaller in Belgium and Canada than in France or the UK suggests that *the budgetary problems of Belgium and Canada may not be quite as severe as many assume* [italics added]."

Not helpful.

And it got worse. The Goldman Sachs report went on to note that even this assessment might overstate the seriousness of the budget situations of these countries. This was because the "budget gaps" being

measured didn't take into consideration how much slack the
an economy (that is, how big the "output gap" was, due to excessively
high unemployment). If a country has too much slack (i.e., too much
unemployment), then its budget gap is bigger than it needs to be. As
the report noted, "Thus, as countries move towards full employment,
the budgetary gap would tend to shrink."

In order to include this factor in its measurement, the Goldman
Sachs report proceeded to calculate something it called the Full
Employment Budget Gap (FEBG). By this, Goldman Sachs was measuring how big the budget gap would be, once Canada achieved full
employment. "On a FEBG basis, the budget gap of Canada vanishes."
Indeed, as the report went on to show, if Canada achieved full
employment, it would have one of the best deficit situations in the
world! "*Only the full employment budget gaps of Canada, Germany and
Japan are negative indicating that their budgetary situations are generally sustainable as long as their economies recover and they approach full
employment.*" (This suggests that Canada could have solved its deficit
problems without massive spending cuts—if it had achieved full
employment. We'll return to this subject later.)

So here was one of the most important Wall Street investment
houses lumping Canada in with fiscal superstars like Germany and
Japan, and arguing a position that would have sent Andrew Coyne
into a tantrum: essentially, Canada had a growth and unemployment
problem, not a government spending problem. Imagine if someone
had tried to float that one at a *Globe* editorial meeting.

This was hardly the kind of analysis that Finance officials were keen
to see bandied about, as they carefully marshalled their arguments for
deep spending cuts in the upcoming 1995 budget. Thus, Dodge felt the
need to send a memo to Martin alerting him to the danger, should the
Goldman Sachs document fall into the wrong hands.

The report also questioned whether Canadian interest rates needed
to be so high. It said that short-term rates were "far higher than what
was justified by the pace of economic activity and inflation." Furthermore, the notion that the Canadian government had to pay a large

"risk premium" to investors in order to get them to buy Canadian bonds—a constant theme of Finance department officials—was exaggerated, according to Goldman Sachs. "We find that the risk premium for Canada seems to be quite high relative to the severity of the budgetary situation."

A copy of the Goldman Sachs report went automatically to Doug Peters's office, although Peters was no longer a meaningful participant in the internal departmental discussion over the next budget. The report was of course right in line with everything Peters had been saying all along. It was gratifying to see these basic principles of public finance set out so nicely in a Wall Street study. "This is exactly the kind of paper we need now," Peters told an aide, his discreet countenance revealing only the slightest hint of glee.

SINCE MARTIN RELIED heavily on his senior departmental advisers—and *The Globe and Mail*—for his economic analysis, the Goldman Sachs report, in the end, had no impact. The direction of the budget was already clearly set by December 1994, when the Mexican peso crisis hit, providing high-octane fuel for the notion that all-powerful markets would punish countries that diverged from market orthodoxy. (Never mind that Mexico was a slave to market orthodoxy. The lesson drawn from Mexico was nevertheless that rigid adherence to market orthodoxy was essential.)

The budget Martin brought down in February 1995 slashed deeply into federal programs and transfer payments to the provinces, producing what would amount to a profound effect on just about every government program and service in the country. By the time all the cuts were to be phased in by 1998–99, Ottawa would have the lowest level of spending on government programs that it had had in fifty years. In case a return to the late 1940s doesn't sound so bad, it is important to remember that we didn't have medicare then, or much in the way of public pensions or unemployment insurance. Furthermore, the unemployment rate today is roughly double what it was back then, so we will have the same level of spending to handle social problems that are clearly much greater.

Double Vision treats the cutbacks as a happy ending. When Martin first became Finance minister, "he felt that markets were holding a gun to his head," the authors tell us. "He needed to build confidence to regain control." After the February 1995 budget, the markets and financial commentators, speaking on behalf of the markets, no longer attacked Martin. At times it even seemed as if he were on the fast track to Bay Street beatification. But was it because Martin had regained control, as *Double Vision* and the Finance department suggest? Or was it because Martin had given Bay Street exactly what it wanted, and there was no need to complain any more? Is that regaining control or is it simply caving in?

Certainly there was a happy ending as far as the *Globe* was concerned. Paul Martin returned for another post-budget session at the *Globe*'s editorial offices, this time to kudos. As Martin was about to leave the *Globe* building for a beer with David Olive, then-editor of *Report on Business Magazine*, William Thorsell himself came bounding down the escalator to present Martin with a giant blow-up of the magazine's next cover—featuring a flattering photo of the Finance minister. As *Double Vision* put it, "All was forgiven."

Just another heart-warming tale, showing that even politicians and journalists can be friends? Perhaps. Except the nagging question remains: were Martin's hands really tied, or did he have an alternative to turning the clock back fifty years, to a far more primitive level of government programs and all the suffering, social dislocation and inequality that that would entail?

We're told we are helpless in the face of pressures from international markets. Yet, after Martin's February 1994 budget, the markets seemed largely accepting. And in the crucial period before the devastating February 1995 budget, sophisticated economists such as Doug Peters, Pierre Fortin and Michael McCracken, president of the economic forecasting firm Informetrica—not to mention those at the

Wall Street headquarters of Goldman Sachs—were clearly saying Canada's budget situation wasn't as bad as many people maintained. Was it really the case that international financial markets dictated that there was no alternative? Or was it more a case of Andrew Coyne— and the other less notable media pundits like him—dictating that there was no alternative.

Is government really impotent, or has it simply been paying too much attention to Andrew Coyne?

THE CUTS IN THE 1995 budget were deeper than anything the Mulroney Tories had dared. The ultimate result, apart from great hardship for many who lost their jobs, was a shrinking of the public sphere. All the programs and facilities in the public domain—universities, schools, libraries, hospitals, community centres, parks, museums, transportation facilities, the arts—were left scrambling to make up for lost funding, reduced to begging for donations from the corporate sector. Furthermore, the removal of some $14 billion of government spending left the economy weak and consumer demand low.

To prop up the economy while it was undergoing these cuts, the Bank of Canada brought interest rates down after the 1995 budget. So, while the government spending cuts were keeping the economy in semi-recession, the lower interest rates were providing some stimulus. By late 1996, the official unemployment rate had fallen to 9.6 percent—a level most people still considered outrageously high. But, in some circles, there was a feeling that it was dropping ominously close to the NAIRU. Thus, it might soon be time for the Bank of Canada to start thinking about pushing interest rates back up to ward off potential inflation. But were Paul Martin and Gordon Thiessen sufficiently committed to low inflation that they would be willing to risk jettisoning the fragile economic "recovery" by raising interest rates?

This question weighed heavily on the minds of a small group of academic economists and policy makers who had provided key intellectual support in the past for the Bank of Canada's war on inflation. As this group was well aware, the existing inflation targets covered only the period up to the end of 1998, so the target would soon once again be up for review. The group therefore made plans to come together for a special meeting at the C.D. Howe Institute in October 1996, in the hopes of once again providing crucial support for the bank's fierce anti-inflation campaign, and ensuring that the Liberal government wasn't pushed off track by popular pressure for things like jobs.

CHAPTER FOUR

Gordon Thiessen and the Machismo Thing

Among the monetary mandarins at the Federal Reserve, it is a long-held dogma that too much employment can be a dangerous thing.
—*Business Week,* November 27, 1995

La meilleure façon de tuer un homme est de le mettre en chômage.
—Felix Leclerc

THE GATHERING AT THE lovely old yellow-brick building of the C.D. Howe Institute in downtown Toronto was as mainstream (one could say "establishment") as the 1993 Sudbury gathering of economic dissidents had been marginal (or "anti-establishment"). The institute boasts that it is "independent," and this is true, in a sense. Certainly, it is independent *of government.* But the flipside is that it is fully dependent on private donations, which come almost entirely from the business and financial sector—all listed in the back of its publications like a who's who of the Canadian financial world.

The participants at this C.D. Howe gathering in the fall of 1996 were economists from major banks, investment houses, the insurance industry, government; those making presentations at the event were mostly academic, university-based economists. Almost all were strong supporters of NAIRU theory and advocates of very low levels of inflation, sometimes called "zero inflation" or "price stability." This group could be said to have played an important role in keeping this low-inflation orthodoxy in place in Canadian public policy, by providing key intellectual back-up and support.

Many of them had contributed to an influential volume published by the C.D. Howe Institute in 1990, explicitly endorsing Canada's decision to take on the ambitious goal of eliminating inflation. Since debate over such decisions is restricted to a small group in rarefied academic, financial and government circles, the enthusiastic support of these academics in *Zero Inflation: The Goal of Price Stability* had had a big impact. Now, six years later, they had come to revisit the territory. With the whole issue soon to be reviewed by government, the economists were keen to once again play a pivotal role.

It would be fair to say that as they discussed the issue at the C.D. Howe gathering, the economists weren't given to a lot of self-doubt or self-criticism. It quickly became clear they had no intention of holding themselves to account for anything that had happened with their active encouragement. While acknowledging that the tight monetary policy they had advocated had had "costs," they indicated that they would not be dwelling on these costs. The tone at the conference was set by Peter Howitt, formerly an economist with the University of Western Ontario and now with Ohio State University, who stuck to the NAIRU theory that the costs were "transient" (short-term pain for long-term gain).

Perhaps what was most striking about the meeting was how loyal the economists remained to the goal of zero inflation—even while acknowledging that there was little proof that it offered any significant benefits. For instance, Howitt, a keen, longtime advocate of zero inflation, conceded that "a good case can be made to the effect that if the transition to low inflation is too hurried or is otherwise mismanaged, the costs can well exceed the benefits." Having tossed out this provocative little bone, however, Howitt moved immediately to close off any further inquiry on this line of thinking: "I shall not consider them [the costs] for the simple reason that they are bygones. Whether or not they exceeded the benefits is an interesting historical question." It is hard to resist adding that to hundreds of thousands of Canadians who lost their jobs in Ottawa's quest for zero inflation, this might seem like more than "an interesting historical question."

It was not surprising that Howitt would decide to let bygones be bygones. The record—after half a decade of Ottawa's efforts to push inflation down close to zero—was not inspiring, to say the least. It was certainly not terrain that Howitt wanted to cover. He was well aware that sitting in the audience was Pierre Fortin, the most academically distinguished critic of the Bank of Canada's zero inflation policy. Fortin was someone who couldn't be ignored on the subject of monetary policy. When the C.D. Howe's book *Zero Inflation* was compiled in 1990, Fortin had been invited to make a contribution, although on the highly technical, relatively innocuous subject of how inflation should be measured. So while the other contributors used their space in the volume to argue the case for zero inflation, Fortin did as he was told and restricted his contribution to a discussion of highly technical issues related to his assigned task, such as "the volatility of the owned-accommodation index" and the "ratio between the consumer price index and the fixed-weight GDP deflator." With Fortin thus deflected to technicalities, he offered no opinion on the key question being discussed in the volume: should the Bank of Canada adopt a zero inflation strategy? As a result, the volume ended up looking like a unanimous endorsement of zero inflation by the leading academics in the field. Anyone reading it could easily be left with the impression that the only debate among serious economists was whether inflation should be reduced to zero or merely to near zero.

Since then, however, Fortin had become very outspoken on the issue. This time, the C.D. Howe gathering had apparently felt obliged to let him make a "comment" on Howitt's presentation—balanced by a comment from former Bank of Canada governor John Crow, who was also attending the conference. Howitt knew that Fortin was going to be forceful in his criticism. It was only four months since Fortin had delivered a devastating critique of Canada's anti-inflation policy in his presidential address to the Canadian Economics Association's annual meeting.

Bank of Canada officials and their C.D. Howe supporters had learned to live with Fortin's barbs, even the particularly stinging attack in his presidential address. However, what they had not been prepared for, only two months later, was a sharp rebuke from a leading U.S. expert in the widely read British magazine *The Economist*. To their horror, *The Economist* had run a three-page article by internationally known economist Paul Krugman, a professor at MIT in Boston. Krugman's piece, promoted on the cover of the magazine, was a harsh critique of the zero inflation policy, arguing that there was little evidence of the benefits and lots of evidence of the costs, and that those who supported it largely did so on "faith." Krugman wrote, "The evidence actually points the other way: the benefits of price stability are elusive, the costs of getting there are large, and zero inflation may not be a good thing even in the long run."

Even more stinging for Bank of Canada officials was the fact that Krugman focused his attack mostly on Canada. So here, in a magazine that was almost a bible to economists all over the world, the Bank of Canada was being singled out as a central bank that had followed this disastrous path, largely on faith. "Consider the case of Canada," Krugman wrote, "a nation whose central bank is intensely committed to the goal of price stability." Krugman argued that because of this, the unemployment gap between Canada and the United States "has continued to widen" and that the "Bank of Canada's anti-inflationary zeal . . . is costing [Canadians] hundreds of thousands of jobs."

Given this kind of recent, high-profile attack on the effects of Canada's experiment with zero inflation, Howitt was careful to keep the focus of his presentation away from the negative evidence of recent years and largely focused on theory. He proceeded to trot out almost exactly the same set of arguments for zero inflation that he had made in the 1990 C.D. Howe volume. And his arguments were as lame this time as they had been in 1990. For instance, he argued, as he had six years earlier, that "the biggest gain from low inflation is that it allows us to avoid the distorting effects of a variable measure of value in conventional accounting practices." And to think we struggled by as a nation all those years with such distortion in our accounting practices! Would it not make more sense to make some adjustments to our accounting methods, rather than to force hundreds of thousands of people into unemployment in order to correct this ghastly problem?

Here's another one of Howitt's key arguments about the horrors of inflation: it has the effect of attracting bright people into socially unproductive work in the financial sector, where they can earn huge incomes figuring out ways to take advantage of the distorting effects of inflation. "In times of low inflation, the best and the brightest become engineers and researchers rather than derivatives traders." Really? After five years of near-zero inflation in Canada, there hasn't been a noticeable exodus from Bay Street financial houses to research and engineering. On the contrary, the financial sector is booming while research and engineering have been depressed—in part because the tight monetary policy, advocated by Howitt and others, has strangled growth in the real economy while making financial assets ever more valuable.

After ten pages of outlining every theoretical argument he could think of, Howitt was left with a pretty lukewarm case, as even he conceded. "Overall, while there is plenty of evidence consistent with the view that low inflation is producing long-lasting economic benefits in Canada, it is certainly not overwhelming, and all of it is open to alternative interpretations." For instance, Howitt became quite excited about the "striking evidence of the beneficial effects of low inflation in the labour market"—that is, the reduction in strike activity. But he also acknowledged that there might well be an alternative explanation for this—namely, that workers weren't striking as much not because low inflation made them content but because high unemployment, caused by the war on inflation, had put them in a very weak bargaining position.

This raises an interesting question. Is the real advantage of low inflation the weaker bargaining position of workers, caused by the anti-inflation crusade? If so, then the benefits of low inflation may be restricted to certain groups in society—such as employers—and may come at the expense of other groups—such as employees. Of course, Howitt, being an academic, would never want to be seen to be openly championing the interests of one group in society—particularly the most powerful—over another. So he steered clear of justifying the zero inflation policy on the grounds that it weakens the power of labour, even though this is clearly one of its main consequences. Altogether, Howitt was left without much to hang his hat on. "In summary, there is some evidence of large benefits from maintaining a low inflation rate, and also some evidence of large costs, but none of this evidence is at all conclusive." Well, there's a policy we can all get behind.

Still, Howitt soldiered on. In a final attempt to come up with some kind of cost–benefit analysis, Howitt turned to a study by Harvard University economist Robert Barro, who looked at inflation and growth in more than one hundred countries over a twenty-five-year period. Barro found that the beneficial effects of low inflation on economic growth were actually quite small. But Howitt figured that since these benefits would last forever, as NAIRU theory alleges, they would end up being very significant over time. Howitt did some quick calculations and concluded that in the long run, the net benefits would be very large—although he twice warned that his calculation of the benefits "must be taken with extreme caution."

Howitt concluded his presentation with an admission that the case for zero inflation is essentially non-existent. "Assessing the costs and benefits of maintaining a low inflation rate is subject to even more uncertainty than is usual in economic policy analysis. . . . It is fair to say that, given the present state of economic knowledge, there is no way to present overwhelming evidence for either a permanent benefit or a permanent cost of maintaining inflation at its current low rate or even reducing it to zero." So why don't we all just fold our tents and go home?

Note that Howitt does not deny that there are costs to maintaining low inflation, namely high unemployment. The question is simply whether these costs would be long term (as critics suggest) or merely short term (as NAIRU theory suggests). But, given that the costs exist—whether short term or long term—why wouldn't one err on the side of caution? Given the short-term unemployment costs alone and the absence of any clear long-term benefits, one might expect a careful academic to conclude that, for now at least, we don't have enough evidence to justify keeping so many people out of work. But no. Howitt, despite his training as a social scientist, is prepared to go on faith alone. Immediately after admitting there was no conclusive long-term evidence one way or the other, he offered his "opinion." Stick with low inflation, he advised, and "await further evidence." Needless to say, this is the kind of position that would be argued only by someone with a full-time job.

The reason, he explained, was that "Canada has by all accounts paid an enormous cost to establish it [low inflation]." Here he skirted awfully close to getting into that danger zone of discussing "bygones," but he quickly moved on. "Thus," he continued, "it would be highly imprudent to throw away all the hard-earned progress against inflation in the hope of achieving a speedier reduction of unemployment." But couldn't one just as easily argue that given the enormous price we've paid in lost jobs and missed growth, perhaps we should cut our losses and bail out before we create even more suffering for those who have borne the brunt of all this extra unemployment?

Howitt's weak case in favour of maintaining very low inflation is even weaker after Fortin has had his chance to comment. Barro's multi-country study—which had perhaps been Howitt's strongest argument (although, as he admitted, an argument that had to be viewed with "extreme caution")—turns out to have little relevance for Canada. As Fortin notes, the vast majority of the countries Barro studied had high inflation rates, above 15 percent per year, whereas Canada's inflation rate has been mostly below 2 percent for the past five years. If these high-inflation countries are left out of Barro's sample, the benefits of reducing inflation become completely insignificant. As Fortin cryptically points out, "It is far from obvious that the recent experiences of Bolivia, Haiti, Nicaragua, Sierra Leone, Turkey, Western Samoa, and Zaire with high inflation contain any useful lessons for the current debate on Canadian monetary policy."

Indeed, there is little evidence to support the assumption that low inflation spurs economic growth—an assumption strongly held in Canadian government circles. A recent IMF study looked at eighty-seven countries from 1970 to 1990. Like Barro's study, the IMF's concluded that high levels of inflation did hurt an economy, while low levels were fairly harmless. The IMF paper, by economist Michael Sarel, concluded that below 8 percent, inflation had either no effect or a slightly positive effect on growth. It found scant evidence of beneficial effects from inflation ranging from 1 to 3 percent a year—the range Howitt was arguing should be maintained in Canada. A study done by two Montreal economists, Steve Ambler and Emanuela Cardia, which was presented at a recent Bank of Canada conference, found no evidence to support the bank's contention that low inflation encourages economic growth.

Fortin also attacked Howitt and the other zero inflation advocates for failing to include in their calculations the real costs of unemployment on individuals. He acknowledged that such an approach might "raise eyebrows among economists," who are far more comfortable discussing the distorting effect of inflation on prices than the traumatic effect of unemployment on people. This blind spot is somewhat curious, though. Even if economists feel queasy getting into what they might consider fuzzy, unscientific areas like measuring the devastating impact unemployment can have on a person's self-esteem or the long-term impact poverty can have on the children of the unemployed, there seems to be no reason economists can't at least take into consideration the straightforward, quantifiable costs of unemployment on an individual's *financial* well-being.

If we consider just these private financial costs, Fortin argued, the costs borne by the unemployed, as Ottawa experiments with zero inflation, are horrendous. After all, workers who end up unemployed suddenly lose their entire incomes. They usually have to wait a number of weeks before they can start collecting unemployment benefits, and the benefits amount to only slightly more than half of their previous incomes. And this is the best-case scenario—the fate of the lucky ones who actually qualify for unemployment benefits. About 40 percent of unemployed workers no longer qualify, leaving them to the mercy of relatives or dwindling welfare programs. All this might have seemed rather remote to those at the C.D. Howe gathering.

There is an added irony in these economists shying away from dealing with the social costs of unemployment, apparently because such costs are hard to measure and therefore are unscientific. In the end, it is Howitt's case that is truly unscientific. As he himself acknowledged, he can't really make a case, on the basis of evidence, to justify his support for a policy of maintaining very low inflation. And yet, even though there is clear evidence of significant *costs* from this policy, Howitt decides to rely on his "opinion" that we should stick with it anyway, since the country has already paid such a high price to get this far. The problem with this, according to Fortin, is that it is a game that goes on forever. "Each passing year is seen as proof that progress against inflation is more and more 'hard-earned' and therefore costly to jettison, and that one more year of pain is needed before the costs begin to go away and the benefits start to take over. . . . In this way we are sure to [ac]cumulate net costs forever."

Fortin's arguments, which might seem compelling to many people, had virtually no impact on the C.D. Howe gathering. As a group, they seemed much more inclined to support the position suggested by Howitt, and even the more extreme one advocated by John Crow. In his comment, Crow argued that inflation should be brought down further, and right away. "[T]here is no need to wait until 1998 to do it," said the former central bank governor, without any indication that he has ever had the slightest doubt about the usefulness of the radical experiment he conducted on the Canadian economy. Crow criticized the more moderate approach to inflation control taken by Alan Greenspan, chairman of the Federal Reserve Board, the U.S. central bank. Greenspan had said that he considered inflation low enough when it "ceases to be a significant factor affecting economic decisions." Crow, in his comments to the C.D. Howe gathering, explicitly rejected this more moderate approach and called instead for "price stability," which he defined as "a state of confidently held expectations about the *absence* of inflation [italics added]."

The final word at the C.D. Howe gathering was given to Michael Parkin, another economist from the University of Western Ontario, which in recent years has been something of a hotbed of anti-inflation extremism. Trying to pull together a consensus from the conference, Parkin offered, "Looking forward from where we now stand, the weight of professional opinion points strongly to the view that the permanent benefits of price stability outweigh any costs." Parkin doesn't even bother mentioning Howitt's caveats that there's no evidence to back up this case, which presumably lies at the heart of what the conference was all about. Better to send everyone home without a lot of doubts in their minds.

Parkin's parting thought is about what he considers "our biggest challenge . . . to find a way of formalizing the relationship between the Bank and the government to ensure that price stability continues to be the Bank's primary concern so that 'a state of confidently held expectations about the absence of inflation' can be established"— John Crow's exact words! This is a bold and astonishing conclusion. Parkin wants to "ensure" that the primary goal of Canada's monetary policy is to achieve John Crow's extreme definition of inflation control. But wait! John Crow is no longer running the Bank of Canada, because the elected government in Ottawa wasn't able to get him to accept more moderate inflation targets, which is apparently more in keeping with what job-hungry Canadians want and what the Liberals campaigned on. Yet Parkin is suggesting that the "biggest challenge" facing this élite little group is to come up with a way to make sure the government and the central bank can succeed in implementing Crow's extremist vision anyway.

As the economists left the C.D. Howe meeting freshly invigorated in their determination to keep the zero inflation dream alive, one thing was clear: they weren't terribly concerned about getting a lot of input from the public on all this.

～

IT IS RARELY OBVIOUS at first glance, but much of monetary policy is about machismo. Or at least one could say that those who govern central banks—almost all of them men, up to this point in history—seem to feel that proving themselves and the fierceness of their resolve against inflation is key to their success. From the beginning of his term heading the Bank of Canada, this posed a problem for Gordon Thiessen, who, fairly or unfairly, was considered by some to be a bit of a wimp.

When Alan Greenspan was appointed Federal Reserve chairman by the Reagan administration in August 1987, he wasted little time proving his manhood. Greenspan's desire to show anti-inflation toughness to his Wall Street audience partly reflected his fear that because of his close Republican ties, the financial markets wouldn't trust him to shore up the unpopular anti-inflation battle while the Republicans were hoping to win re-election. Market lore had not forgotten Arthur Burns, the Nixon-appointed Fed chairman who was often criticized for tolerating inflation in the 1970s in order to co-operate with White House calls for faster growth.

Out of an apparent desire to show he was nobody's patsy, Greenspan jacked up interest rates half a percentage point almost as soon as he found his way to the spacious chairman's office inside the grand, columned Federal Reserve Building just down the way from Congress. The move caught markets by surprise; it is often said in glossy business magazines that that rate hike contributed to the stock market crash in October 1987. But all was forgiven on Wall Street when Greenspan made it clear that he would pump needed money into the system to prevent the collapse of financial institutions. He did so, and the markets quickly recovered. Greenspan was viewed as being off to an impressive start, having passed through his rite of manhood without bringing down a single bank or creating a major recession.

It may seem odd that Greenspan felt the need to prove his independence, as some of his close associates believe. In reality, he has always been his own man, an enormously strong and self-possessed character. After growing up in poverty in New York during the Depression and quitting a Ph.D. program in economics for lack of tuition, he had become an economic forecaster, quickly excelling through sheer brilliance. Sadly, there wasn't an ounce of charisma in the man. But he spoke about the economy with such a breadth of understanding and a grasp of detail that he quickly intimidated just about everyone he met—including Richard Nixon, who was introduced to Greenspan by Leonard Garment, Nixon's law partner and former manager of a jazz band that Greenspan had briefly played in years earlier. This would have seemed like the crucial break for the young economist, deeply impressing a man who was in the process of running for president. Greenspan did some volunteer work on Nixon's campaign, and when Nixon won, Greenspan was well positioned for the perks generally offered to brilliant young men who put in voluntary campaign service for the winning presidential candidate. But Greenspan declined attractive offers to work in the Nixon administration. As it turned out, he hadn't worked on the campaign to get a plum White House job. Rather, he had been drawn to the campaign simply because he liked Nixon's strong rhetoric about the need to control inflation.

Greenspan was like that: principled, independent, marching to his own drum. If there was another drum he marched to, it didn't belong to those in power but to the writer Ayn Rand, who wrote novels to popularize her fervent free-market beliefs. Greenspan had been heavily influenced by Rand in the 1950s when he joined an intense group of intellectuals who met regularly with Rand to discuss her ideas and review her work. Rand's novels usually included a hero-entrepreneur who triumphed in his dream to achieve some grand personal goal— building a steel mill or founding a railway empire—despite the interference of small-minded bureaucrats or do-good social activists.

Inflation was seen as an evil that would strip these natural-born leaders of their well-deserved financial rewards. Greenspan remained a devotee and promoter of Rand's philosophy, even writing articles and making speeches to spread her ideas. Although he apparently lacked the personal greatness of a Rand hero himself, Greenspan could make an important contribution in the years ahead, particularly after his appointment to the top job at the Federal Reserve. By keeping a firm grip on inflation as chairman of the Fed, he could help make the world a safer place for a Rand hero.

The task of proving himself was more daunting for Gordon Thiessen. Unlike Greenspan, Thiessen, who became governor of the Bank of Canada in February 1994, had to fight all the way to head off a reputation as a wimp. Born in the small northern Ontario mining town of South Porcupine, Thiessen grew up mostly on the prairies. After high school graduation, he joined the Royal Bank, working at branches in small communities like Wapella and Eyebrow, Saskatchewan, before heading off to study at the University of Saskatchewan and eventually to England to do a Ph.D. at the London School of Economics.

Like another small-town prairie banker who ended up in a high-level economic policy position in Ottawa in the 1990s, Thiessen was soft-spoken and very pleasant to deal with. But it wasn't just his manner that branded him as a softie. It was the difficulty of emerging from the shadow of his predecessor, John Crow, who had ruled over the bank with an imperiousness and arrogance that left no question in anyone's mind who was in charge.

The central bank was a very hierarchical place to begin with. (When guests are invited for lunch in the bank's dining room, they are seated at the end of a long, formal table, next to the governor's seat at the head. Bank officials are arranged on both sides of the table—in descending order of rank.) Under Crow, the bank had been even more hierarchical than usual. Crow simply dominated everything within the bank. Secondary officials rarely voiced an opinion. Although the bank boasted a research staff of several dozen specialized economists,

Crow largely ignored the work they turned out, relying on his own interpretation of economic developments.

At the regular Tuesday luncheon meetings between senior bank officials and senior Finance staff, it was rare for anyone from the bank but Crow to speak. On one such occasion, Don Drummond, assistant deputy minister of Finance, arrived at the bank for the luncheon and went to sit on a large empty sofa at the side of the reception room. A number of senior bank officials were crowded onto loveseats or less comfortable chairs. Drummond sat down at one end of the sofa. Embarrassment all round, until someone explained that that was where Crow sat. The following week, Drummond sat at the other end of the same large empty sofa, and was again told he was in Crow's seat. The next week, Drummond was foolish enough to sit in the middle before realizing that despite the limited seating capacity of the room, the entire sofa was for Crow.

No one ever questioned Crow's commitment to inflation control. It was under Crow in 1988 that the Bank of Canada adopted a radical policy aimed at eliminating inflation. Even among central bankers Crow was an extremist, rigidly adopting Milton Friedman's notion that economic growth and employment must be sacrificed to the greater good of inflation control. As *Canadian Banker*, the banking industry's magazine, put it, "He [Crow] was the first central banker of a major nation to insist that monetary policy should not be designed to promote economic growth; rather its sole objective should be price stability." While this set of priorities had meshed nicely with those of former Conservative Finance ministers Michael Wilson and Don Mazankowski, it seemed likely to pose problems for Liberal Paul Martin, who had spent much of his time both in business and politics extolling the virtues of economic growth.

There turned out to be less friction between Martin and Crow than many had anticipated. Martin spoke well of Crow at the *Globe* editorial board meeting. Under intense questioning from Andrew Coyne, Martin insisted, "I've got a lot of time for John Crow." Just as, once in power, Martin came to see the importance of deficit reduction, so he also became much more willing to see merit in what Crow was trying to accomplish with his high interest rates. By the time Martin became Finance minister in the fall of 1993, much of the really brutal work had already been done. With inflation now subdued by Crow's gladiator-like performance, it seemed that the road ahead would be somewhat easier.

The key financial players on Bay Street felt strongly that Martin should reappoint Crow as governor when his term expired in January 1994. The chairmen of the big banks had made the trek to Ottawa as a group to meet with Martin and Peters to advise the new ministers of the importance they attached to Crow's reappointment. (Even Richard Thomson, the TD chairman who had had to endure the most insulting one and three-quarter hours of his life in Crow's presence, was there as part of the unified bankers' front.) With such a heavy-weight crowd backing Crow's reappointment, Martin set about trying to make it work.

Martin and Crow weren't really that far apart as negotiations got underway. The existing targets, which Crow had negotiated with Michael Wilson, were for an inflation rate ranging between 1 and 3 percent. But Crow wanted to tighten the monetary screws a little fur-ther, replacing those targets with more stringent ones. He had in mind 0.5 to 2.5 percent. This may sound like splitting hairs, but in fact the discrepancy was important. It meant the difference between the bank aiming for about a 2 percent inflation rate, the midpoint of the exist-ing target range, or just 1.5 percent, the midpoint of the proposed range. The difference is significant because as inflation moves lower, it is harder and harder to squeeze out the last remaining traces of it. Bringing it down an extra half percentage point, when it was already under 3 percent, could require painful interest rate hikes.

Still, Martin was not ruling out the new targets, which he felt he might be able to live with. Indeed, by early December 1993, after weeks of discussions, Finance and the central bank were still locked in nego-tiations over the new target zone. As Martin chaired an unusual meet-ing of several dozen economists he had summoned to Ottawa's

Congress Centre to discuss the economy, senior Finance officials were still faxing proposed drafts of the inflation agreement to Crow, in a last-ditch attempt to hammer out acceptable terms. In the end, Crow wasn't satisfied.

Martin's decision to appoint Thiessen—Doug Peters had proposed someone right outside the bank, like respected Bay Street economist Lloyd Atkinson—was as close as one could come to appointing Crow without actually doing so. With his years of service at the most senior levels of Crow's administration, Thiessen was clearly no maverick. Little was known about him and his views, since he had not had much of a public presence, always lurking in the darkness of Crow's shadow. Thiessen's pleasant, non-aggressive manner had made him seem particularly demure next to the haughty governor. Still, it was a safe bet that as Crow's second-in-command, Thiessen must have either enjoyed being subjected to a good lecture or shared the governor's fervour for inflation control. It seemed clear that one could comfortably assume that Thiessen, having survived as second-in-command for seven years under Crow, was a bit of a yes-man.

The financial community was satisfied by Thiessen's credentials as an anti-inflation zealot who had risen through the ranks under the tutelage of the great master, but there were still fears that he might prove to lack backbone on his own. What if he simply transferred his obedience to a new master—Paul Martin, whose campaign talk of "growth" and "employment" still haunted those on Bay Street? When Martin finally announced Thiessen's appointment in late December 1993, those in the Finance department braced themselves, fully expecting the financial community to show its disapproval by selling Canadian dollars, driving down the price. When the dust settled the next day, inexplicably, the dollar had risen.

But Thiessen still hadn't proven himself. In cocktail conversations at the National Club, in lunches at Canoe, even at the chip wagon in front of the Finance department building, the term "wimp" was often carelessly bandied about. Proof to the contrary was needed and, thankfully, an opportunity soon presented itself. In March, less than two months after Thiessen had taken over at the bank, the U.S. Fed raised interest rates slightly to head off fears of imminent inflation there. U.S. unemployment was dropping, getting awfully close to the magic 6 percent rate that many economists considered was the NAIRU for the United States.

The Canadian situation was dramatically different, however. Unemployment was still above 10 percent, only slightly below its alarming 1993 average of 11.2 percent. With such a huge reserve army of the unemployed to keep inflation at bay, few sensible Canadians feared inflation. Still, the Canadian financial community always grew concerned whenever U.S. interest rates went up, fearing that if Canadian rates didn't follow, there would be a drop in the value of financial assets denominated in Canadian dollars, which were held in large numbers by themselves and their clients. For most ordinary Canadians, who held little in the way of financial assets, this was of little concern. What was of great concern to these ordinary Canadians was jobs, and jobs would be greatly threatened if the Bank of Canada followed the Fed in raising interest rates.

For Thiessen, however, the moment had arrived. Here was an opportunity to show the financial community just how tough he could be. After all, any pantywaist could raise interest rates when there was full employment and serious inflation to contend with. But it took someone with real swagger to raise interest rates at a time like this, when there were already so many people out of work—and there was no realistic fear of inflation! That took guts. It was high noon and Thiessen, tall in the saddle, pushed up Canadian interest rates. "He had to do it, or be viewed as a wimp," said one high-level Finance official in a matter-of-fact way. It apparently worked; the financial community was impressed. Thiessen had shown that his new master would be the market, and that he would serve it as faithfully as he had served John Crow.

In fairness, Thiessen had agreed to the "looser" inflation targets of 1 to 3 percent, which had been rejected by John Crow. In practice, however, he has kept monetary conditions tight, and inflation generally below 2 percent—where Crow wanted it kept. This hasn't involved high interest rates. On the contrary, Thiessen has brought interest rates down significantly. This may seem a little confusing and has perhaps led the public to believe that the bank has abandoned its extremism under Thiessen. In fact, the bank has not abandoned the central obsession that motivated Crow—achieving very low or no inflation. The high interest rates that Crow imposed on the economy were never an end in themselves, but a means for achieving low inflation. Crow kept interest rates high in order to slow down the economy and kill inflation.

Thiessen, on the other hand, inherited the economy after Crow had succeeded in rendering it virtually lifeless—and inflation-free. By the time Thiessen took over in early 1994, Crow's fingerprints were all over the economy; his high-interest-rate medicine had succeeded in bringing down inflation (from 4.5 percent to under 2 percent), while driving unemployment up (from 7.5 percent to above 11 percent). Having swelled the ranks of the unemployed so greatly, Crow passed on to Thiessen an economy that faced little danger of inflation. Since the reserve army of the unemployed has remained so large, Thiessen hasn't had to do much to keep inflation low. Even so, he's been quick on the trigger, pushing interest rates up in the latter part of 1997, despite the lack of any realistic prospect of inflation. In a speech in Boston in September 1997, Thiessen talked openly about the need for such "pre-emptive" strikes in order to "maintain a low and stable rate of inflation in the period ahead." So the Bank of Canada under Thiessen has not really changed its stripes.

Back in the United States, Greenspan seems to have done things differently. Although he came to office with a reputation as an inflation hawk, he has led the Federal Reserve on a more moderate course than the Bank of Canada. He has never set explicit inflation targets. And in practice, he has let inflation run at just below 3 percent a year—almost double the Canadian rate of the past few years. Furthermore, Greenspan has even defied NAIRU orthodoxy. As U.S. unemployment dropped close to—and then even below—the generally agreed NAIRU, Greenspan resisted cries for interest rate hikes to pre-empt a feared upsurge in inflation. As the U.S. unemployment rate dipped below 5 percent in the spring of 1997, Greenspan still refused to budge. And, interestingly, inflation just kept chugging along at just below 3 percent. The fabled acceleration of inflation, much heralded by Friedman, didn't materialize.

One must be careful, of course, not to view the United States too favourably. To say unemployment dipped below 5 percent can be misleading. One has only to walk through any U.S. inner city to see that the percentage of adults who are not gainfully employed is well above 5 percent, and it's not because they've chosen to spend more time in cultural pursuits. Clearly, millions of Americans have simply fallen, or been pushed, out of the mainstream and now live horrible, deprived lives on the margins of society. But these people do not fit the official definition of "looking for work" and therefore don't show up as unemployed in the statistics. Furthermore, one of the reasons for the lower U.S. unemployment rate is that a much larger percentage of the American population is in prison, where they no longer qualify as "unemployed" since, by definition, they can't be looking for work. Americans are imprisoned at a rate five times higher than Canadians. This is not exactly a desirable method of reducing the national unemployment rate.

Besides, just because the United States has a lower unemployment rate doesn't for a moment mean that its citizens are better off, even in a material sense. They are not. Indeed, low-income Americans are much worse off than low-income Canadians because the U.S. social welfare system is so glaringly inadequate. A study done by Michael Wolfson of Statistics Canada, with the co-operation of the U.S. Census Bureau, reveals that most Canadians are financially better off than most Americans. This may come as a surprise; we tend to think of Americans as richer. In fact, the rich in the United States are considerably richer than the rich in Canada, so when they are added into the overall picture, it appears as if Americans are generally richer. But it is simply that the American rich are so well off that they bring up the

U.S. average. When the rich are left out, Canadians are doing better than Americans. As Wolfson notes, "[R]oughly half to two-thirds of Canadian families had disposable incomes in 1995 giving them higher purchasing power than their U.S. counterparts."

The superiority of Canadian living standards for most of the population is even clearer when we add in benefits that are difficult to measure in dollar terms, such as access to health care. One interesting measure of this was a 1997 study, published in the *American Journal of Public Health*, showing how low-income Canadians have much higher cancer survival rates than low-income Americans, largely because they have more access to public health care. Not only do most Canadians have more disposable cash than most Americans, they also have better access to vital services.

It is important to keep this kind of difference in mind in any Canada–United States comparison. The ultimate goal, surely, is to create a society that benefits its citizens. Keeping unemployment low is one very important way to do this, since it provides people with a means of support and also a sense of purpose and belonging to the community. Providing adequate social systems—particularly when the private marketplace generates such inequality even when people are working—is another crucial feature of a well-functioning society. To achieve low unemployment without improving the lives of the nation's people is a hollow victory.

Although the United States has much to learn from Canada (or even more from European countries) when it comes to social welfare systems, Canada has something to learn from the United States when it comes to the crucial area of monetary policy and its impact on unemployment. Many critics—including the late William Vickrey— have argued that U.S. unemployment could be lower still, especially when one considers how much unemployment fails to show up in the official figures. Still, compared with the extremist approach taken in Canada since the late 1980s, the United States has been more moderate, more willing to find a balance between the competing goals of controlling inflation and generating employment.

It is interesting to note that no one in this debate ever argues that high or even medium-level inflation isn't a problem, or that central banks shouldn't be watchful on the inflation front. Rather, the debate is whether to allow a little bit of inflation (perhaps up to a maximum of about 5 percent a year), in order to allow for more growth and employment. In other words, the "popular" approach is to advocate what would seem like a fairly moderate position: that both controlling inflation and generating employment are important goals in a healthy economy, and therefore a middle ground should be found to accommodate these often competing goals. On the other hand, the "market" position, which is championed by the Bank of Canada and the Finance department as well as by the key players in financial markets, supports a position that can only be described as extremist. It rejects the possibility of balancing the goals of inflation control and employment growth, and advocates that controlling inflation must take precedence. (This is reflected in the fact that Ottawa sets very specific inflation targets, while refusing to establish even vague unemployment targets.) The extremism of this position is illustrated by the fact that even the chairman of the U.S. central bank comes closer to the "popular" approach. So does the original mandate of the Bank of Canada, written in the early 1930s, which calls for the bank to use its powers to both control prices and promote employment.

The Canadian extremism, under both the Conservative and Liberal governments, can be illustrated best by a quick return to the NAIRU. While NAIRU theory has been central in both countries (although lately less so in the United States), Canada has applied NAIRU theory in a particularly aggressive way. As we've seen, the NAIRU is a theory that aims at keeping the inflation rate from *accelerating*—that is, keeping it stable. The NAIRU doesn't spell out what the inflation rate must be; an economy could, for instance, have a stable rate of inflation of 3 percent per year—or 8 percent or 20 percent, for that matter.

But there's another use of the NAIRU. The theory shows us not only how to keep the inflation rate steady or stable, but also how to *reduce* it. This is a more radical goal and calls for more radical action. To achieve a reduction in the inflation rate, it is not enough to keep unemployment up to its natural level. Rather, it is necessary to drive the unemployment rate *above* its natural level, thereby making workers scramble even harder for jobs and negating some of the security they have won through government support programs. We can even calculate, using NAIRU theory, how much higher the actual unemployment rate must be pushed above the natural rate, and how long it must be held there, in order to achieve a specified drop in the inflation rate.

This goal of reducing or even eliminating inflation—as opposed to merely keeping it stable—is more ambitious and involves more active use of high levels of unemployment as a tool for inflation control. In the past decade, the United States has tended towards using the NAIRU to keep inflation stable, while Canada has opted for the more extremist purpose of actually reducing it. This radical approach has taken Canada down a different path. Indeed, there is a great deal of evidence to suggest that this approach is the biggest single reason why Canada's unemployment rate has been roughly double the U.S. rate throughout the 1990s.

Many Canadian media commentators and Reform and Conservative politicians have tried to put a different spin on the United States–Canada unemployment gap. They have argued that the difference can be attributed to Canada's more generous unemployment insurance system, higher minimum wages and higher rates of unionization. But a two-year study by the Ottawa-based Centre for the Study of Living Standards found that these factors were relatively minor contributors to Canada's higher unemployment rate. The most significant factor was the lower level of demand in the Canadian economy, which was attributed to Canada's more aggressive anti-inflation policy. "The Bank of Canada's tougher stance on inflation was considered to be the key factor in depressing Canadian demand," said Andrew Sharpe, an economist who heads the centre and co-ordinated the study.

This conclusion was in keeping with Pierre Fortin's assessment in his presidential address to the Canadian Economics Association. Fortin argued that Canada's more extreme anti-inflation policy was "the only factor that has been sufficiently important, persistent and powerful to explain the coincident sharp and prolonged divergence between the output and employment performances of Canada and the United States in this decade." For Canadians, Fortin argued, this fierce anti-inflation campaign has meant economic losses in the previous six years that "exceed everything we have known since the Great Depression of the 1930s."

One critic has dubbed this type of anti-inflation extremism, which Canada has pioneered, "sado-monetarism."

IF PAUL MARTIN IS aware of Pierre Fortin's gloomy conclusion—and he is, by the way—there is no hint of it in his joyous expression as he delivers his key "fiscal update" speech in Vancouver in mid-October 1997. It would be hard for the Finance minister to have a much bigger smile on his face. And it is not hard to imagine why he is so happy. He is announcing that the federal deficit is virtually gone and expected to be completely gone by next year. For more than a decade, Bay Street and the media have treated the deficit as the most important problem facing the nation. And now Paul Martin has achieved what no other Canadian Finance minister seemed capable of achieving: a deficit no-show.

"The strategy is working," beams an understandably delighted Martin.

Certainly, if we check the two key items on the "market" agenda—low government spending and low inflation—we see that Martin has achieved strong results in both. Indeed, one could say he has performed superbly in achieving these "market" goals. On the other hand, if we check the two key items on the "popular" agenda—full employment and strong social programs—we'd have to be less charitable in our assessment. So far, then: market agenda, 2; popular agenda, 0.

For that matter, if we were to use other standard measures of economic performance, we'd find that Canada performed badly in the 1990s. Andrew Sharpe notes that between 1989 and 1996, Canada had the lowest overall per capita growth of the thirteen industrial countries surveyed by the U.S. Bureau of Labor Statistics. Canada was the only country to experience an absolute drop in real per capita growth. As a result, our relative standard of living declined significantly; we fell from second place to seventh place among the thirteen countries, over the course of the 1990s. Sharpe comments, "The 1990s have been a watershed. The great progress in improving the standard of living of Canadians has been reversed." Although not all this can be blamed on Martin, who only became Finance minister in late 1993, it hardly seems like an appropriate time to crow about Canada's performance.

However, in the mainstream media, which subscribes to the market agenda, Martin's achievement was treated as near-godlike. Nobody of consequence even stopped to ask the question: were all those cuts really necessary? Given the lightning speed with which the deficit disappeared, is it not possible that Martin indulged in overkill? Wouldn't a more moderate course—such as the one long urged by Doug Peters, Pierre Fortin or the economists who contribute each year to drawing up something called the Alternative Federal Budget—have achieved sufficient deficit reduction, without destroying much of the country's social infrastructure in the process?

The alternative course was never that the deficit should be ignored. Any serious member of the "popular" camp always argued that the deficit was an important economic problem—among several important economic problems—that Canada needed to address. The question was always *how* to address it. Whereas the "market" camp favoured cutting the deficit only through spending cuts, the "popular" camp favoured a more moderate, gradual approach. Once again, it is interesting to note that those in the "popular" camp favour moderation over the more extremist deep-cutting actions promoted by the "market" advocates. In this case, the gradual approach favoured by the "popular" camp involved a deliberate lowering of interest rates to produce more economic growth, which would also bring down the deficit by generating more tax revenues. As Doug Peters, in his days as an outspoken Bay Street economist, once succinctly put it in testimony to the House of Commons Finance committee, "Unemployed people pay less tax. That is one of the most certain laws of all in economics. It should be inscribed on plaques and hung in the offices of prime ministers and premiers across the country."

In fact, this "growth scenario" approach to deficit reduction—not the deep spending cuts—seems to have been the key cause of the deficit's rapid decline in Canada after 1995. Jim Stanford, an economist with the Canadian Auto Workers, used the federal government's own numbers to show that reduced spending on government programs accounted for about 40 percent of the decline in the deficit, and tax increases contributed another 8 percent. But the biggest factor in shrinking the deficit was the growth scenario: lower interest rates and stronger growth, which together accounted for about 52 percent. So while financial commentators were heaping all the credit on the deep spending cuts, the real hero was the much-reviled growth scenario, so disdained by, among others, the *Globe and Mail* editorial board.

This is of more than passing interest because it suggests that Ottawa's deficit reduction could have been achieved without the drastic cuts. Of course, the deficit wouldn't have fallen quite so quickly; rather, it would have declined at a more gradual pace in keeping with the deficit reduction timetable that Martin himself set in his 1995 budget. (This would still have given Canada the fastest pace of deficit reduction among G-7 countries, for whatever that's worth.) A possible side-effect of this growth-oriented approach might have been a little bit of inflation, although, given the weak state of the economy and high levels of unemployment, this is unlikely. Stanford, who is co-chair of the macro-policy committee, which draws up the annual Alternative Federal Budget, comes to a startling conclusion: "Martin's program spending cuts could have been *avoided altogether*, yet Martin's original deficit-reduction timetable still have been met, on the strength of lower interest rates and economic growth."

Of course, there will be an immediate objection to this from those in the "market" camp. They insist that the lower interest rates were possible only because of the decline in the deficit. Indeed, Martin regularly takes credit for the lower interest rates. He said in Vancouver, "The current favourable interest rate environment would not have been possible without the substantial improvement in public finances." This apparent connection between smaller deficits and lower interest rates is repeated regularly in the media. Business reporters even refer to it in their news stories without attribution, as if it were uncontroversial fact. Thus, *Globe and Mail* business reporter Angela Barnes wrote that, in the days of Ottawa's big deficits, many foreign investors "demanded a substantial risk premium [higher interest rate]," but now the interest rate on Canadian bonds has fallen "largely because of Canada's sharp improvement on its deficit problem." The Finance minister, the media and just about everyone else on Bay Street refer to this "risk premium" theory as if it were self-evidently true.

And, on the surface, it seems plausible enough. It seems logical that if people buying government bonds feel they are at risk that the government won't repay them, they will demand a higher premium. But how risky are the government bonds of major industrial nations? In truth, the "risk" is largely imaginary in the developed world; major western nations have an almost flawless record in repaying their creditors. This trend has not gone unnoticed in the financial world, which looks at such government bonds as a kind of unadventurous but extremely safe place to put money. Recall that the Goldman Sachs report, which irritated those in the Finance department so much, noted back in 1994 that the Canadian deficit situation was not severe enough to justify such a high risk premium on Canadian bonds.

In fact, the relationship between deficits and interest rates is much more complicated than the Finance minister or the media imply. Despite constant deficits and debt build-up in Canada over the past twenty years, Canadian interest rates have fluctuated considerably during this period, suggesting that there is not a straightforward relationship between indebtedness and interest rates. To examine the relationship more closely, Jim Stanford looked at extensive data for OECD nations in the past two decades and found a high degree of overlap between big deficits and high interest rates, just as the theory suggests. But, in an article published in *Canadian Business Economics,* Stanford raises a provocative question: which caused which? Did the big deficits cause the high interest rates, as popular theory holds, or did high interest rates cause the big deficits?

The case for the latter is stronger than it seems, even if it is rarely acknowledged in popular business writing. It can be quickly summarized: high interest rates slow down the economy, throwing people out of work. With this increased unemployment, the deficit grows because tax revenues decline and social assistance costs rise. The deficit also grows because the high interest rates add to the government's borrowing costs. As Pierre Fortin, Doug Peters, Michael McCracken, Lars Osberg and many other economists have argued, the dramatic rise in the Canadian deficit in the early 1990s was thus the direct result of John Crow's decision to push interest rates so high.

Similarly, the decline in interest rates in the past couple of years may have less to do with Ottawa's shrinking deficit and more to do with the simple fact that the Bank of Canada decided to ease up on interest rates, largely because the economy was so weak. In other words, interest rates fell not because investors had more confidence in Canada, but because the Bank of Canada decided to let them fall. Thiessen himself suggested that he had deliberately brought down interest rates after 1995 because the Canadian economy "needed a substantial amount of monetary stimulus to respond to the degree of fiscal restraint and problems associated with a major restructuring of the economy." Thus, lower interest rates were not really a "dividend" that Canadians had earned for all their deficit-fighting sacrifices, but rather the symptom of an economy so weak that even the Bank of Canada felt the need to revive it. Indeed, if lower interest rates were the "dividend" for our stellar performance on the deficit front, why did interest rates start rising again in the summer and fall of 1997, just as the good news on the deficit was reaching a fevered crescendo?

The purpose of this discussion is not simply to rain on Paul Martin's Deficit Victory parade. It is to help us get a proper understanding of what happened in the past so we can behave more wisely in the future. The popular interpretation of history greatly influences the actions that will be possible in the future. Thus, *The Globe and Mail* is anxious to make sure that Canadians have drawn the appropriate lesson "from the long struggle with the deficit." It asks in an editorial, "Will we surrender to the old logic that a cheque-writing machine will solve every social ill, or have we learned that our fiscal pain was a direct outgrowth of that failed philosophy?" Similarly, Paul Martin continues to talk as if excessive government spending was the source of our deficit problem, and as if his drastic cutting of government spending was the source of the deficit cure.

But if Peters, Fortin, Stanford and others are correct, the real cause of the deficit and debt build-up of the past decade was the Bank of Canada's extreme anti-inflation policy. And the real cause of the recent decline in interest rates has been the bank's willingness to bring interest rates down, largely because the economy, by the mid-nineties, was desperately gasping for air. If Thiessen now pushes interest rates back up—in order to keep inflation in its near-zero state or to satisfy the C.D. Howe gathering's desire to see inflation go lower still—the repercussions for the economy and the nation's finances will be enormous.

In fact, the Bank of Canada's actions will largely determine how much of a "fiscal dividend" we can expect to see in the coming years—or whether we'll see a fiscal dividend at all in the near future. Stanford considered two scenarios. In the first, the Bank of Canada keeps interest rates low for the next five years, allowing unemployment to fall to about 7 percent while inflation rises to about 3 percent. Under this moderate growth scenario, we could expect an accumulated fiscal surplus over the next five years to total about $152 billion. This money would be available for either rebuilding social programs, reducing taxes or paying down the debt, or any combination of these. In

another scenario, the central bank sticks to its current very low inflation plan, which will almost surely result in higher interest rates,
thereby keeping unemployment up around 9 percent and inflation
down around 1.5 percent. The result of this tighter monetary policy
will be an accumulated fiscal dividend that will be much smaller—*by
at least $70 billion*. Once again, Stanford makes a provocative point.
Imagine the reaction of Canadians, he writes, "if the bank were to present the federal government with a bill for $70 billion, as the ultimate
fiscal cost of its emphasis on continued low inflation."

Then again, if the C.D. Howe crowd gets its way and succeeds in
pushing the bank's inflation targets even lower, the bill is likely to be
considerably larger.

AS THE FESTIVE SEASON set in, the business press was increasingly full of ads for pricey designer jewellery. In *The Globe and Mail*,
one could find plenty for that hard-to-buy-for person: a Paloma
Picasso necklace for $22,400, with a matching bracelet for $12,200 and
clip-on earrings for $2,500, available at the Tiffany store in Toronto.
There was also an ad for a Chopard watch, available from the Royal de
Versailles shop on Bloor Street. No price was mentioned, but a quick
call to the store revealed that the watchband was "standard crocodile"
with a watchface of 18 karat gold, and a price of $8,900. For $10,595,
you could get the same watch with seven small diamonds clustered on
the face, making it easier, presumably, to tell the time.

It didn't have to be the Christmas season to draw attention to the
growing richness of the rich in Canada in the late 1990s. Car dealers
reported difficulties keeping luxury cars on their lots throughout
1997. In Vancouver, there was a six-month waiting list for a certain
Porsche model, and stockbrokers were reportedly paying an extra
$18,000 to buy out the person ahead of them in line. There was also,
of course, the familiar procession of ever-higher bank profits and CEO
salaries reported in the media until, by the end of the year, a kind of

"bank-profit fatigue" was setting in. When critics repeatedly drew attention in the press to the obvious contrast between the growing richness of the banks and the growing ranks of the homeless, a *Globe and Mail* article referred to the critics as "bank bashers."

Certainly, inequality seemed to be on the rise. In the United States, inequality was reaching levels not seen in fifty years. The U.S. Census Bureau reported a pronounced increase in the gap between the incomes of the poor and the well-to-do. It found the average income for the top 20 percent of Americans grew from $73,754 in 1968 to $105,945 in 1994—a 44 percent jump, after being adjusted for inflation. Yet over the same time period, the bottom 20 percent of Americans saw their income increase by only 7 percent—from an average of $7,202 to $7,762.

Well-to-do Americans didn't seem bothered—or even particularly aware—of the growing gap. A Republican congressman from North Carolina, Fred Heineman, described his sense of the term "middle class" in the following way: "When I see someone who is making anywhere from $300,000 to $750,000 a year, that's middle class. When I see anyone above that, that's upper middle class." The lower middle class, Heineman suggested, consisted of those making between $100,000 and $200,000 a year. And the poor would obviously be easy to spot—they'd be the ones wearing the plain "standard crocodile" watches.

Ominously, the same sort of attitude seems to be found in some members of the Canadian élite. "My definition of a millionaire now is a guy who earns $1 million *a year* [italics added]," the owner of a Calgary oil and gas exploration company was quoted as saying. In the same article, the author of a study on Canadian millionaires notes that most well-to-do Canadians now believe they need assets of about $5 million to retire on comfortably.

Generally, however, the story is quite different in Canada than in the United States. The sharp increase in inequality so evident south of the border—except perhaps to U.S. legislators—has not happened here. Statistics Canada data showed that over the past two decades, the gap between the rich and the poor actually decreased slightly in Canada. The poorest 20 percent saw their incomes (in inflation-adjusted dollars) rise from $7,230 in 1973 to $10,073 in 1993—a rise of 39 percent. Over the same two decades, the incomes of the highest-earning 20 percent rose from $80,029 to $93,207—a rise of 16 percent.

However, the Canadian situation wasn't quite as reassuring as these numbers might suggest. Statistics Canada prepares another set of data to show the distribution of income *before* social transfers—such as unemployment insurance, welfare payments and pensions—are added to incomes. In other words, this set of data measures the way the market distributes income, and here the Canadian story is more similar to that of the United States. It is one of dramatically rising inequality. The poorest 20 percent of Canadians saw their *market* incomes actually fall (in inflation-adjusted dollars) from $1,961 in 1973 to $925 in 1993—a drop of 52 percent—while the top-earning Canadians saw their market incomes rise from $78,233 to $91,714—an increase of 17 percent.

This clearly suggests that Canadian social programs have played a crucial role in acting as a bulwark against the rising inequality in the private marketplace. It also suggests that as these social programs are diminished through cutbacks, they will be able to play this bulwark role less effectively, and the rich–poor gap in Canadian society will become more pronounced, more like the rich–poor gap in the United States. The data cited above only go up to 1993. The deepest cuts—Paul Martin's 1995 budget and Mike Harris's slashing of Ontario welfare rates in 1995—have taken place since then.

The presence, up until recently at least, of fairly strong social supports in Canada has masked the devastating impact of the extreme anti-inflation medicine served up by the Bank of Canada. While this anti-inflation extremism is supposedly good for the economy, in fact its only clearly established impact is on the distribution of resources in society. The inflation of the 1970s eroded financial wealth, while easing the burden of debt. The result, according to a study by New York University economist Edward Wolff, was that "[t]he poor and middle-class gained relatively to the rich. . . . The biggest losers [were] the large stockholders." It was this bad experience with inflation in the 1970s that prompted the rich to move inflation fighting to the top of their agenda.

The resulting purge of inflation, starting in both the United States and Canada in 1981, ushered in a new era in which, as we've seen, high levels of unemployment became a tool for warding off a repeat of the inflationary 1970s. The impact of this new anti-inflation toughness was a redistribution of resources in the other direction: from poor to rich. Sadettin Erksoy, an economist at Dalhousie University, did a study of the impact of higher levels of unemployment in Canada in the early 1980s and concluded that "those in the Atlantic provinces, those who have little education, those with smaller incomes, those with blue-collar jobs, females, the married, and the young appear to be by far the biggest losers." In other words, Erksoy summed up, "one may conclude that those who are already economically disadvantaged are the most affected by the disappearance of jobs."

So can those who defend zero inflation possibly present themselves as anything other than the valets of the rich? Well, they certainly try to. Of course, they insist that the entire economy benefits from low inflation—a case they admit they can't prove. But they also have a new argument: that the growth in the value of financial assets is much more widely shared these days, owing to the rise of popular invest-ment vehicles such as mutual funds and pensions. So, the argument goes, when the central bank protects the value of financial assets from erosion through inflation these days, the beneficiaries include work-ers as well as wealthy investors. This argument has the advantage of seeming very up to date; the old argument about central banks protecting the rich can be tossed aside as just another out-of-date, left-wing shibboleth. In the exciting new world of global markets, we're all winners.

Or are we? To actually answer this question, we need to introduce a new yardstick. To the extent that the subject of economic inequality is discussed at all these days, the focus is almost always restricted to a discussion of inequality of income. But there's another measure of economic power in society: *wealth*. When business magazines do annual surveys of the richest individuals in the country, they aren't measuring them by their incomes but rather by their wealth, which includes their stocks, bonds and real estate holdings. In fact, wealth is a more meaningful measure of true economic power and command over the country's resources. The other interesting thing about wealth is that it is even more concentrated in a small number of hands than is income. Indeed, while the *income* gap between the haves and the have-nots is certainly large, it pales in comparison to the *wealth* gap between the two groups.

Dutch statistician Jan Pen came up with a graphic way to illustrate this. Pen's idea was to create two imaginary one-hour parades, in which all the citizens of a country would participate. In the first parade, called an "income" parade, the size of every citizen is determined by his or her income, from the smallest citizens—with the lowest incomes—at the front of the parade, to the tallest—with the highest incomes—at the end. Then the citizens are reassembled for a "wealth" parade. Everything is the same in this second parade, except this time the size of the marchers is determined by their wealth, not their income. What is most noticeable in both parades is how many very small people there are in the country, which is why Pen described them as parades "of dwarfs (and a few giants)."

When I adapted Pen's idea for Canada in a 1987 book, the result was striking. In the income parade, people at the front of the parade were exceptionally tiny, only a few inches high. The height of the marchers rose very gradually; by the halfway mark, people were still only five feet tall. It is only in the last five minutes of the parade that the marchers became very large, standing more than fifteen feet tall. In the last minute, and then the last few seconds, we saw the real giants, standing as high as three hundred feet tall.

The Canadian wealth parade was similar, but more dramatic. This time, the parade was going on for ten minutes before we even realized it had started. That's because the people at the front of the parade were so small they were actually under the ground. These underground people represented Canadians who owned nothing of value, had no savings and were overall in debt. The rest of the wealth parade was much the same as the income parade, with heights rising only very gradually—until we came to the end. By the last second of the wealth parade, we were witnessing some colossal people—Conrad Black and brother Montagu, with assets of $200 million, walked past at an astonishing height of six miles. Shoe baron Thomas Bata was twelve miles high; Galen Weston, twenty-nine miles high; Charles Bronfman, thirty-two miles high. Finally we got to the last man in the parade—the wealthiest man in Canada—Ken Thomson, 198 miles high.

Needless to say, many Canadians are keen to know what the Canadian wealth parade looks like in 1998. How long would the updated version of the parade be going on before we saw signs of life above the ground? Would the senior members of the financial élite tower over their fellow Canadians from heights of three hundred miles or more? All this is not only fun to contemplate but relates directly to our question: have we all benefited from the central bank's war on inflation? When central banks protect financial assets against inflation, the result is an increase in the asset holder's wealth. So if we want to test the theory that we're all winners in the new anti-inflation era, we must check out the 1998 wealth parade to see how our relative sizes have changed.

Oh, that it were so easy! Sadly, it must be said that it is no longer possible to accurately design a wealth parade for Canada. Wealth data have always been very hard to come by. My 1987 Canadian parade was based on data drawn from the Consumer Asset and Debt survey of Canadian households, which used to be conducted by Statistics Canada. But Statistics Canada stopped the survey in 1984, apparently owing to a shortage of funds. The country no longer had the money to find out how its money was distributed. A cynic might suggest that politicians were only too happy to do away with this potential political hot potato. And since there was no popular outcry of "Bring back

the Consumer Asset and Debt Survey!" it has simply disappeared into
the annals of Canadian statistical history. But without it, we unfortunately cannot determine too much about the distribution of wealth in
Canada. Yes, we know from business magazines that the wealthy have
increased their wealth, but what we need to know is have other Canadians as well? Without the data from the wealth survey, we can't properly answer this question. The parade of dwarfs has turned into a
parade of ghosts.

We can, however, make some guesses, based on wealth data for the
United States. The Federal Reserve Board makes calculations about
U.S. wealth distribution based on data it collects through its national
Survey of Consumer Finances, as well as data it has access to from the
U.S. Internal Revenue Service. In the past, the Fed published these
calculations in its principal journal, the *Federal Reserve Bulletin*.
Although the bulletin is not exactly available in supermarkets, it is
fairly accessible. But in recent years, the subject of wealth distribution
seems to have become as touchy a subject in the United States as it
apparently has in Canada. The Fed still collects the data, but it releases
it in a much more obscure form.

In March 1996, for instance, the Fed revealed its most recent wealth
findings in a highly technical, unpublished working paper. Too bad
that almost no one—outside of readers of the business press—heard
much about its findings, which suggested that there is no truth to the
popular notion that wealth is becoming more evenly distributed these
days in the era of popular investing. On the contrary, the Fed working paper found that the top 1 percent of wealth-holders boosted their
share of the nation's wealth from 30.2 percent in 1992 to 35.1 percent
in 1995. Most of that colossal increase actually went to the top half of
1 percent, a group whose average net worth rose from $8 million to
$11.3 million—all in the course of three giddy years! It might have
interested supermarket shoppers to learn that at the same time, the
share of wealth held by the bottom 90 percent of Americans slipped
from 32.9 percent to 31.5 percent.

Another U.S. study, by MIT economist James Poterba and Dartmouth

College economist Andrew Samwick, helped explain why that wealth distribution was so unequal, even in the face of more popular investing. The study noted that stock ownership by individuals has climbed steadily in the past decade, but it is still not widely held; some 71 percent of U.S. households still own little or no stock. "So juicy market returns do little for the average person. Instead, they fatten the wallets of the top quarter of households, which owns 82 percent of all stock," *Business Week* commented in a write-up on the Poterba-Samwick study. Remember these words come from *Business Week*, not *The Progressive Worker.*

While the U.S. situation is likely more pronounced, the same broad trends seem to be evident in Canada. A 1996 national survey of Canadian households, conducted by a firm called Marketing Solutions, found evidence that a growing number of Canadian families own mutual funds. *The Financial Post* commented in an article about the survey, "The growth of mutual funds has brought Canadian ownership in line with the 40 percent rate in the U.S." The *Post* went on to note another similarity to the U.S. situation: that Canadian ownership of mutual funds is concentrated among well-to-do households: 70 percent of families earning above $75,000 a year own mutual funds, compared with 14 percent of families earning less than $20,000. The significance of this finding was not lost on the *Post*, which quoted Marketing Solutions manager Dan Richards as saying, "High ownership among wealthier families flies in the face of conventional wisdom that mutual funds appeal largely to unsophisticated investors with lower income." Richards continued, "The data clearly turns that theory on its head, demonstrating exactly the opposite."

Moves are apparently afoot within the bureaucracy of Statistics Canada to revive the wealth survey. Until then, we can only guess the true picture of Canadian wealth distribution in this era of tight money. But I suspect that those who anticipate a great levelling of Canadian wealth in recent years may be disappointed. Indeed, I would bet my entire bond portfolio that if the wealth survey were to reappear, we would see a new parade with more Canadians farther under the ground and a small number with a bird's-eye view that would truly take your breath away.

SO THE SCORE SEEMS stuck at market agenda 2, popular agenda 0. But, if playing by market rules leaves governments impotent to deliver items on the popular agenda, why not change the rules?

Of course, that's easier said than done. Recall the currency trader from Bermuda who considered laws restricting international capital flows tantamount to a declaration of war. An exaggeration, no doubt. Still, the point is: there are many people—rich and powerful people—who share the fierce pro-market views of the currency trader. They like the system as it is. As we'll see in the next chapter, the only thing market advocates find more unacceptable than the notion that governments should ignore market power is the suggestion that governments should even consider taking steps to bring markets under democratic control.

How Rodney Schmidt
Tried to Save the World

◇

Almost anybody who has a sense of human understanding and compassion takes views that oppose the views of the Department of Finance.
—Finance Minister Paul Martin, November 21, 1996

◇

RODNEY SCHMIDT WAS ABOUT as low as you could be on the Finance department totem pole and still have a Ph.D. in economics. After doing his doctorate in international finance at the University of Toronto, Schmidt had joined the department in Ottawa as an entry-level economist, and after two years, he had risen one notch to a slightly more senior but still low-level rank. It wasn't exactly a meteoric rise, but Schmidt could be said to be doing relatively well for someone his age in the hard-pressed 1990s. At thirty-six, married with two young children, he already owned a house in the pleasant, shady-treed neighbourhood of Holland Cross in western Ottawa. In many ways, he had all the characteristics of a young up-and-comer in the Finance department: bright, articulate, anglo, white, male. There was only one characteristic that made him seem a little different from the others in the department—a tendency towards independent thinking.

Certainly in the sensitive areas of the Finance department's mandate—like spending or tax policy—any thinking that deviated much from the accepted views of the department was distinctly discouraged. Since Schmidt worked in the section that dealt with international economic analysis, independent thinking seemed less of a problem. After all, his focus was on other countries, not Canada. While this made things a little freer than elsewhere in the department, it also made them perhaps a little duller. The international economic analysis section wasn't exactly churning out material that was on the daily firing line in the parliamentary Question Period.

So Schmidt was particularly pleased in the spring of 1994 to get what promised to be a very interesting assignment. He was to investigate the feasibility of something called the Tobin tax. Schmidt knew vaguely about the Tobin tax—the idea that had been proposed by economist James Tobin as an ambitious method of taxing the vast sums of money that swirled around the world each day in international currency transactions. Although Schmidt hadn't really given the tax much serious thought, the idea of it appealed to him. As we saw in Chapter 1, it was the kind of idea that the international financial community hated, so it had little chance of ever being implemented. But it was intriguing, nonetheless, because it appeared to offer such enormous benefits for those outside the financial community—in other words, for most of the world's population. What made Schmidt's little research project particularly fascinating was the fact that, as he was to discover, it came about because Paul Martin himself had expressed an interest in the tax.

This was easily the most exciting assignment Schmidt had been given since he'd first walked through the doors of the Finance department. As he settled in to work on it, Schmidt knew there was only one problem: his superiors had made it clear that his task was to come up with reasons to convince the minister that the tax was *not* a good idea.

This, then, is the story of how Canada almost played a role in nurturing a fledgling idea to reform world financial markets.

~

DESPITE THE ALMOST ceaseless efforts of Peter Nicholson, David Dodge and other senior officials of the Finance department, there remained a small part of Paul Martin's brain that hadn't been fully won over to Finance department orthodoxy. It was something about the make-up of the man. He was, above all, an enormously self-confident individual with a taste for success and an eye on the prime minister's job. These traits helped him to see the wisdom of the Finance department's point of view, which was also, of course, shared by the powerful interests of Bay Street. But there was another, less-developed but still important trait in Martin—a slightly contrary populist, almost anti-establishment, idealistic strain. It fit with his lively mind and his interest in new, slightly off-beat ideas.

So, for instance, while Martin's past boasted an impressive array of standard business achievements—vice-president of Power Corp., CEO of Canada Steamship Lines, director of such corporate giants as Redpath, Manufacturers' Life Insurance and Imasco, he had also become involved with a more eclectic group of organizations—the Canadian Council for Native Business, the Canadian Centre for Arms Control, and the Centre for Research and Action on Race Relations.

Another organization, of which Martin was actually co-founder, was the North–South Institute, an Ottawa-based think tank dedicated to helping develop solutions to Third World poverty and underdevelopment. Under director Roy Culpeper—a former Finance department economist who had concluded that the department was not the best place for someone hoping to make at least a tiny contribution to the betterment of humanity—the institute had evolved into a fairly influential member of Ottawa's circle of non-governmental agencies, with the board of directors including such notables as Joe Clark and Sylvia Ostry.

As Finance minister, Paul Martin had remained interested in the work of the North–South Institute, signalling this interest by fitting into his busy schedule the occasional appearance at the organization's annual board of directors meeting. As further evidence of Martin's unorthodox bend of mind, he also took an interest in the

Tobin tax, which was being actively pushed by the North–South Institute and by many other agencies interested in problems of international development.

In a way, the Tobin tax was right up Martin's alley. The notion of such a grand, visionary scheme as taxing affluent speculators in order to feed Third World children, fund the clean-up of international disasters like Chernobyl or assist in Canadian deficit reduction downright appealed to Martin's innovative, idealistic side. Perhaps it gave him a feeling of potency. Cut off from doing anything constructive to strengthen social programs or create jobs in the country where he actually wielded considerable power, Martin could at least cheer himself up by dabbling in remote, impossible schemes to make the whole world a better place.

Martin's interest in the Tobin tax may have been further piqued by an article supporting the tax that Culpeper had written in *The Financial Post* in the spring of 1994. When Martin ran into Culpeper the following month at an IMF reception at the State Department in Washington, Martin commented on the article and indicated an interest in the subject. Martin suggested getting Culpeper and a small number of other experts together to discuss ideas of this sort as a way of planning for the upcoming G-7 summit, to be held in Halifax the following year.

If the Tobin tax were to fly, it would likely have to be with the agreement of at least the leading industrial nations. So the G-7 meeting was the perfect place to begin the process. Martin knew there would be plenty of resistance to such a radical idea, particularly because it involved taking on the worldwide financial community, which is not known for its obsequiousness. Furthermore, even getting a subject—let alone a highly controversial subject like this—onto the agenda of a G-7 leaders' meeting was a daunting task involving much international consultation. But Martin had one thing going for him. As host of the upcoming summit, Canada had considerable say over the agenda.

Martin was also aware that there was some high-level support for the tax in other countries. Lloyd Bentsen, who was at the time secretary of the U.S. Treasury, was supportive, as Martin discovered when he began raising the subject informally at the regular meetings of G-7 finance ministers. Furthermore, Lawrence Summers, deputy Treasury secretary, had vigorously endorsed the idea of the Tobin tax in his academic writing before joining the Clinton administration. Support also existed at high levels within the French government. On the other hand, other countries—notably Britain, which at the time had a Conservative government—were opposed. As with any controversial issue, there was a wide range of positions.

Inside Canada, there was also some political support, beyond Martin. The House of Commons committee on Foreign Affairs and International Trade, chaired by Liberal Bill Graham, studied the Tobin tax and concluded, "[T]he objectives of a tax on currency speculation at least have sufficient merit and promise to deserve serious longer term examination within a G-7 context." And Lloyd Axworthy, then minister of Human Resources Development, was sufficiently interested in the idea to raise it in a speech to the World Summit for Social Development in Copenhagen in March 1995. "An examination of innovative measures such as the Tobin tax is required," Axworthy said. Even Chrétien was initially interested in the tax, and an official of the Prime Minister's Office was assigned to prepare a memo on the subject.

But if there was some support—or at least willingness to examine the issue further—in political circles, senior Finance department officials in Ottawa resolutely resisted the tax. "I raised the issue at one of my first meetings of the G-7 finance ministers, and I think it led during the next three meetings to not letting me out of the sight of Finance officials," Martin quipped in later comments to the North–South Institute's board. He went so far as to jest, "Almost anybody who has any sense of human understanding and compassion takes views that oppose the views of the Department of Finance!"

When he first asked the department to do some research on the Tobin tax, Martin was well aware that it would respond by assembling a powerful set of arguments against the idea. If he harboured any scheme for someday taking his case to cabinet, Martin knew the department would provide him with a weapon that would shoot only blanks. So he wasn't surprised when the department's paper on the matter, written by Rodney Schmidt, supported the department's case against the tax. Despite his own misgivings, Schmidt had concluded, as instructed, that the tax was a bad idea. "[T]axes on international short-term capital flows would not be effective and would impose higher costs on domestic markets," his report said. A meeting of senior officials from the Finance department and the Prime Minister's Office had no trouble deciding that the idea was not worth pursuing at the Halifax Summit.

Despite the naysayers within the bureaucracy, Martin kept one small part of his mind slightly open to the idea. In January 1995, he followed through with his plan and assembled a group, which included Culpeper, Bill Graham, a handful of officials and academic experts, as well as Gordon Thiessen, to discuss possible agenda items for Halifax. When the subject of the Tobin tax was raised by Graham, there was little support for it around the room, except from Culpeper and Graham. Thiessen was strongly opposed and even suggested that it would be wiser for the government to raise environmental issues at the summit (as someone at the meeting had advocated) than to raise the Tobin tax. It was clear that Thiessen was not saying this because of a deep concern about the environment.

Yet, even as the idea of the Tobin tax was being quietly put to rest at the senior levels of the Canadian government, a development thousands of miles away provided the perfect illustration of why such a tax could help the world.

FOR CANADIANS LYING on sun-drenched Mexican beaches during the 1994 Christmas holidays, the biggest worry had likely been whether they had applied enough sunscreen to their pale Canadian skin, all too suddenly uncovered after months encased in sweaters and coats. As news of the sudden collapse of the peso spread to the beaches just days before Christmas, tourists didn't have a sense of being in the eye of an international financial storm. The most immediate effect was that with the peso abruptly worth about half its previous value, Canadian dollars could buy a whole lot more than the day before. Canadian tourists suddenly had even more bargaining power in haggling with underfed Mexicans for beachside trinkets and brightly coloured local blankets. But for these "merchants"—as well as for all the Mexicans who raked the beaches, served the tequila and made the beds—it was a bleak picture. As they went about their lowly tasks as unobtrusively as they had the day before, they were quietly aware that their struggling lives were about to become even more problematic.

There was an irony in all this that was probably not evident to the tourists loading up on extra shark-tooth necklaces to take home. Although it certainly seemed that Mexico was being punished by international investors who were pulling their funds out of the country, it wasn't clear what Mexico was being punished for. In the world of international finance, Mexico had not been "bad." Quite the contrary. It had done exactly as it had been told.

Indeed, after earlier wayward behaviour, culminating in its massive default on international loans in 1982, Mexico had become a textbook model of free-market economics. It had repudiated its deep-rooted protectionist, nationalistic traditions that had so irritated U.S. business interests. Under Mexican leaders trained at Harvard's business school, it had opened up its markets to foreigners, sold off many of its publicly owned enterprises, reduced its deficit to a modest 2 percent of GDP and raised interest rates relentlessly until inflation was reduced from 150 percent in the late 1980s to a mere 7 percent in 1994. The reforms were wildly popular with foreign investors, who poured some $30 billion into Mexican stocks and bonds in 1993 alone.

For the vast majority of Mexicans, however, the reforms had actually made conditions worse. By 1992, average real Mexican wages were about one-third lower than they had been a decade earlier, before the reforms. And while Mexico had never offered much in the way of social services, its minimal programs to subsidize the price of tortillas, milk and school breakfasts were all but eliminated as part of the cut-backs apparently required to attract investment. Public spending on health and education was cut in half. Not surprisingly, parents faced with higher education costs and lower wages pulled their children from school, providing fresh recruits for the already-strong army of child street vendors. During the decade of reforms, the top one-fifth of the population increased its share of national income by 13 percent; Mexico's richest man, Carlos Slim Helu, was reported to have more money than all the 17 million people crowded at the bottom of the country's income ladder put together.

The reforms not only made things worse for the Mexican people, they also seem to have contributed to the collapse of the peso. The flood of foreign money into the country kept the value of the peso artificially inflated. A high value for a nation's currency can be a good thing, if it reflects a strong economy and growing wealth. This was not the case with Mexico in the early 1990s. Mexico's overall economy was not stronger but weaker, with a large external trade deficit. Although a few Mexicans were getting richer, the national income as a whole was not increasing. But, with vast amounts of money pouring in to buy Mexican stocks and bonds, which were denominated in pesos, there was plenty of demand for pesos, keeping their value high.

Thus Mexico ended up with a falsely high—or overvalued—currency, which created problems. Once-cheap Mexican products were all of a sudden more expensive abroad, making them uncompetitive in foreign markets. Similarly, imported goods suddenly became more affordable to Mexicans, making Mexican-produced goods less competitive in their own home market.

The result was rising unemployment and sluggish growth. Faced with an election in 1994, the unpopular Mexican government knew it had to do something to help out the stalled economy. But what to do? The answer seemed to be to lower interest rates and let the value of the peso drop. This action would stimulate exports and give a break to the local economy. And yet it would be extremely unpopular with foreign investors, in that it would cut the value of their investments. If the peso were to be revalued to, say, 85 percent of its existing value, investors would find their investments suddenly worth only 85 percent of what they had been. Considering the large profits they had been making, this might not seem like an unreasonable concession to ask. But investors were not in the habit of accepting such losses lightly.

Terrified to do anything that would upset foreign investors, whose large cash injections into the Mexican stock market seemed to be one of the few bright spots in the alleged Mexican miracle, the government decided not to devalue the peso. Instead, it tried to alleviate rising unemployment by pumping money directly into the economy with increased government spending. As it turned out, this wasn't any more acceptable to investors, who saw it as a sign that the Mexican government might lack the backbone to stick with its reforms. As investors began to lose confidence in the government's adherence to market orthodoxy, a vicious circle developed. Nervous investors began to sell their Mexican financial assets. Anxious to prevent a further sell-off, the Mexican central bank raised interest rates to make it attractive for investors to keep their money parked in Mexico. The higher interest rates further paralysed the economy and drove up unemployment. As the economy turned down, the high value of the peso became even more artificial, making investors more worried that there would be a devaluation. And on and on.

The backdrop to all this was the stunning nineteenth-century-style peasant rebellion in the southern Mexican province of Chiapas that began in early 1994. Out of nowhere, it seemed, a peasant army had risen up to champion the rights of the poor and, in a few days of bloody fighting with the Mexican army, had taken control of six southern towns. Contributing to the romance of it all was the fact that this band of revolutionary bandidos was led by a dashing, handsome and highly articulate guerrilla leader, identified only as Commandante Marcos, whose mysterious manner and scarf-covered face had all the drama of the TV character Zorro.

Commandante Marcos became an overnight sensation and hero to millions of impoverished Mexicans, as well as to elements of the Mexican middle class who felt badly squeezed by the eroding wages and high interest rates of recent years. Foreign journalists, allowed by the rebels to make the trek deep into the woods to view the makeshift camps and talk to the masked Marcos, reported high tales of adventure that only fuelled the magic and mystique of it all. For foreign investors—including managers of faraway pension and mutual funds, who often fail to appreciate the romantic appeal of peasant rebellions—it was simply another signal that Mexico was not a safe place to put billions of dollars.

By November 1994, investors, both foreign and local, were selling off their Mexican assets in earnest, creating a stampede to move money out of the country into safer currencies. In mid-December, newly elected Mexican president Ernesto Zedillo finally devalued the peso by 15 percent—a move that seemed to create even more fear and uncertainty and urgency to shed pesos. Two days later, with money virtually hemorrhaging out of the country, Mexico dropped all pretence of being able to maintain a fake value for the peso and allowed it to float openly on currency markets so that private investors could determine its value. With some $25 billion having fled the country over the previous few weeks, the peso promptly sank to about half its value.

The Mexican crisis sent shock waves through the financial world. The collapse of the peso meant that the Mexican government's enormous debts were suddenly that much more difficult for it to repay. With hundreds of billions of dollars owed to creditors around the world, the prospect of Mexico defaulting on these loans suddenly loomed as a terrifying prospect to investors and promised to have a ripple effect throughout western economies. To head off such major financial repercussions, the Clinton administration orchestrated a $50-billion international bail-out package, with $20 billion coming from the U.S. government and $30 billion from the IMF and a number of western countries, including $1 billion from Canada. In exchange for this package enabling it to repay its creditors, Mexico was required to impose an even harsher version of market economics—a fierce austerity program that included even deeper government spending cuts and still higher interest rates.

While Mexico's creditors around the world were thus spared a devastating blow, the "tequila effect" continued to rattle the world's wealthy. If Mexico, so well schooled in the market orthodoxy, could come crashing down, where was money safe any more? The boom in Third World "emerging market" funds suddenly evaporated, as money came rushing home to the safety of strong, well-grounded currencies, such as German marks and Swiss francs. Even countries like Canada felt the pinch. Although Canada bore no real resemblance to Mexico, its relatively large debt made financial experts suddenly nervous and uneasy. Moody's Investors Services, one of the big international debt rating agencies in New York, decided to undertake a fresh assessment of Canada—along with several other advanced nations with big debts. Although nothing had changed in Canada—the deep-slashing February 1995 budget was still a few weeks off—Moody's announced that Canada was on credit watch, under consideration for a possible downgrade of its credit rating. This news, as we've seen, helped the Finance department make its case that Ottawa had no choice but to undertake massive spending cuts.

The general commentary in the media and in official circles was that the Mexican crisis served as a perfect example of how deeply integrated the world financial system had become, and how powerless we were to escape its claws. Peter Nicholson advised Paul Martin that Mexico revealed the urgency of proceeding with billions of dollars' worth of government spending cuts in the upcoming February 1995 budget to satisfy nervous markets about Ottawa's intention to reduce the deficit. Looking back on the events several years later, Nicholson says that Mexico provided an important "lesson" of "how unforgiving capital markets can be when they turn against you." The authors of *Double Vision* echoed this view: "Mexico would provide a lesson for nation-states in just how dependent they were upon the vagaries— even potential irrationalities—of the financial markets."

So is Mexico just a cautionary tale from the trenches of the new global economy, showing us the need to placate international investors? Was the peso crisis just an inevitable casualty of the new realities, a revelation of the ultimate powerlessness of the nation-state? Or could a different set of rules have produced a different result?

NO ONE IN THE audience at Princeton University that day in 1972 realized they were hearing an idea that was to take on almost mythical proportions in some circles over the following decades. The Princeton event was pure Ivy League, not unlike the visit of Milton Friedman to the University of Pennsylvania that had got Sidney Weintraub so exercised a few years earlier. This time it was James Tobin, a respected economist from Yale, who had come to Princeton to give a guest lecture.

Tobin had done his Ph.D. at Harvard and then moved to Yale as Sterling Professor of Economics in 1950, becoming a major figure in the debate between Keynesianism and Milton Friedman's monetarism that flared in academia in the 1960s and 1970s. With expertise in finance and financial theory, Tobin maintained that the monetarists placed too much emphasis on measuring the money supply and not enough on measuring real variables like employment. Highly articulate and prominent in debate over national economic policy, Tobin had chaired President Kennedy's Council of Economic Advisers in the early 1960s. It wouldn't be until 1981 that his brilliance was finally rewarded with the Nobel Prize in Economics for his work in financial market theory and the nature of investment choices.

The auditorium at Princeton was full for Tobin's lecture. It was the prestigious Janeway Lecture, and with the national stature he had attained in the Kennedy years, Tobin was quite a draw. In addition to a keen crowd of faculty and students, there were plenty of notables from the senior ranks of the university administration. The focus of Tobin's lecture—like the focus of most of his work—was how to use government policy to achieve key goals, particularly full employment.

He proposed a number of measures, one of which became known as the Tobin tax. Tobin's remarks were well received by the Princeton crowd, and he was treated with the adulation appropriate for someone of his academic stature and semi-celebrity. At the reception afterwards, there was a great deal of intelligent commentary about his remarks, but no particular focus on his tax idea.

It wasn't until six years later that Tobin decided to try again to flog the idea publicly. By 1978, he was president of the Eastern Economic Association, and in the intervening years, he had become even more convinced that financial markets were operating in a way that was dangerous to the public interest, and that his tax idea had the potential to curb some of the worst excesses. Tobin devoted his presidential address—his keynote speech of the year—to his tax idea. But, once again, the audience of high-powered economists greeted the notion without much interest. "[O]ne might say it sank like a rock," Tobin later recalled. But while the community of academic economists exhibited little interest—and Wall Street financial experts would show even less—Tobin had planted the seeds of an idea that was to develop a considerable following over the years in less mainstream circles.

It was Tobin's concern about the waning commitment of western governments to full employment that led him to propose his tax. He recognized that it was difficult for nations to pursue full employment policies when investors could move large amounts of money effortlessly around the globe in search of quick returns. If interest rates were higher in Mexico, then investors would borrow money at lower rates in New York and move the money into higher-rate Mexican bonds. It therefore became necessary for countries to maintain high interest rates in order to compete for mobile capital. But maintaining high interest rates was a sure way for a country to choke its domestic economy; it made full employment policies virtually impossible. While Mexico would later serve as a dramatic example of what could happen in extreme circumstances, all countries were affected in that all had to compete, to some extent, for mobile capital.

The essential idea behind the Tobin tax, then, was to hinder this easy movement of capital across currencies in search of the highest rate of return. By taxing capital mobility, Tobin was trying not to stop it, but simply to run some interference, to slow it down. To do this, he advocated imposing a small tax whenever money was exchanged from one currency to another. What was ingenious about this idea was that it would have the effect of discouraging less desirable sorts of investments, while not really affecting desirable ones. It would have virtually no impact, for instance, on long-term foreign investments or the one-time purchase of foreign goods—transactions that were necessary for the healthy functioning of an international economy. Like the perfect cancer drug that leaves healthy tissue alone, the Tobin tax would not impinge on the healthy flow of capital involved in nations trading and investing in one another. But the tax could be quite punitive towards the kind of quick-moving, in-and-out transactions across currencies that earn investors huge profits, such as in Mexico in the early 1990s. For money constantly moving in and out of currencies in search of quick profits, the tax would have to be paid constantly and would become quite onerous.

It's easy to see how onerous. Let's imagine a Tobin tax of 0.2 percent. This sounds very small, but watch what happens in practice. If $100,000 is exchanged into another currency, a tax of $200 would be owed—not overly punitive for someone wanting to make a $100,000 long-term investment in another country. But the picture changes significantly if that $100,000 is simply parked for a short while in another currency, with the purpose of earning a quick profit, and then the money is exchanged back into the original currency. Under this scenario, the Tobin tax would become a heavier burden, because it would have to be paid each time the $100,000 crosses into another currency. So, for instance, if the money makes a round trip every month, the cost will be $400 a month, or $4,800 a year. If the money makes a round trip every week, the $400 will have to be paid each week, amounting to a charge of more than $20,000 a year. If the money makes a round trip every day, the yearly cost of the tax becomes staggering—more than $100,000.

Thus the Tobin tax would have significant power to slow capital movements. Had the tax been in place in the early 1990s, there would probably have been less speculative capital flowing into Mexico. As a result, the peso would not likely have become so overvalued and its crash might well have been avoided. Even if the peso had become overvalued and the crash had happened, a Tobin-style tax could have prevented the situation from escalating into a massive hemorrhage of funds out of the country. In such times of crisis, the Tobin tax could be raised on capital leaving the country, making its departure more costly.

Of course, there is also the issue of the vast amounts of money that could be raised through the tax. Even if the tax were set at 0.2 percent or lower, the revenue potential is dramatic because of the sheer volume of money that is exchanged on world currency markets—some $1.2 *trillion* dollars *a day*. Certainly, the revenue collected wouldn't amount to 0.2 percent of $1.2 trillion a day, because the tax would have the effect of discouraging a lot of the short-term, speculative transactions—which is exactly what the tax is supposed to do. Either way, the world community benefits: either it collects a huge amount of tax that can be put to good purpose, or it collects a smaller amount of tax but succeeds in discouraging disruptive capital flows.

And what makes the prospect of a Tobin tax all the more compelling is that the vast majority of this money moving across currencies is doing so for questionable purposes—that is, for the kind of quick in-and-out transactions that can wreak havoc in an economy. Indeed, only a small fraction of the daily world currency transactions are carried out for the purposes of trade or long-term investment. This leaves hundreds of billions of dollars a day being traded for purposes that are potentially harmful to the world economy.

It is hard not to like the idea of the Tobin tax, particularly when one puts the whole issue in some kind of perspective. Essentially it boils down to this: by scooping a small percentage of the enormous amount of money traded daily on foreign exchanges, the Tobin tax would help improve the functioning of the world economy *and* collect hundreds of billions of dollars, which could be handed over to a good cause. And these are the side benefits! Don't forget the main benefit: giving countries greater freedom to pursue full-employment policies. If only the Tobin tax could do something really useful, like cure the common cold, perhaps the Finance department in Ottawa would give it some serious consideration.

～

AFTER RODNEY SCHMIDT had completed his paper, producing the negative results his superiors wanted, that should have been the end of the matter. The only problem was that Schmidt felt ashamed of himself.

It was a feeling he was not easily able to shake. Schmidt was inclined to be sympathetic to the Tobin tax. After all, one would have to be an automaton or a thoroughly indoctrinated clone of the Finance department *not* to see an inherent appeal in the tax. But did the dream fall apart because of technical problems?

Schmidt was well aware of the case against the tax. There were two lines of argument. First, it was sometimes asserted that the whole concept of the tax was wrong because it interfered with the natural workings of the marketplace, which was necessarily more efficient left on its own than subject to human intervention. Supporters of this line of argument didn't deny that unrestrained capital mobility created some treacherous situations, like the one in Mexico. But they insisted that these difficulties were necessary and even healthy, that they provided a form of "discipline" for countries, pushing them in the direction of managing their economies properly. Crucial to this argument was the assumption that mobile capital moved to nations with healthy economic fundamentals, that investors put their capital in countries with good long-term prospects and shunned investing in countries with poor long-term prospects.

According to this argument, then, investors put their money into Mexico not just because they figured they could quickly pocket a great deal of money. Rather, they did so because, after carefully studying the direction of Mexican economic policy, they concluded that the long-term prospects for the Mexican economy looked good and therefore Mexico was a wise choice for long-term investments. But on closer examination, this explanation of the Mexican boom seems unsatisfactory. It is difficult to imagine that investors were particularly concerned about the long-term prospects for Mexico when a good deal of the money they "invested" was on a short-term basis, generally no more than three months, often no more than a few hours. It is hard to see how this amounted to much more than a get-your-money-and-run strategy.

To the extent that they had longer-term horizons, investors favoured a particular type of policy on the part of the Mexican government. They were very enthusiastic, for instance, about Mexico's adoption of a tough anti-inflation stand and its cutbacks in government spending. But it is a large jump to assume that these sorts of policies form the basis of healthy economic fundamentals. To a large extent, they really amount to a set of policies that favour investors at the expense of ordinary Mexicans and the general health of the Mexican economy. So when investors "discipline" countries by withholding their capital, are they necessarily providing incentives for nations to follow healthy economic policies, or are they simply providing incentives for nations to put in place policies that favour investors? Is the so-called discipline that markets impose really just self-serving—a means of forcing nations to pander to the interests of investors?

If this is the case—and one can certainly make an argument that it is—then this objection to the Tobin tax seems to have little merit. Why would we want to give already powerful international financial capital even more power—the power to punish countries for not favouring its interests? If the Tobin tax reduces the power of financial capital to force countries to do its bidding, this would seem to be a compelling argument *in favour* of a Tobin tax.

The second line of argument against the Tobin tax is more problematic, and hence the one more frequently raised—that the tax is simply unfeasible. Desirable as it may be, it just won't work.

There are several different strains to the unfeasibility argument. First, the tax is simply uncollectable because investors will devise ingenious ways to evade it. Second, even if it were technically feasible to outsmart wily speculators, the tax could never work because it would be impossible to get the nations of the world to agree to it.

In his paper, Rodney Schmidt leaned heavily on the feasibility argument. It was clearly the more compelling argument, and one could advance it while still sympathizing with the basic goals of the tax. Thus, he simply concluded that tax evasion presented a "devastating practical problem." This statement was undeniably true, given the fact that the immensely powerful international financial community was dead set against the tax and would likely do everything in its power to kill the idea.

So Schmidt hadn't really compromised himself at all. He'd acknowledged some positive aspects of the Tobin tax, but concluded it was simply not feasible. Still, somewhere deep down, he felt lousy. What was he doing? Had he suffered through five difficult years of postgraduate work in international economics, then steered clear of a more lucrative future on Bay Street, only to end up in Ottawa pussyfooting around an issue that he cared deeply about? In fact, it was worse than that: he had written a paper that helped kill any faint hope that the tax might have made it onto the international political agenda.

On his own initiative, Schmidt began working on a second paper. And this time he decided to say what he really believed.

WORKING ON HIS OWN, freed from the deadening supervision of the department, Schmidt threw himself enthusiastically into the task of analysing the feasibility of the Tobin tax. Legitimate concerns about the tax needed to be addressed, and Schmidt had no intention of producing a whitewash endorsing the tax. He wanted to carefully review the issues and present a balanced critique. In other words, he wanted to investigate the issue with an open mind and honestly try to assess whether the tax was worthy of serious consideration by the Canadian government. He wanted to produce the paper he should have been assigned to produce in the first place.

The sheer drama of the changes taking place in the foreign exchange market made the subject fascinating. In the first three decades after the Second World War, the world's nations had participated in an international financial system, known as the Bretton Woods system, in which their currencies were set at fixed rates of exchange. Although there were circumstances under which the rates could be adjusted, for the most part currencies remained stable. After the breakdown of Bretton Woods in the early 1970s, international financial markets were very turbulent. Exchange rates were no longer fixed and were therefore subject to dramatic swings as capital moved swiftly from currency to currency, shopping for the highest rate of interest. As we saw in the Mexican situation, this had the potential of creating enormous difficulties for vulnerable economies, saddling them with high interest rates and volatile exchange rates that made trading difficult.

On the other hand, the new situation created enormous profit-making opportunities for those buying and selling currencies. From almost nothing, a huge market for foreign currency exchange developed. By the mid-eighties, daily trading in foreign exchange markets around the world amounted to $150 billion; by 1992 that had risen to $880 billion, and by 1995 to $1.2 trillion.

Schmidt set all this out in his paper and provided details of the nature of the vast new market, in which sophisticated traders developed complex new financial instruments. There were spot trades, currency options, outright forward swaps—all simply variations in the game of betting on the changing value of currencies. Increasingly exotic in their design, they were also increasingly divorced from the real world of trade in goods and services. Most of the transactions had nothing to do with this real world of goods and services moving across borders, or with investors making real long-term investments in a foreign country. As Schmidt noted, in two-thirds of all the out-right forward and swap transactions the money moved into another currency for fewer than seven days. In only 1 percent did the money stay for as long as one year.

This rapid movement contributed to the volatility of exchange rates, which, as we've seen, posed serious problems for national economies. But, as Schmidt noted, this volatility was the bread and butter of those playing the currency markets. Without constant fluctuations in the currency markets, there was little opportunity for profit. This certainly seemed to suggest that the interests of currency traders and the interests of ordinary citizens were operating at cross-purposes.

Schmidt also noted another interesting aspect of the foreign exchange market: the dominant players were the private banks, which had huge pools of capital and access to information about currency values. Since much of the market involved moving large sums of money (typically in the tens of millions of dollars) for very short periods of time (often less than a day), banks were perfectly positioned to participate. Among swap transactions, which represented a major chunk of the foreign exchange market, 86 percent of the transactions were actually between banks. In Canada, the private banks carried out some $30 billion *a day* in currency trades. This was in fact part of the banks' business. International currency trading was, for instance, the major component of the fastest-growing part of the Bank of Montreal's 1995 income.

As Schmidt put the research together, the political nature of the problem became increasingly obvious. Whatever the technical problems with the Tobin tax might be, there was clearly another problem of political dimensions. Volatile currency markets were bad for the national economy, but they were advantageous to key elements in the financial community, particularly the banks, which were not generally shy about making their views known to government. Although a Tobin tax might offer real benefits to the economy, Schmidt noted, "[b]anks will be the clear losers from the tax."

As for the evasion problem, Schmidt had decided on further consideration that it wasn't the insurmountable obstacle it was often made out to be. It was true that hot-shots in the financial world were sharp as a pin when it came to devising new schemes for avoiding taxes. Surely, the Tobin tax would be easy grist for their mill, a mere plaything that they would effortlessly bat around for sport, with no real power to hurt them. On the other hand, devising complex avoidance schemes had its own costs and risks, since it often involved adding extra steps to the transactions, and this meant adding to the number of problems that had to be anticipated. Besides, this is exactly what goes on in any area of corporate taxation: governments impose taxes, clever corporate tax lawyers devise loopholes, governments plug loopholes, clever corporate lawyers devise new loopholes, and on and on. Since when has the ingenuity of highly paid tax lawyers been grounds for not imposing taxes on corporations?

The more serious evasion problem—and this was always presented as the real clincher—was the problem of getting world-wide participation. It was frequently argued that the Tobin tax would be unenforceable unless every country in the world agreed to collect it, which was about as likely as the world's nations agreeing to hand over all their military weapons to an international peace authority. If even a few small countries opted out of collecting the Tobin tax, it was argued, all foreign exchange business would migrate to these countries.

But this was likely overstating the case. There are already plenty of financial reasons to locate operations in low-tax jurisdictions, but other considerations keep the major investment houses in places like New York, London, Tokyo and Toronto. It's unlikely that a low-rate Tobin tax would make them move. If firms stayed in the major centres, but simply transferred their currency transactions to subsidiaries located offshore, the tax could be imposed on all funds transferred to and from these offshore locations. Furthermore, the IMF, which is controlled by the world's dominant powers, could require all nations to impose the Tobin tax as a condition of membership and, therefore, a condition of borrowing privileges. Access to IMF loans—an insurance policy few nations would want to be without—would be available only to nations collecting the Tobin tax. In other words, the real problem was not getting every nation in the world to agree, but getting the major nations of the world to agree. Was this really so impossible? We'll come back to this question later.

In January 1995, Rodney Schmidt completed his second paper before Paul Martin held his meeting with Culpeper and the others about the Halifax Summit. Although longer and more detailed than the first one, Schmidt's second paper was actually not that different; both were technical and academic in tone, and came complete with bibliography. But there was one key difference. Schmidt had concluded in his first paper that the Tobin tax was not feasible. This time, without the careful supervision of the department, he had come to a different conclusion: the Tobin tax was desirable *and* feasible.

Schmidt submitted the second paper for departmental consideration, in the hopes that it would be passed up the line and land on Paul Martin's desk. But the department considered this paper unsuitable, and it was not approved for distribution up the chain of command. As he prepared for the Halifax Summit, Paul Martin was to be spared the confusion of knowing that the Finance department expert who had been assigned to investigate the Tobin tax had decided, upon greater reflection, that the tax was indeed worthy of further study.

NO ONE HAD WATCHED more intently as the Mexican peso crisis unfolded than officials inside the government of Chile. The peso crisis sent much of Latin America into a tailspin. Foreign investors who had sunk billions of dollars into so-called emerging markets in Latin America and elsewhere in the Third World started pulling their funds out as rapidly as they had put them in. Latin American markets lost almost 40 percent of their value in two months.

As fear and uncertainty spread through much of the continent, Chile had been able to watch the fiasco with a slight feeling of detachment.

Foreign investors who had put money into Chilean stocks and bonds weren't just able to grab their money and run. Chile had a law that required investors to keep their investments in the country for at least one year. The Bank of Chile enforced this by requiring investors to make reserve deposits, which would be forfeited if their investments were withdrawn in less than a year. The Chilean law was just a different way of addressing the problem that the Tobin tax tries to address. By requiring capital coming into the country to stay there at least a year, the law prevented the sudden departure of capital from creating serious problems for a country's domestic economy. And the Chilean law had the added advantage that it didn't rely on the co-operation of other countries. Chile had put in place a form of capital controls entirely on its own. As a result, Chileans had been able to watch in relief as the peso crisis swirled around their country but didn't touch it. Yet, only a year later, this Chilean law was under attack. Strangely, the attack was coming from Ottawa.

Canada was negotiating a bilateral trade pact with Chile. In negotiations in the summer and fall of 1996, Ottawa was pushing Chile to abandon its law on reserve requirements. Canada wanted the law to go because it interfered with the free movement of capital, which offended some Canadian investors. Ottawa's position was reflected in a policy paper, written by Prakash Sharma, a senior economist with the Trade and Economic Analysis Divison of the Department of Foreign Affairs. In it, Sharma argued that "the benefits of capital controls are uncertain" and it is "not prudent to adopt a policy that jeopardizes economic gains expected from freer trade and investment." The paper concluded that "potential NAFTA partners, who currently regulate capital movements, should be prepared to reform their policy toward foreign investment and meet the NAFTA standards."

While Ottawa officials considered the benefits of this sort of capital control "uncertain," analysts in Chile were more enthusiastic about the results. In a paper for a United Nations conference on globalization of financial markets in New York in 1996, two economists with the central bank in Chile found considerable merit in the Chilean law, as well as a similar one in Colombia: "Both Chile and Colombia have registered an impressive performance compared to their historical record and to the contemporary results of other countries in the region.... Overall the reserve requirements and other capital account regulations, with all their limitations, have played a very important role in these successful macroeconomic experiences." In another research paper prepared for the UN, U.S. economist Rudi Dornbusch concluded, "The experience of Chile indicates that prudent, flexible, moderate management of [capital flows] is an effective strategy."

Indeed, these laws have helped limit the inflow of capital into developing countries in recent years. Gerald Helleiner, professor of economics at the University of Toronto (and father of previously quoted Eric), notes that "surges in private capital in amounts much larger than they could handle" have been a major problem for Latin American and Southeast Asian countries in the 1990s. The excessive funds were often poorly invested. Furthermore, when investors suddenly withdrew their funds, the national currencies would plummet, as they did in Southeast Asia in the fall of 1997.

So why was Canada so keen to kill the Chilean experiment? For that matter, why was Ottawa so wedded to defending the free movement of capital, which clearly had the potential to create enormous problems, not only for desperate countries like Mexico, but also ultimately for Canadians as well?

If Canada's resistance to the Tobin tax was based on its lack of feasibility, surely the Chilean experiment represents an interesting alternative route for accomplishing the same goal: regaining control over our economy. It's striking, then, that Canadian officials, who are quick to point out how capital mobility has rendered us powerless, show so little interest in exploring this avenue for re-empowerment. Why wouldn't all the Finance officials who have lamented our impotence grab on to the Chilean experiment like a lifeline? Yet not only do these types appear to have no interest in studying the results of the Chilean experiment to see what we might learn, they are adamant that the experiment must be stopped.

A TALL, SLIGHTLY STOOPED James Tobin makes his way through the cavernous, charmless building in downtown Ottawa that houses the Finance department. In his late seventies, Tobin is still a busy man, still teaching at Yale, still writing books about macroeconomics and speaking publicly about his tax proposal. He has just finished addressing a luncheon meeting organized by the Canadian Centre for Policy Alternatives. He is now on his way to see a high-ranking Finance department official at a meeting arranged by the Canadian Labour Congress, which likes the idea of the Tobin tax and has paid for Tobin's visit to Ottawa. With only a few weeks to go before the G-7 leaders gather in Halifax in June 1995, the congress has asked for the meeting, in a last-ditch, far-fetched attempt to convince the government to put the Tobin tax on the Halifax agenda.

It's a slight nuisance to the Finance department. Senior officials know where they stand on the Tobin tax, and that's not going to change no matter what this near-octogenarian whiz-kid has to say. But it's a bit awkward having to deal with him. After all, he is a distinguished senior professor from Yale and a former chairman of President Kennedy's Council of Economic Advisers. And then there's that business about him winning the Nobel Prize in economics—an honour that has the power to leave other economists in a room feeling weak.

Indeed, there isn't an economist in the Finance department who wouldn't be intimidated by Tobin, if confronted in person. Most of the department's economists, however, are too busy to attend Tobin's luncheon address. In fact, Tobin will meet only with Louise Frechette, associate deputy Finance minister and the highest-ranking woman in the department. Her office is large and well-decorated enough that this will seem like a sufficiently prestigious reception for a Nobel laureate. But no one would mistake this for rolling out the red carpet. And so it is that on his visit to Ottawa, a man whose counsel was once sought by President Kennedy in the Oval Office will have to content himself with a rather uninterested hearing from Louise Frechette.

Frechette wastes no time making it clear that the department is solidly opposed to the tax. She trots out the usual objections that have been conveniently culled from Rodney Schmidt's first paper: nice idea, but it just won't work because of the evasion problem. Tobin has heard this before and has given it a great deal of thought. He quickly runs through his responses, noting that an IMF requirement obliging member states to collect the tax would almost certainly solve the evasion problem. Frechette, who in fact knows little about international financial markets and has not spent years of her life trying to figure out how to get control of them, repeats the department's position. The meeting is quickly brought to a close. With the Mexican peso crisis still very much in the air and the G-7 meeting in Halifax only weeks away, it does seem that an opportunity for action has somehow been missed.

Tobin, perhaps a little more stooped and cranky than before the meeting, heads back to New Haven, Connecticut. Increasingly, it seems clear that if there is ever to be a Tobin-like solution to the world's dangerously volatile international financial markets, it won't be in his lifetime.

HILLHOUSE AVENUE, New Haven, Connecticut. The tree-lined street in the heart of Yale University is the best that New England has to offer, with its lovely old street lamps and stately three-storey buildings set back from the quiet road. Number 30 houses the Cowles Research Foundation, a spacious old mansion with hardwood floors and leather couches. On the third floor, in a cramped office overcrowded with books, James Tobin sits at his desk. On one side is a small window, which is mostly taken up with an air conditioner. Evidently, looking out on the charming surroundings below is not a high priority.

James Tobin has done this before. Clearly, he's sat still for many an interview about his tax. His impatience is clear; he arrives an hour late and cuts the interview short from the allotted time.

We talk about the tax. He explains that his central concern is to create the possibility for countries to have their own monetary policies, thereby preserving their economic sovereignty in the face of international markets. "The proposal is to make a little bit more room for interest rate differentials between countries" to allow them "to go for full employment."

Perhaps he blames me for the slight from the Canadian government. I ask him about his encounter with Louise Frechette in Ottawa. "She was negative, absolutely," he says. He recalls that she trotted out all the standard objections to his tax.

The entire situation is familiar to Tobin—the keen interest of a journalist who has made a special trip just to hear the great man talk about his tax, fresh on the heels of a brush-off from those in power. Since the 1960s, Tobin has commanded enormous respect within the profession and within establishment circles for his accomplishments, yet this respect has not translated into much interest in exploring his tax idea—just as William Vickrey was able to win the Nobel Prize but never able to get mainstream economists willing to consider his ideas about full employment.

It is true that there has been plenty of interest in the Tobin tax outside professional and élite circles. Since he first floated the idea in 1972, a steady momentum of support has been building among activists, reformers and academics, including even some economists with less of a mainstream bent. That support culminated in 1995 in an international conference, organized under the auspices of the United Nations, where academic experts from around the world presented highly technical papers analysing virtually every aspect of the Tobin tax and its feasibility in international markets. Their conclusion: although there are problems, the tax is desirable and feasible. Nevertheless, when it comes to official circles, the interest is limited. Perhaps this explains why Tobin seems a little impatient and even cranky around those who show an interest in his tax; he's seen their interest before and knows it leads to nothing.

"I haven't tried to be a crusader. I don't have the time or the inclination," he says matter-of-factly, trying to wrap up the interview. He wants to get back to his work. I take the hint.

～

IF TOBIN IS TOO jaded to make an impassioned plea for his tax, Rudi Dornbusch is more than happy to step into the breach. Dornbusch, Ford professor of economics and international management at MIT, is highly respected in the profession and sufficiently mainstream to have a regular column in *Business Week*. Dornbusch argues eloquently and forcefully for the Tobin tax, partly on the grounds that it would make the capitalist system function better. "The economy needs a favourable environment for capital accumulation," he writes. "Often chief executives from non-financial businesses divide their time between litigation and speculation, rather than focusing on investment in research and development of technology, products and markets. Capitalism blossoms when business takes the long view. . . . Innovation and competition have undermined the blessings of capitalism by turning financial markets into overly trigger-happy institutions with an emphasis on debt leverage, capital gains and the short horizon."

This distinction between harmful short-term speculation and badly needed long-term investment was an important one for Keynes as well. As Keynes noted in one of his most widely quoted passages, "When the capital development of a country becomes the by-product of the activities of a casino, the job is likely to be ill-done." Keynes expressed disdain for the tendency of the financial community to direct its efforts towards quick, highly lucrative profit-making rather than investing in the long-term development of the nation's enterprise. It was with this in mind that Keynes, more than three decades before Tobin, called for "a substantial transfer tax on all transactions . . . to mitigate the dominance of speculation over enterprise."

Dornbusch considers today's highly liquid capital markets, with their emphasis on speculative profiteering, to be badly in need of some kind of control. He compares it to the need for gun control in the United States: "Most sane people believe that gun control is desirable because an uncomfortably large number of people carry guns. Whatever they may be maximizing, it surely is not social welfare. Gun control disarms an overly trigger-happy world, just as speed limits cool overly aggressive driving. Liquidity is of the same nature: it cries out for a tax that curbs the excess. We all want to be totally liquid, all the time; yet the economy's capital must be held. Too sharp a focus on the short-run means that the capital stock will . . . not [be] the most productive."

The Tobin tax, according to Dornbusch, offers the prospect of introducing some degree of control, some hope of redirecting capital markets from speculation into longer-term investment. Dornbusch is not suggesting that the Tobin tax alone would curb the excesses of today's capital markets. Other supporters such as U. of T.'s Gerry Helleiner argue that the Tobin tax is simply "one of a whole range of things we need to be thinking about. . . . It would be useful as part of an armoury of policy instruments." Some critics suggest that if Tobin's idea for throwing "sand in the wheels" of capital markets isn't enough, we should try rocks. As Dornbusch notes, "A financial transactions tax is no panacea, just as gun control would not stop all murder; poison and knives would make a comeback. . . . A financial transactions tax will not stop speculation altogether. But it certainly will help lengthen the horizon and focus the mind of capital markets on enterprise and investment rather than [speculative] trading."

Dornbusch's wise comments also help put the political issues surrounding the Tobin tax in perspective. He acknowleges "the vehement backlash from Wall Street," but argues that even with this opposition, the tax could be made to work. "Opponents of a cross-border financial tax will be quick to claim that it cannot work. Business will simply move offshore. . . . True, some trading would move offshore. But the risk is easily exaggerated, and in any event it can be checked."

Dornbusch comes to the refreshing conclusion that we are not impotent to control world capital and argues that the G-7 is where action should begin. "The G-7 has not done anything useful for years. Why not surprise the world with a genuine innovation. . . . [A] financial transactions tax can tame capital flows, thus unenhancing their productivity and [making] the world capital market safe for development finance."

BACK IN OTTAWA, there was no such breadth of vision, only thoughts of impotence. In the face of opposition from the Finance department and Bay Street, the Chrétien government decided not to include the Tobin tax on the agenda of the Halifax Summit.

But if the peso crisis failed to push Ottawa to consider new approaches for dealing with the power and capriciousness of financial markets, the Chrétien government was quick to co-operate with the request from Washington for a $1-billion line of credit as part of the $50-billion bail-out package. The speed with which Washington cobbled together that $50-billion deal turned heads in the U.S. Congress, where there was considerable opposition to the costly plan. Maxine Waters, a Democrat representing a very poor section of Los Angeles, pointedly asked U.S. Treasury Secretary Robert Rubin why such resources are never available to deal with the crisis situations that exist in U.S. inner cities. "We marvel at the ability of all you guys just to get together in a room and solve a crisis of this magnitude," she told Rubin at a hearing of the House banking committee. "We just wish you could apply some of that creativity and thinking and find some loan guarantees for us."

It did seem ironic, on the face of it, that the United States was hustling to hand over $50 billion to help out a country whose citizens were regularly rounded up by U.S. border patrols and treated little better than dogs. The irony disappears when we remember that the $50 billion was not actually to help the Mexican people, but rather to make sure that investors, mostly from the United States, Japan and Europe, didn't suffer huge losses on their Mexican holdings. Essentially, western nations were offering up their tax dollars—collected from all their cit-izens—to make sure that their wealthiest and most powerful citizens did not suffer significant investment losses.

It's interesting to note just how smoothly and efficiently the world's leading nations responded to this crisis, enabling the world's financial markets to simply continue operating as before, barely skip-ping a beat. Indeed, the peso crisis seemed to stiffen the resolve of the advanced nations to make the existing system work. In the immedi-ate aftermath of the crisis, the IMF took on an assertive role of super-vising the international financial system—something it already was doing, but planned to do more aggressively in the future. IMF man-aging director Michel Camdessus told a Washington audience that the IMF had decided to step up its "surveillance" of the global finan-cial system.

What is intriguing is how far all this strays from the notion that international capital markets are simply free markets out there oper-ating on their own. As we've seen, the investors who stood to lose money in the peso crisis were not left to the mercy of the market, to be tossed about capriciously by the Invisible Hand. On the contrary, a highly organized international rescue effort, worth $50 billion, was orchestrated by the most powerful nations of the world, almost overnight, to insulate these investors from any potential harshness the market might deal out. No similar treatment, of course, was afforded to the Mexican people, who were left to make "adjustments."

Compare this with what might have happened if, for instance, the powerful nations of the world had not provided the $50-billion bail-out. Mexico would have been forced to default on its loans. According to popular wisdom, this would have been catastrophic for Mexico. But is this really true? Certainly, defaulting on loans is never an ideal solu-tion, but, in some ways, it might have been a better alternative. The point here is not to advocate default, but rather to note that the real beneficiaries of the bail-out were not the Mexican people but the international financial community.

After all, those who had lent Mexico money—including major

international banks—would not have simply been able to abandon
Mexico if it had defaulted. They had already loaned Mexico too much
money to wash their hands and walk away. Rather, they would have
been forced to renegotiate the loans, on terms that were more
favourable to Mexico, so that Mexico would have been in a position
to repay at least some of the money. This is exactly what happens
when large corporations get into debt situations they can't manage.
When the Reichmanns were no longer able to pay the interest on
Olympia & York's bank loans in the early 1990s, the banks came up
with easier terms. When Eaton's got into severe financial trouble in the
spring of 1997, its creditors were forced to take a write-down on their
loans; for every dollar Eaton's owed, a creditor was lucky to get sixty
cents. It's a well-known principle that if a creditor has loaned enough
money to a particular debtor, that debtor enjoys a certain power. A
creditor cannot afford to let a major debtor go under.

For months after the peso crisis, the Mexican press was full of commentaries about these sorts of possibilities, written by leading Mexican political, business and academic figures, who well understood
how disastrous the implications of the bail-out were for Mexico. None
of this commentary appeared in the mainstream North American
media, where the bail-out was presented as almost a humanitarian
gesture, or at least a necessary measure to restore the soundness of the
international financial system. What was not pointed out was that the
bail-out restored a particular type of international financial system.
And of course the question was never posed: whose interest does that
particular type of international financial system serve?

When we look at the massiveness of the intervention in the private
marketplace that took place in the peso crisis, we can't help but notice
how much less intrusive something like the Tobin tax seems. Or for
that matter, the Chilean law that requires capital to stay in the country for one year. Do these sorts of solutions really represent more
intervention in the workings of the private marketplace than a $50-
billion government bail-out and the imposition of severe adjustments
that essentially redesigned the entire Mexican economy, or the IMF's

increased "surveillance over the international monetary system and members' exchange rate policies"?

All these measures—whether government bail-outs, IMF surveillance, the Tobin tax or the Chilean law—interfere hugely in the operation of the private marketplace. What distinguishes them, however, is whose interests the intervention serves. To a bank that trades millions of dollars' worth of currency per day, a tiny transaction tax on those trades seems like a gigantic intervention, even an affront to the very principles of freedom and democracy. On the other hand, to a Mexican peasant whose income has just been drastically cut because of the severe adjustment policies imposed on his country as a condition of the $50-billion loan, the Tobin tax would hardly seem intrusive or onerous at all.

It's pretty clear where the burden falls in the case of international banks and Mexican peasants. But what about ordinary Canadians? We certainly haven't had to suffer the brutal adjustments experienced by ordinary Mexicans. However, the existing international financial system—with its obeisance to capital mobility—does impose real costs on us too, as we've seen. It's the fear of capital mobility that drives us to put in place policies that please international investors, even though these policies prevent us from achieving full employment and maintaining the kinds of social programs we want.

The point is that, contrary to popular lore, international financial markets are already subject to heavy intervention, in the form of supervision, regulation and surveillance. But all this intervention is currently carried out in the interest of financial investors. Why not carry it out instead in the public interest?

To even suggest that international financial markets be regulated in the public interest sounds like pie-in-the-sky dreaming. Or does it? In fact, it's been done before—for several decades. And those decades, interestingly, coincided with the most prosperous era in the history of the world.

How John Maynard Keynes (Briefly) Did Save the World

It is the absence of the threat of individual starvation which makes primitive society, in a sense, more human than market economy.
— Karl Polanyi

I've come to the conclusion that we should not trust any economist under the age of 65—those who know first hand the 1930s and the Great Depression.   — Duncan Cameron

AMONG THE RANKS OF those fighting for the rights of the com-mon man in the early part of the twentieth century, Sidney Webb cut an impressive figure. Although born into the British aristocracy in the mid-nineteenth century, Webb—or Baron Passfield—was an avid reformer who dedicated his life to fighting poverty. A lawyer by train-ing, he spent many years in Parliament as an MP and cabinet minister in the Labour governments of the late 1920s and early 1930s. Webb's commitment to social justice was shared by his wife, Beatrice, who was also born into wealth and privilege. Together, the Webbs served on a royal commission studying Britain's poor laws and produced an important dissenting opinion. They also jointly founded the London School of Economics and Political Science, as well as the journal the *New Statesman.*

But for all Sidney Webb's education, his involvement in political debate and his years of activism in progressive causes, he was taken aback by the news, on September 21, 1931, that Britain had gone off the gold standard. "Nobody told us we could do that," he remarked.

To Webb, as to just about everyone else outside the clubby little world of international banking, the gold standard wasn't something one chose to be on or off. It was simply the way the world worked, the only way the international financial system could be organized. There was no alternative. Gold was precious. It had an eternal value. Therefore it seemed only logical, only natural, that the value of every nation's currency should be set in relation to the value of gold.

If the gold standard seemed like part of nature, it wasn't. It was an artificially constructed system that was tightly managed by the central bankers of the major trading nations, with the help of the important private banking houses in London, Vienna, Paris and New York. And its abandonment was the crucial first step for the common people in gaining any hope of economic betterment.

CONTRARY TO WHAT ONE might think, hunger as a serious social problem is a relatively recent phenomenon. As the economic historian Karl Polanyi has pointed out, individuals were not in danger of starving in primitive or traditional societies, unless the whole community was threatened by some adverse condition. In feudal Europe, for instance, everyone had had work to perform on the manor, and everyone was fed. The principle of freedom from want was sanctioned, notes Polanyi, "under almost every and any type of social organization up to about the beginning of sixteenth century Europe." It was only at this point in history, with the emergence of "individuals unattached to the manor," that the problem of hunger really began to take shape as a social ill. Without the security of the manor, some individuals were able to make it on their own as independent craftsmen or workers in the cottage industries; others fell into pauperhood and near-starvation. With the coming of the Industrial Revolution, the fate of all these unattached individuals became more uncertain. By the end of the eighteenth century, the condition of a large number of them had become quite desperate.

It was because of this that a group of local magistrates gathered at the Pelikan Inn in the town of Speenhamland, England, on a lovely day in early May 1795. Outside the inn, the scene was lush and pastoral, the air fresh with the smell of the English country garden below. But inside, things were gloomy, as the magistrates, after eating roast beef and drinking French wine, pondered the devastation of the people in the countryside. They did not like what they had seen. As representatives of the old patriarchal world of landed privilege, the magistrates regarded the chaos and despair all around them as evidence of the dysfunction of the new industrial order, which was increasingly being foisted on the country by the aggressive new capitalist class of merchants and industrialists.

In the interests of avoiding an actual famine, the magistrates at the Pelikan Inn decided to put in place a new allowance system guaranteeing that the poor would have bread. The allowance was to be determined by the price of bread: when a loaf of bread "shall cost one shilling, then every poor and industrious person shall have for his support 3 shillings weekly . . . and for the support of his wife and every other of his family 1 shilling, 6 pence." This allowance, which was to ensure a minimum income, was an attempt to re-establish a traditional principle that had once been taken for granted, "the right to live."

Less than forty years later, as the Industrial Revolution gained momentum, the "right to live" was seen as a horrible impediment standing in the way of progress.

THE "RIGHT TO LIVE" did, in fact, represent a serious impediment to progress, or at least, progress towards the kind of economic system that the newly influential merchants and industrialists were keen to put in place in the early decades of the nineteenth century. The essence of the problem was that the Speenhamland allowance system ensured that everyone had bread to eat, regardless of how hard they worked or even whether or not they worked at all. If they worked but their wages were below the minimum necessary to buy bread for the family, the allowance system would top up their wages. If they didn't work, they'd still receive enough allowance to buy bread. The Speenhamland system greatly reduced the desperation level of the worker.

This was a dramatic departure from Elizabethan times, when there had been a sharp division between the working poor and destitute paupers. Under Elizabethan Poor Laws, support was available only to these destitute paupers who lived in "poorhouses"—hellish barracks, little better than jails, where the truly destitute were spared from actual starvation. The working poor, on the other hand, were the independent craftsmen and domestic workers who enjoyed a status in society considerably above those confined to the poorhouse. Indeed, in the days before the emergence of a "middle class," the term "poor" did not mean that someone was in desperate circumstances; it simply referred to the "common people." As Polanyi notes, "the gentlemen of England judged all persons poor who did not command an income sufficient to keep them in leisure." The poor belonged neither to the gentry nor to the poorhouse; they were those who had to work for a living.

The Speenhamland allowance system changed all this. It meant that public relief was available even to those who did not enter the dreaded poorhouse. For the first time, "outdoor relief" was to be generally available. It was now possible to live an independent life (of sorts) outside the poorhouse and not starve. The result was, Polanyi notes, considerable demoralization for the working poor, who effectively lost their somewhat higher position in the social hierarchy. Their once-proud, independent status was gone, as they were suddenly not much different from the poorhouse crowd.

This demoralizing situation could have been avoided. A guaranteed "right to live" wouldn't have been demoralizing if there had been opportunities to improve one's condition and raise one's status through working. But rigid anti-combination laws prevented workers from unionizing or organizing in any way to push for better wages, so they had little hope of improving their situation, and therefore little material incentive to work. No matter what they did—whether they worked hard or even whether they worked at all—the result was the same: bread.

But the real problem with the "right to live," at least from the point of view of the factory owners and industrialists who wielded increasing power in early-nineteenth-century England, was that it prevented the labouring classes from feeling desperate enough to want to work in the wretched factories and mines where their labour was badly needed. The lack of a desperate labour force was seen as holding back the advance of the Industrial Revolution, which was bursting to proceed. It's not surprising that the powerful figures in the new industrial class found much merit in the arguments put forward by a group of social commentators and philosophers who, anticipating later NAIRU theory, favoured withdrawing the "right to live."

These commentators advocated the abolition of the paternalistic Speenhamland allowance system, thereby putting the labouring classes in a sufficiently desperate position to "freely" sell their labour. As long as the poor were lolling about, feasting on bread, there would be little to motivate them to perform the tasks at hand. What was needed was more hunger. It was an essential element; it spurred the poor to work. As William Townsend noted, "Hunger will tame the fiercest animals, it will teach decency and civility, obedience and subjection, to the most perverse. In general it is only hunger which can spur and goad them [the poor] on to labour."

Hunger, then, was seen as the key to human motivation—at least the key to the immediate problem of getting available bodies to work in the factories. Even in times of prosperity, the poor were not to share in the bounty, lest a lessening of hunger sap their motivation. Philosopher Jeremy Bentham argued that even in the best of times, "the great mass of citizens will most probably possess few other resources than their daily labour, and consequently will always be near indigence." As long as the working man was near indigence, hunger would remain an effective tool to goad him to labour. In an interesting twist, Bentham argued that an important task for government was to *ensure conditions of deprivation*, thereby guaranteeing that hunger would work its magic and allow progress to proceed.

By the mid-1830s, the British government was finally called upon to perform this important task. It did so by implementing the Poor Law Reform of 1834, which wiped out the Speenhamland allowance system. The general "right to live" was withdrawn; relief was once again to be available only to those willing to check themselves in to the poorhouse. The results were brutal, as a mass of desperate humanity was herded into the unregulated world of the marketplace, with child labourers sweeping chimneys and pulling heavy carts of coal in unventilated mine shafts at all hours of the day and night.

If this seemed like an awfully mean-spirited way to treat the common people, contemporary commentators were quick to point out that society was simply acting on the laws of nature. They explained that the poor were confined to this rather brutal state by their own deficiencies and lack of useful abilities. A foresighted God had apparently put them on earth because they were necessary; how else would the filthy, degrading and endless toil needed to run the world get done? Certainly, the poor were needed to go to sea and to fight England's battles. "For what is it but distress and poverty which can prevail upon the lower classes of the people to encounter all the horrors which await them on the tempestuous ocean or on the field of battle?" asked Townsend. The only impediment to the smooth working of the natural law of hunger was the natural generosity of the rich, who, according to Townsend, were never lacking in charitable sentiment towards the poor.

This charitable spirit apparently didn't interfere too much, however. The charity of the rich was not enough to actually alleviate the plight of the poor, whose situation did not improve in the early decades after the Poor Law Reform, despite the growing prosperity of England. (It would take another few decades and the rise of unionization before there was a general improvement in the lives of the poor.) This failure of the poor to improve their situation in the 1830s and 1840s was attributed to the workings of natural law, or what became known as the "iron law of wages"—the notion that the wages of the common people were permanently low because of natural laws that created an ever-growing population and a scarcity of food.

Some man-made laws also helped keep the poor in a weak and vulnerable state. In addition to the Poor Law Reform, which ensured hunger for those who didn't work, there was the gold standard. An integral part of the international financial system that developed in the nineteenth century, the gold standard created an orderly world for international trade, which contributed to Britain's prosperity. The gold standard also had the effect of suppressing workers' wages.

In its simplest form, the gold standard was a system that made it easy for nations to trade with each other. Unlike domestic trade, which was carried out in the same currency, international trade involved the problem of establishing the value of different currencies. How many French francs would be worth the same as a British pound? Without a systematic way of establishing the value of one another's currencies, trade would be hopelessly complex.

The gold standard system offered a simple answer: the entire trading system was anchored to gold—a scarce metal with a universally recognized value. The value of each country's currency was established in relation to gold, roughly based on the nation's wealth. (This fixed rate was backed up by real reserves of gold held in the nation's treasury or central bank.) With the value of each national currency fixed in relation to the price of gold, it could be fixed in relation to other national currencies as well. Thus, under this system, the value of the British pound was always the same vis-à-vis the French franc, facilitating trade between the two countries.

This did have a nice simplicity to it. But it also meant there was no way to adjust the value of a nation's currency. This could pose problems. Let's say French products improved and France was therefore able to increase its sales to Britain, while at the same time France purchased fewer British products. This would create relatively more demand for French francs, since French products had to be purchased in French francs. So French francs would suddenly be more sought after; in essence, they would have become more valuable. But the problem was that French francs *couldn't* be more valuable; their value was fixed under the gold standard. They always had to be worth the same in relation to the British pound. As a result, a gap would develop between the values fixed by the gold standard and the real values. The question then became: what adjustment could be made to accommodate this new reality so that Britain and France could still trade easily with each other? Since the relative values of the currencies were set and could not be altered, there had to be some other form of adjustment. The only other possibility was for the British to cut their *prices.* With lower British prices, the French would need fewer francs to buy the same volume of British goods. The British price cut would have the same effect as a cut in the value of the British currency would have had, had it been allowed under the gold standard. In both scenarios, there would be a correction of the imbalance that had occurred because the British were buying more goods from France than they were able to sell to France.

But there was a crucial difference in the two methods of correcting this trade imbalance, or trade deficit. A cut in the value of the British currency meant the British pound would be worth less when it came to buying foreign goods. Essentially, everyone in Britain would be a little poorer, in relation to everyone in France. But in relation to one another in Britain, nothing much would have changed.

Under the second method—a cut in British prices—there would be a significant difference in the relative well-being of those within Britain. To see this, it is necessary to consider how the drop in prices would be achieved. Basically, the mechanism for driving prices down was for the nation's central bank to raise interest rates. Higher British interest rates would attract foreign capital into the country, thus strengthening the pound to help it maintain its required value under the gold standard. But these higher interest rates also had the effect of slowing down the economy. This had a general depressing effect on wages as well as prices. If companies were to still sell their products at a profit, they would have to cut wages to compensate for the lower revenue they were receiving owing to their lower prices. Workers had little choice but to agree to a wage cut. If they resisted, their employer might not be able to make a profit any more and might well be driven out of business. Companies operating at a marginal profit would probably be forced out of business anyway, thereby driving up unemployment even as wages were dropping. This additional unemployment put a further downward pressure on wages; with large numbers of desperate, unemployed workers, employers could get away with paying even lower wages.

For the rich, this situation had some definite advantages. They could now pay their workers less. And they also benefited from the higher interest rates, which meant a higher rate of return for people like themselves who had excess money to lend. The rich also benefited from the general drop in prices. The common people, who lived at a subsistence level, experienced no benefit from the lower prices, because their wages fell too. But for those who had large accumulations of money, the lower prices were an advantage. The cost of a carriage or a setting of fine china was suddenly less, even though the rich had the same amount of money. This made them relatively even wealthier than before. Thus, deflation—the falling of the price level—benefited those with money, and hurt those without it. And deflation, the means by which central banks corrected trade deficits, was a constant reality under the gold standard.

All this meshed nicely with the thinking of classical laissez-faire economics, the prevailing orthodoxy in the nineteenth century and forerunner of modern "market" theory. Largely derived from the late-eighteenth-century writings of Adam Smith, the classical school of thought held that the private marketplace functioned with wonderful efficiency if left on its own. There was a buyer and a seller for everything, and the market would determine the price based on supply and demand for any particular product or service. According to this theory, everything always naturally found the right price, which was what someone was willing to pay for it. In practical terms, this meant that if workers were unable to find work, they were simply pricing their labour too high. The answer was for them to lower their expectations to what employers were willing to pay.

Thus, the gold standard and classical economic theory reinforced each other: both favoured the idea that workers should be prepared to adjust their wages and their expectations downward. Although Adam Smith had argued that workers would eventually benefit by the general rise in prosperity due to economic growth, he held that the means of achieving this economic growth was the acceptance of the often harsh rules of the marketplace. Those rules were clear: if there were too many people unemployed, the answer was for workers to accept less. Any interference—from government or unionization—would only disturb the mechanism by which the economy achieved its maximum efficiency, which, ultimately, would benefit all.

The role of government in the economy, then, was to be limited to maintaining the external value of the currency, through hikes in interest rates when necessary. The other necessity for government was to keep its budget balanced, since government deficits were considered potentially inflationary, and inflation threatened to erode the external value of the currency. So the fate of the domestic economy, and the workers who participated in it, was not something government was supposed to concern itself with. Government's role in economic affairs—a role that was required under the gold standard—was strictly to maintain the external value of the currency. For those with an accumulation of financial assets, this meant the value of their fortunes would be maintained.

It's not hard to see why the rich found a lot of merit in the gold standard. It offered wage restraint for the common people, high rates of return for themselves and a restriction on the role of government to maintaining this agreeable situation. And it achieved all this effortlessly, invisibly, without requiring any apparent meanness or lack of consideration. It all happened automatically, in accordance with international law, in the cause of maintaining stable currencies to facilitate world trade.

One thing the gold standard was not, however, was natural or self-regulating. The system worked only because of the full co-operation and trust of the tiny group of players who dominated international finance. There was absolute confidence within this exclusive world of banking and investment that the major central banks would do what the gold standard demanded: that is, raise interest rates to protect the external value of the currency, no matter how dreadful the impact on the domestic economy. This confidence meant that those with capital knew exactly what to expect at all times. Thus, they were happy to lend money to a country with a trade deficit, secure in the knowledge that its central bank would raise interest rates as required. So, private capital would flow almost automatically into a gold-standard country experiencing a trade deficit, thereby helping that country solve its deficit problem. The result was a fair degree of international stability and a lot of capital mobility.

The key to all this co-operation by the financial élite was the knowledge that the central banks would behave exactly as they were supposed to—imposing discipline on the lower orders and rewarding those with money. The perfect little system might still be operating today, if it hadn't been for the rise of democracy.

THE DANGER POSED by democracy was a constant theme among the established orders in the nineteenth century. In its early form, before universal male suffrage, democracy was primarily a vehicle for the new capitalist class of industrialists and merchants to challenge the power of the landed aristocracy. This new class scored a major political victory in the 1830s when it succeeded in pushing the aristocrats in the British House of Lords to surrender considerably more power to the House of Commons. This was essentially a transfer of power from one privileged group to another, since the House of

Commons was largely made up of well-to-do members of the new capitalist class.

But after wresting more power from the aristocracy, this new part of the élite felt things had gone far enough in the name of democracy. Certainly, they had little interest in extending the franchise to the roughly 85 percent of the male population—and 100 percent of the female population—who failed to meet the strict property, education and gender requirements necessary to qualify to vote. Extending the franchise was loudly denounced by such well-known thinkers as Thomas Macaulay and Herbert Spencer. In a renowned speech to the House of Lords, Macaulay called for the rejection of demands for universal (male) suffrage on the grounds that it would put at risk the institution of property, which Macaulay argued was the basis of civilization. This was a view that was widely shared by all those who held property—the newly rich liberal capitalists as well as the old, landed aristocracy.

Thus, there was little empathy for a popular movement for greater democracy that emerged in the late 1830s, shortly after the "right to live" was withdrawn by the Poor Law Reform. Starting out as the London Working Men's Association in 1836, a group of workers, led by charismatic William Lovett, quickly decided that the answer to their desperate plight lay in achieving a voice for the working man in Parliament. The idea spread like wildfire through the dismal, overcrowded tenements of working-class London, full of once-independent artisans and craftsmen from the countryside who now found themselves virtual prisoners in the factories and mills. Within two years, Lovett had drafted a people's charter and, with virtually no political experience and no resources, he and his supporters had organized what amounted to a national campaign for full male suffrage. Known as the Chartists, they organized mass meetings in various parts of the country to elect delegates to a kind of people's assembly. The following winter, the General Convention of the Industrious Classes assembled in London. In June 1839, Lovett led a delegation up the intimidating steps to the Parliament buildings to present their petition—with 1.28 million signatures.

The gentlemen in Parliament were not impressed. To underline their request to vote, the Chartists held demonstrations, which turned into riots in Birmingham. When Lovett promptly published a pamphlet attacking the harshness of police methods during the riots, he was arrested and thrown in jail for a year. With this lawlessness as a backdrop, the Parliamentarians voted overwhelmingly—235 to 46—to reject outright the petitioners' demands.

More disruptions, strikes, boycotts and riots followed. Four months after Parliament's rebuff, fourteen Chartists were killed in clashes with police in a riot in Newport, and mass arrests and trials followed. As the movement spread and became more volatile, Parliamentarians consoled themselves that they had done the right thing in keeping their unkempt, unruly, uneducated countrymen at bay. When a second, even larger, national Chartist petition was rejected by Parliament in 1842, there were more riots, strikes in the coalfields and a general strike that briefly paralysed the north.

With the rejection of the second petition, the Chartist movement started to lose some of its clarity. It became split between those, such as Feargus O'Connor, who wanted to take it in a more militant, working-class direction, and those, like Lovett, who sought an alliance between the working class and sympathetic members of the emerging middle class. There were others, too, who saw it as more of a working-man's self-improvement course, taking on the form of Knowledge Chartism, Bible Chartism and Teetotal Chartism.

Despite the divergent strands, the movement had no trouble organizing a third national campaign around its unifying theme of universal male suffrage. Against a backdrop of violent popular uprisings on the Continent in 1848, the Chartists geared up once again to challenge the privileged men running the country who surrounded themselves with a massive army of special constables stationed around the Parliament buildings and throughout the streets of London. The Chartists had mustered more than 5 million signatures on this third petition. But the answer from Parliament was the same. There were no riots this time, however, and the crowd was dispersed by nothing more than driving rain.

Parliament had once again survived an assault by the people. But at the same time, the move towards more inclusive democracy was starting to seem unstoppable. The 1848 uprisings led to the extension of full male suffrage in France, Germany, Switzerland and some other European countries. Britain finally succumbed to the pressure, gradually relaxing its property and education requirements somewhat in the 1860s, and relaxing them further in the 1880s. Attempts were made to subvert this trend towards democracy; in Belgium and the Netherlands, for instance, the impact of full suffrage was diluted by the fact that property owners and those with higher education were given additional votes. But by the turn of the century, the general march towards democracy seemed unstoppable. By the 1920s, even women had been included.

The gradual inclusion of the broad mass of the population in the electoral process changed the political picture dramatically. Labour and social democratic parties, which promised to champion the political cause of the less powerful, quickly emerged. The Social Democrats in Germany became a major electoral force as early as the 1890s and formed a government in 1919. The British Labour Party first entered electoral politics in the 1900 election; in 1924, with universal suffrage, it briefly formed a government. That same year, France elected a left-leaning government for the first time.

The masses used their new-found power to press for changes: regulations protecting them in the workplace, minimum wages, the right to unionize, even the first rumblings of pressure for social programs. In Britain, union membership doubled over the years of the First World War; in France, the growth was even more pronounced. By the early 1920s, huge strikes were becoming a common feature on the economic landscape of Europe, claiming more than 30 million work days in Italy in 1920, and 36 million in Germany in 1924. The 1926 general strike in Britain cost the economy 162 million work days. The lower orders were showing a spunkiness that would have seemed inconceivable only about a century earlier, when it was left to others to decide how much bread they needed to survive. If they didn't fully have the power to run the country, at least they had the power to disrupt it.

All this did not bode well for the gold standard. Not that it was a hotly debated topic in union halls or a rallying cry with protesting mobs. Outside the banking community and government finance departments, there was little understanding of the role played by the gold standard in keeping wages down and unemployment up. Even among those who grasped the serious deflationary regimen imposed by the gold standard, there was little appreciation that there could be any other way of organizing international finance. So the gold standard, which threatened to crush the dreams of the newly enfranchised workers, was a hugely powerful—but almost invisible—force.

The gold standard was abandoned during the First World War, along with just about all international trade and co-operation. But with the end of the war, the economic élite was adamant about the need to restore it. The traditionally powerful banking houses in London joined forces with the increasingly influential New York bankers to push behind the scenes for a restoration of the important elements of their pre-war world: independent central banks, balanced budgets, free capital movements and—the key enforcement mechanism for the whole package—the gold standard. The London and New York bankers worked closely together, managing to turn the restoration of the gold standard into a top priority at international post-war conferences in Brussels and Genoa. The bankers offered more than advice on the matter. They also willingly supplied large loans at attractive rates to governments thinking along their lines. To European nations struggling under crippling war debt, the bankers' vision of the post-war world seemed more and more compelling.

Nowhere was the compulsion to return to gold felt more acutely than among the financial élite in Britain. A committee headed by Lord Cunliffe, governor of the Bank of England, recommended immediately after the war that Britain return to gold as soon as possible. After all, London had served as the capital of the world financial system, which was anchored by gold. Foreign governments, central banks and international firms held significant deposits in London, conducted international business there and looked to London for financial leadership. The gold standard was seen as the stabilizing centrepiece of the world trading system, which Britain had dominated so well in the late nineteenth century. Restoring the gold standard seemed synonymous with restoring Britain's dominion over its glorious international trading empire, even with restoring the world that had been lost. To some, it was practically synonymous with Britain's honour.

And yet, seven years after the end of the war, Britain hadn't yet returned to gold. The reason was clear: it would be a wrenching adjustment, and Britain was now a very different place. The difference was the emergence of a newly empowered working class whose members were no longer willing to have their incomes sacrificed for the sake of preserving someone else's notion of what the national currency should be worth on foreign markets. The adjustment involved in moving back onto the gold standard would be horrendous, especially since it was assumed that Britain would have to return to gold with the value of the pound set at its old pre-war value. This would be extremely difficult, since prices in Britain had risen considerably during the war. Those prices would have to be driven down. The only way to do this was for the Bank of England to raise interest rates and for the British government to cut spending, thereby pushing the country into austerity and recession and eventually causing a reduction in the general price level. But times were already hard enough. The postwar recession in 1920–21 had been grim and had come hard on the heels of four brutal years of war and deprivation. More austerity was hardly what the British people had in mind.

They had something very different in mind—a much better deal for themselves. They showed their collective muscle right after the war by using their trade unions and new parliamentary power to press for—and win—a 13 percent reduction in the working week, with no change in pay. This was an enormous victory for labour, which reflected its new power on the economic and political landscape. But it was a victory that also made the return to gold even more difficult. If prices were to be driven down, as the gold standard demanded, workers would have to accept less. If they didn't, their employers would have to cut profit margins, which in some cases would drive them out of business. But workers had just won more. And they also had their sights set on getting more from government too. Wartime leaders had promised pensions, health care and housing for veterans in the post-war world. Now veterans—most of the male population— were focused on seeing government deliver some of those benefits. Once again, the gold standard, which required balanced government budgets, stood in the way.

All this revealed the great gap between Britain's conservative financial élite and the mass of working people—a gap that had always existed but seemed more of a problem now that the two groups found themselves uncomfortably sharing power in the new post-war world. While the working people felt entitled to much more than they'd ever had and were determined to see how far they could push their new-found rights, the élite was determined to crush those expectations and take Britons back to the more limited, confining world they'd lived in under the gold standard.

Indeed, the élites increasingly came to regard the gold standard not just as a desirable way to run the world, but as a powerful vehicle for holding the masses at bay. Returning to gold would have the automatic effect of keeping democracy in check, insulating those in power from the pressures and demands of the new electorate, and acting as an iron wall against which the people would be powerless to push. The gold standard had always provided that iron wall. But the wall hadn't really been necessary before, since power had been concentrated in the hands of a small élite, whose views on economic management reinforced the principles of the gold standard. In the post-war world of greater democracy, power was now shared with many who had little taste for deflation and austerity. Therefore, in order to ensure sound money policies and head off demands for excessive government spending, an external force would be needed to undermine the power of ordinary people. The gold standard appeared to be the answer.

This was clearly understood by the people most keen to return to gold. At hearings of the Chamberlain committee, set up in Britain in 1924 to determine how to finally take steps to return to gold, experts from the financial and business world virtually all expressed their support for the gold standard. And their reasons for supporting it had much to do with its ability to impose limits on democracy. The key benefit, according to their testimony before the committee headed by Sir Austen Chamberlain, was the power of the gold standard to prevent elected governments from being pushed by the electorate to deliver costly programs or reduce interest rates. Employers also saw it as a way of disciplining the growing power of unions. No matter how much the electorate pushed for new government programs or unions pushed for higher wages, both goals would be rendered impossible by the need to suppress domestic prices in order to maintain the external value of the currency, as the gold standard required. The politicians' hands would be tied. It wouldn't matter what the electorate did or said. The final decision about their hopes and their dreams would rest not with a person or a group of persons who might be swayed or coerced, but with an international requirement that the value of the British currency would be precisely 3 pounds, 17 shillings, 9 pennies per ounce of 11/12 fine gold.

The anti-democratic power of the gold standard was perhaps captured best by Lord Bradbury, an influential senior official in the Treasury department and enthusiastic supporter of the gold standard. Bradbury testified before the Chamberlain committee that the gold standard was "knave-proof." The knaves he had in mind were clearly the ordinary people of Britain, who were increasingly demanding a say over issues such as whether they would be able to find employment or whether they could count on the government to deliver them a pension. Such knavish behaviour was seen as a threat to the established orders and their property, and the élite felt no qualms trying to squelch it. The beauty of the gold standard was that it rendered the knaves harmless; they could flail away all they wanted, but their aspirations would ultimately run aground on the immovable rocks of the gold standard. The country would be "knave-proof."

The urgency of the problem was revealed starkly in 1924 with the election of Britain's first Labour government. This underlined the true threat to the established orders. Not only could the knaves put seemingly unbearable pressure on reasonable governments, but they could even elect fellow knaves to form a government! Certainly, the election of a Labour government made the idea of operating without the gold standard more perilous, since it put the management of the currency into potentially irresponsible hands. Economist Edwin Cannan advised the Chamberlain committee that in times when responsible officials were in charge of protecting the currency, there might be some advantages to staying off the gold standard. However, with the Labour government in power, staying off the gold standard was very risky. As Cannan concluded, "I don't think it is practicable for this country at present."

Certainly the gold standard was viewed as the best way to enforce discipline on a demanding population. In the words of Arthur Kiddy, editor of *Bankers' Magazine,* the gold standard would "prevent 'unsound' experiments by Socialist Governments which might divert the English people from the only real solution of their problems—economy and hard work." Montagu Norman, governor of the Bank of England, felt the behaviour of governments was so unreliable in a democracy that the truly important questions of financial management should be left entirely in the hands of central bankers, who should have complete autonomy from popularly elected governments. According to Norman, the interests of all members of society on financial questions should be considered, "but not consulted any more than about the design of battleships."

Ironically, despite the intense fears of the established orders, the Labour government proved surprisingly meek in challenging the orthodoxy of the gold standard. Philip Snowden, Labour's Chancellor of the Exchequer, turned out to be no knave at all. Rather, he became a major defender of the gold standard, and even a supporter of Norman's view that the central bank should operate free of interference from elected governments. "Parliament is not a competent body to deal with the administration of such highly delicate and intricate matters," said Snowden, echoing Norman, as well as the rest of the financial élite.

One of the few dissenting voices in this resounding chorus of support for the gold standard was that of John Maynard Keynes. For some time, Keynes had been using his regular column in *The New Statesman* to spell out the foolishness of pushing an already depressed economy further into recession in order to return to the gold standard. Keynes's heretical economic views kept him quite outside the mainstream of accepted opinion, but his enormous intellect and wide circle of highly placed friends made him at least a force to be reckoned with. So it was no surprise that Keynes was invited to give testimony before the Chamberlain committee, some of whose members regarded him as little more than a traitor to his class.

They were particularly keen to confront him with the "knave" problem. Chamberlain asked Keynes how, in the absence of the gold standard, there would be any means of preventing the Chancellor of the Exchequer (the British finance minister) from running large budget deficits to finance expensive programs demanded by the electorate. "I do not think there is any means of strapping down a really wicked Chancellor of the Exchequer," Keynes shot back, his playful eyes revealing the enormous pleasure he experienced tormenting the stuffy members of the financial élite. "Well, you could try to stop him as much as possible," retorted Chamberlain, who had served as Chancellor of the Exchequer himself immediately after the war and understood the kinds of pressures that chancellors were now subjected to.

Keynes responded that the Bank of England could be counted on to keep a watchful eye over inflationary pressures inside the country, with the option of raising interest rates if prices rose unduly. But the committee members were clearly worried that without a gold standard to tie his hands, even the governor of the central bank himself might not be able to resist the pressure to ease up on the austerity campaign. "Do you think we shall have to breed a superman [to run the central bank]?" asked committee member Gaspar Ferrer, a private London banker. But Keynes blithely pushed such concerns aside. "I should not have the smallest hesitation in thinking that there would always be a half dozen persons in the City [London's financial district] well competent to look after it."

When the Labour government proved short-lived and the Conservatives returned to power in late 1924, the increasingly pressing issue of the gold standard was handed to the new Chancellor of the Exchequer, Winston Churchill. Ironically, Montagu Norman was slightly disappointed to discover he would no longer be dealing with Labour's Philip Snowden, who had proved such an oddly reliable fan of the gold standard. Churchill, by contrast, was an unknown quantity, regarded as ignorant in the field of financial matters and lacking in technical sophistication. However, Churchill proved co-operative, and within two months Norman—a strange, secretive man who travelled abroad under the name "Mr. Skinner," his secretary's surname—had set off to visit key bankers in New York to set the stage for Britain's transition to gold.

Particularly important on Norman's agenda were meetings with his close friend Benjamin Strong, a dominant force both in the world of private New York banking and in the Federal Reserve, the U.S. central banking system. Strong was a "Morgan man"—a kingpin in the vast financial empire of J.P. Morgan. In addition, he was president of the New York Federal Reserve Bank, which, as Wall Street's voice, dominated the Federal Reserve System. It was through Strong that Wall Street, and the Morgan financial empire, largely ran U.S. financial policy in the 1920s. After the governor of the Bank of England had visited all the key players in New York and Washington—including J.P. Morgan himself—Benjamin Strong offered "Mr. Skinner" a $500-million loan to help ease Britain's transition back to gold, with $200 million coming from the Federal Reserve System and $300 million from J.P. Morgan & Co.

In April 1925, with Keynes railing loudly from the pages of the *New Statesman*, Churchill put Britain back on the gold standard. The already-tightened belts of British workers had to be tightened another few notches. Among the hardest hit was the coal industry, as the value of the British pound rose to its old, pre-war level, making British coal uncompetitive on foreign markets. The mine owners immediately demanded a 10 percent wage cut from their workers to allow companies to drop their prices and restore their competitiveness. The workers dug in their heels, and the giant Trades Union Congress, the umbrella organization for the labour movement, promised to turn the conflict into a general nationwide strike.

The Conservative government offered a temporary subsidy to the industry and a royal commission to study the matter. But there wasn't really much to study; the gold standard had effectively determined that costs had to be cut and labour was too big a cost to escape the hatchet. In the end, the result was a humiliating defeat for labour. With their bargaining power essentially removed by the gold standard, the leaders of the Trades Union Congress led the labour movement out on a general strike in 1926, but the strike lasted only twelve days. The miners held out longer, until sheer desperation drove them back to work on the terms demanded by their employers. It was a victory for the ruling élite. The masses had been contained and even beaten back. As country after country followed Britain back to the gold standard in the late 1920s, the power of capital seemed greatly strengthened everywhere. It seemed the old world had been restored.

But any sense of a world restored was fleeting. With the crash of the New York stock market in October 1929, the true contradictions between the gold standard and democracy came into sharp relief. As the effects of the crash quickly spread, the industrialized world entered a slump the likes of which had never before been seen. Yet there was virtually nothing that governments could do, given the constraints of the gold standard. What was needed was some kind of break for consumers, something to breathe life into the dying economies. But lower interest rates or more government spending—which offered the hope of kick-starting the faltering economies—were the opposite of what was required under the gold standard. Thus, even in the depths of the Depression, the Macmillan committee—yet another committee investigating Britain's dire economic situation—argued that prices had to be pushed down lower still. This was necessary, the committee said, in order to maintain the gold-standard value of the currency—despite the fact that 2.63 million Britons were already out of work and such a move would only add to their ranks.

As the Depression deepened, Keynes's attacks grew more insistent. "We have the savings, the men and the material. The things are worth doing. It is the very pathology of thought to declare that we cannot afford them." It would take another decade of crippling economic stagnation and six long years of war before the genius of this simple insight was—for a while at least—acknowledged.

IN THE GRIM WINTER of 1933, only months after the election of Franklin Roosevelt to the White House, the U.S. Senate finance committee came up with a plan to try to head off the implementation of the New Deal. With roughly a quarter of the American work-force idle and tens of millions of Americans slipping into desperate poverty, Roosevelt had had little trouble defeating the do-nothing government of Republican incumbent Herbert Hoover. But the conservatives who dominated the Senate finance committee were now keen to prevent the new administration from actually proceeding with its radical proposals for national recovery. The senators figured that their committee could provide a forum for the captains of industry and commerce to warn the public of the dangers of Roosevelt's legislative plans. The captains of industry and commerce readily made themselves available.

But the carefully designed plan turned into a fiasco. As the prominent figures—a virtual who's who of the corporate and financial world—got up one after another at the Senate committee hearings, it became painfully obvious that they had no solutions to offer the

American people, nor did they even seem terribly concerned about the plight of Americans. Typical was the response of Jackson Reynolds, of the First National Bank of New York, who, asked if he had a solution, simply replied, "I have not, and I do not believe anybody else has." This was echoed by Myron C. Taylor, chairman of the U.S. Steel Corp., who commented, "I have no remedy in mind, except that the government should put its own house in order as an example to the community, balance the budget and live within its income." There was general agreement that government could—and should—do nothing beyond balancing the budget.

Some of the prominent figures went further and suggested the Depression was a refreshing tonic to restore the nation to health. Bernard Baruch, former head of the War Industries Board, portrayed the Depression as a cure for the nation's wayward behaviour: "Natural forces are at work to cure every evil, but what have we done to aid the cure? . . . We have set every legislative force against the economics of a cure." General W.W. Atterbury, president of the Pennsylvania Railroad, painted the Depression as a moral struggle that required pain. "There is no panacea for a resumption of prosperity except the slow, painful one of hitting the bottom, and then slowly building up with a sane and economical foundation on which to build."

Although these sorts of attitudes hadn't been quite so clearly showcased until the Senate committee hearings, they were perfectly in line with the views of those who had run the U.S. government and central bank so ineffectively through the first few years of the Depression. Indeed, what is striking about the early days of the Depression was how little action was taken by U.S. authorities, despite the fact that levers were available to them. While the gold standard really did limit the possibilities for the indebted European nations trying to dig their way out of the Depression, it imposed fewer constraints on Washington, since the United States was a creditor nation. Because other nations owed money to the United States, it wasn't obliged to deflate its prices in order to maintain the external value of its currency the way European nations were. This meant there was no reason that the

U.S. Federal Reserve Board couldn't lower interest rates substantially to ease the severity of the Depression. Had it done so, it would have eased the burden on the European nations as well, since they would have been able to lower their interest rates somewhat also, without fearing capital would flee to the United States.

But, trapped in the logic of classical laissez-faire economics, those who ran the Federal Reserve concluded that it was better to leave the Depression to work itself out. The strong and the good would survive. As the economy collapsed all around them, the governors of the Fed had maintained high interest rates, convinced that the brutal medicine they were administering would serve the country well in the end. The only answer was austerity, learning to do with less. As senior Fed official George W. Norris put it, "We believe that the correction must come about through reduced production, reduced inventories, the gradual reduction of consumer credit, the liquidation of security loans and the accumulation of savings through the exercise of thrift." The answer, then, was to shrink the economy, to starve the public body back to health.

Towards the end of the Senate committee hearings, after almost four dozen captains of industry and commerce had paraded their bleak views, a banker from Utah was called to the stand. Unlike the previous witnesses, who were all prominent men, known to the senators on the committee, this man was hardly recognized by anyone in the room, nor was his name—Marriner Eccles—familiar to them. But as Eccles began his testimony, the curiosity in the room turned to utter surprise. Here was a banker who sounded completely different from every other figure from the financial world. The others had all called for government restraint, balanced budgets and learning to do with less. But Eccles stunned the room by calling for a new government activism that would involve massive spending on public works projects and unemployment relief, minimum wage laws and tax reform to redistribute income, as well as changes to the Federal Reserve System that would strip power from the hands of Wall Street. "We shall either adopt a plan which will meet the problem of unemployment under capitalism," Eccles told the hushed room of senators, administration officials and reporters, "or a plan will be adopted for us which will operate without capitalism."

Eccles's appearance before the committee had largely been an accident. He had been invited because a junior senator on the committee was from Utah, and Eccles was an important banking figure in the state. But no one had had any idea what he was going to say. Certainly his testimony was not at all what the senior members of the committee wanted to hear. But it struck a highly responsive chord among the more innovative members of the new administration, who were trying to push Roosevelt into taking dramatic action along the lines that Eccles had just outlined. Here was a banker who was defying Wall Street orthodoxy, who actually had a bold plan to overcome the paralysis of the Depression.

Almost immediately, Eccles was drawn into the inner circle. He quickly became a key architect of the New Deal as well as a close Roosevelt adviser, who helped push the president towards the big-spending initiatives of the early years of his administration. Eccles also had little trouble convincing Roosevelt that it was essential to reform the Federal Reserve System, which he argued concentrated too much power in the hands of Wall Street bankers who were quite content to keep a chokehold on the gasping economy. Roosevelt agreed and decided that Eccles was the man to oversee the reform, in the position of Fed chairman.

The New York bankers bitterly fought Eccles's confirmation, but failed to block it. Although he was a banker, Eccles was clearly not one of them. Owner of a chain of twenty-eight banks in Utah, Idaho, Wyoming and Oregon, Eccles had little in common with the Wall Street crowd that had dominated the hearings. In the highly stratified world of U.S. banking, there were a small number of extremely powerful banks, mostly located in New York and led by the Morgan financial empire. Beneath this upper tier, there were thousands of smaller regional banks, many of which went down in bankruptcy in the early Depression years. Their demise went unlamented by the Wall Street crowd; these were exactly the kinds of weak, improperly managed enterprises that the Depression was fortunately purging from the American economy.

There was little love lost between the two banking worlds, which were almost totally different in orientation. The New York banks maintained close ties to the sophisticated international banking scene in London, Paris and Vienna, and were focused on goals like maintaining the gold standard and squashing inflation. The regional banks, which had played a key role in financing the development of the American west over the previous hundred years, were expansionist, entrepreneurial, even reckless, often relying on the larger banks to bail them out.

Eccles was very much a product of this frontier culture. His father, David Eccles, had emigrated from Scotland with nothing and, in one generation, lived the American dream to the fullest. Through hard work, entrepreneurialism and a good deal of luck, he had accumulated a considerable frontier fortune in timber, coal mining and construction, building each new business with the savings he had carefully accumulated in his previous endeavours. A Mormon polygamist with two wives, David Eccles left twenty-one children when he died. Marriner, at the age of twenty-two, managed to gain control of a significant part of his father's business ventures and developed it into an even bigger empire, particularly in banking. In the state of Utah, the name Eccles became synonymous with power and wealth. To Marriner, it all seemed to come down to a simple code: work hard, be thrifty, watch out for your own interests, get rich. Had Marriner Eccles been asked to testify at a Senate finance committee hearing only a couple of years earlier, his advice would have been much the same as the Wall Street crowd's.

But the Depression changed everything for Eccles. For three years, he watched the panic and pain spread through the American heartland. Although he had not suffered personal hardship, he had witnessed great suffering. What's more, he had caused great suffering, by ensuring that his banks were as aggressive and uncompromising in their collection policies as was necessary to stay afloat. In the end, none of his banks went under. But the experience transformed him. The conservative economic views that he'd absorbed from his father, and that seemed to fit with his own life's experience, now seemed deeply alien and unsatisfying to him. All of a sudden, all around him, he saw hard-working, thrifty people losing their farms and unable to keep up the payments on their business loans. It wasn't that they had changed; rather the world had changed. In the 1920s, the engine of growth had seemed unstoppable on the frontier, bringing new roads, housing construction, public utilities and oil production to the west. Now everything had stopped, and it seemed impossible to get it going again.

The hopelessness of the situation led to a sense of panic that fed on itself, creating an ever-greater paralysis. Eccles witnessed this first-hand in his bank in Ogden, Utah, in the summer of 1931. When another bank in town failed to open one morning, news quickly spread and a line-up of customers, all wanting to take their money out, began to build in Eccles's First National Bank of Ogden. Eccles knew that to close the bank would simply create more panic, so he instructed his tellers to give the people their money, but to do so very, very slowly. Hour after hour, the besieged tellers carried on at an infuriatingly slow pace, as the crowd grew bigger and more restless. Eventually, an armoured truck arrived at the bank, delivering cash from the local Federal Reserve office in Salt Lake City. After ceremoniously ushering the armed guards with their bags of money to the vault, Eccles jumped onto the counter in front of the crowd and tried to seize the moment to quell the panic.

To everyone's surprise, he announced that the bank would actually stay open late, as long as was necessary to deal with anyone who wanted to take his or her money out. "There is no justification for the excitement or the apparent panicky attitude on the part of some depositors," said Eccles, projecting a mood of confidence and control that masked his own panic. "As all of you have seen, we have just had brought up from Salt Lake City a large amount of currency that will take care of all your requirements. There is plenty more where that came from." While there was indeed plenty more where that came from, in fact, Eccles wouldn't be able to get any more. But since the crowd didn't know this, most of them were satisfied by his show of bravado and left without withdrawing their money.

In many ways, the little Ogden episode was symbolic of the larger Depression drama. There was no shortage of money in the country, but it was locked up in vaults where people couldn't get access to it and where it was doing nothing for the economy. What was needed was a way to unlock these savings and use the money to put the country back to work. Lower interest rates would help, since businesses then could afford to borrow and invest. Under Eccles, the Fed brought interest rates down and became an active source of assistance in the reconstruction of the shattered economy. Gone were the days when the Fed officials would sit back and watch with indifference—even approval—as the nation's weaker members bobbed helplessly in the water until they were no longer able to keep themselves afloat. The role of the Fed, according to Eccles, was "to assure that adequate support is available whenever needed for the emergency financing involved in a recovery program."

But the economy was in such disastrous shape that low interest rates on their own weren't enough. With little prospect of profits, even low interest rates wouldn't prod the private sector to invest. Eccles insisted that given the severity of the Depression, government had to take some initiative; it had to actively intervene with massive spending programs. He was particularly inspired by the research work being carried out by a young economist named Lauchlin Currie, the director of research at the Fed and later Eccles's own economic adviser. Currie argued that massive government spending would have secondary benefits of economic stimulation well beyond the amount of the initial spending. This meant that government could "prime the pump," that is, get things going until the people could continue on their own. If government made the initial outlay of cash, it could revive the economy to the point that business would start spending again. Once that was achieved, government could scale back its own spending and let business carry the can. In this way, the increase in government spending could be reversed without reversing the recovery. Keynes had made almost an identical argument years earlier in testimony before one of Britain's many commissions. The "pump-priming" metaphor, which helped to clarify it, was Currie's, apparently developed without any awareness of Keynes's statements.

As the boldness of the responses necessary became increasingly clear to Eccles, Roosevelt drifted into uncertainty. Rather than getting more radical, Roosevelt seemed to be withdrawing into traditional thinking. In his first few years in office, Roosevelt had defied economic orthodoxy, taking the United States off the gold standard, easing up on credit and, most significantly, experimenting with massive government spending on public works and relief programs. The results had been encouraging. There were definite signs of improvement in 1935 and 1936. But in 1937, focused on balancing the budget, Roosevelt drastically cut back the flow of public funds, sending the struggling economy into a tailspin. By the beginning of 1938, the situation seemed bleaker than ever. Somewhere between eight and eleven million Americans—nobody knew exactly how many—were now out of work with little means of support. With conservatives battling New Dealers inside the administration, Roosevelt had retreated into the security of classical economics.

Eccles was finding it harder and harder to even get the president's attention. Desperate to communicate the urgency of what he felt, he had pressed for a private lunch with the president at the White House. Eccles arrived, buoyed up for the meeting, anxious to convey some of his excitement over the possibilities suggested by Currie's work. But Eccles found Roosevelt distracted, apparently more interested in showing off the new tricks his dog, Fala, could perform than in trying to figure out how to restart the world's biggest economy. When Fala capped her performance by defecating in the corner of the Oval Office, the president seemed even more caught up in the drama, as White House staff crowded in to take care of the mess and provide the necessary discipline. By the time the Fala episode was dealt with, there seemed to be no time left for the president and the chairman of the central bank to make any headway in solving the nation's staggering problems.

It would take the war to finally, unequivocally, demonstrate the need to mobilize the economy, no matter what the cost. And it would take John Maynard Keynes to show that what Eccles and Lauchlin Currie were getting at went to the heart of the problem with classical economics.

ALTHOUGH KEYNES HAD never set foot in Utah and was not the type to jump on a counter to sweet-talk an unruly mob, he and Marriner Eccles ended up with roughly the same formula for ending the Depression.

Whereas Marriner Eccles was a frontier capitalist who struggled to stave off bankruptcy when his safe, secure world seemed to crumble all around him, John Maynard Keynes was a highly intellectual academic with a probing, restless mind and a comfortable seat at the heart of England's self-confident élite. Born in 1883, Keynes was the son of a Cambridge don and grew up in a close-knit, high-powered academic community where his father became the chief administrator of the university. Along with the sons of the country's upper class, Keynes went to Eton, where he won prizes for mathematics, classics and English, and later went on to King's College, Cambridge, where he graduated with a first in mathematics and became a prize pupil of the leading economist of the day, Alfred Marshall. But Keynes was more than just a very impressive student. He mixed easily with the élite crowd at Cambridge, becoming a key social and intellectual figure on campus with active involvement in numerous select campus societies. Although he had no athletic abilities and considered himself homely, he was deeply involved and accomplished in just about every area of life at the university.

For someone who was to tear down much of the edifice of established thinking in Britain, Keynes was, to an astonishing extent, an insider—both at Cambridge and throughout his life. Although an iconoclast whose ideas often piqued members of the establishment, Keynes moved easily among them, entertaining them, dazzling them, infuriating them. He was at the very centre of the economics establishment, taking on the leading economists and economic wisdom of his day with such vigour and brilliance that his views were sought after even by those who disliked them. He was also a successful financier who became independently wealthy from his investing and served as chairman of a large insurance company.

In addition, the lanky, witty Keynes cut a considerable figure in the political world, where he was closely associated at different times with two men who served as Liberal prime ministers, Herbert Asquith and David Lloyd George. Even after years of publicly pillorying Winston Churchill for his decision to put Britain back on the gold standard, he was sufficiently intimate with Churchill to make a private bet with him about the outcome of the 1929 election. Keynes was also associated with some of the leading cultural and literary figures of the day, including Virgina Woolf, whose husband, Leonard, was one of Keynes's oldest friends, T.S. Eliot, E.M. Forster, Lytton Strachey and others in the Bloomsbury group. His marriage to ballerina Lydia Lopokova was a widely publicized social event.

It was from these elevated social and political circles that Keynes was to champion a cause dear to the heart of the common people: the fight against unemployment. But Keynes came to this cause by what might be considered a circuitous route—not through union halls or mass demonstrations but via a crisis of declining religious faith among the philosophical crowd at Cambridge. It was the late Edwardian age and the intellectual élite of England was struggling to deal with the moral vacuum created by the collapse of religious beliefs. The firm moral anchor that Christianity had provided only a generation earlier had given way to a mood of questioning, of moral and spiritual confusion, exemplified by the ultimate challenge posed in

Darwin's *The Origin of Species*. For some at Cambridge, this loss of religious moorings had frightening implications, not least of which was the prospect of a breakdown of the social order. Henry Sidgwick, an influential professor of moral philosophy and contemporary of Keynes at Cambridge, expressed concern that "the general loss of such a hope [of Christian immortality] from the minds of average human beings as now constituted, would be an evil of which I cannot pretend to measure the extent."

For Keynes and some of his close friends, however, this demise of religion was liberating. Keynes was, above all, a man of enormous intellectual scope and breadth. He was highly rational and logical, with an iconoclastic mind that bristled under the constraints of dogma and refused to bow to established ways of thinking. While the loss of religion did create a void and moral uncertainty, it also created an opening—an opening for the discovery of a new meaning, based on human decency and rationality. Keynes was heavily influenced throughout his life by the thinking of G.E. Moore, another Cambridge professor of moral philosophy, who sought to create a new moral world based on individual reasoning and the achievement of "good states of mind." Moore was a powerful teacher who had a dominant influence at Cambridge. He never used notes or seemed to be delivering a prepared lecture. With each class, he appeared to be grappling for the first time with some difficult philosophical dilemma, bringing the students right with him in his search for truth and an understanding of the nature of good.

Running through Moore's thinking, as well as through that of the Bloomsbury group, with which both Moore and Keynes were loosely affiliated, was a cynicism about the narrowness of the Victorian vision. Keynes strongly believed that the social restraints and dogmas of the past could be replaced by a new world of public duty based on human rationality and the desire to achieve good ends. He was deeply impressed, for example, by Sidney and Beatrice Webb, the wealthy activists who created their own moral order and made a lifetime commitment to fighting for human betterment.

Essentially, Keynes sought to bring this aspiration to human betterment to the world of economics, which was dominated by an orthodoxy every bit as rigid as the Christian one but was somehow more adept at surviving in an age of doubt. As the British economy limped from crisis to crisis in the 1920s and 1930s, the men supervising the economy seemed no more willing to have the underlying tenets of their economic faith examined than the clergy welcomed a rigorous analysis of the underpinnings of their religious beliefs. Those running the economy struggled to simply restore the only world they understood—the classical world of the gold standard with all its disciplinary and stabilizing powers.

But as Keynes watched their efforts through the 1920s, he grew more and more sceptical of their approach and the very foundations on which it was built. With their determination to resurrect the gold standard, they had directed their efforts to deflating prices and wages through deliberate measures to contract the economy. Keynes was appalled at the way this slow-torture method seemed to be only increasing the level of unemployment and human misery. The economic authorities, relying on the classical theory, maintained that this was not cruel. On the contrary, this was the only way to increase employment: once wages came down enough, employers would start hiring again.

This solution clearly gave employers immense bargaining power and provided workers with little protection against a serious gutting of their wages. But apart from considerations of fairness, Keynes had a more fundamental objection to the theory: it didn't work. As he told a startled audience at the Institute of Bankers in 1922, the strategy was "almost hopeless" as a method of restoring economic health.

To begin with, the strategy was based on a misunderstanding of the problem, according to Keynes. The reason employers weren't hiring was not because the price of labour was too high, but because there was no demand for their products. No one was investing in any kind of productive enterprise and for good reason: with so much unemployment and the economy so flat, there was little prospect of making a profit. So the problem was circular. As long as the economy was flat, investors wouldn't invest, and as long as they wouldn't invest, the economy stayed flat. And so the slump continued, and even became worse.

If this analysis sounded fairly straightforward, in fact it was an attack on one of the most basic premises of classical economics: the belief that the economy was self-correcting. As we've seen, classical theory held that the economy would naturally achieve full employment; once wages dropped low enough, employers would start hiring again. Keynes disputed this, arguing that as long as there was no demand for their products, employers wouldn't start hiring, no matter how low wages fell. The classical theory failed to account for a crucial element: human psychology, particularly human reticence and fear.

The nature of capitalism involved people taking risks with their money. But, at times like this, it made little sense to put one's money at risk, rather than, say, putting it in a bank account or buying a bond with a fixed rate of interest. Capitalism only worked well—and employed large numbers of people—when those with money were able to overcome their fears, suspend their natural caution and boldly invest their money in some risky venture, out of an enthusiastic expectation of large future profits. But this involved some reason to believe, some hope. When things slowed down and everything was stalled all around them, where would this hope come from? Rather than seeing depression and high rates of unemployment as an aberration, Keynes saw them as a natural and recurring state of affairs. Under laissez-faire capitalism, the economy would tend to sink often into such periods of high unemployment and underemployment. Capitalism, left on its own, was far from self-correcting. On the contrary, said Keynes, it was inherently unstable.

Something else was needed. When humans were nervous and uncertain, as they are during a recession, it wasn't enough to rely on the unpredictable "invisible hand" of supply-and-demand forces in the marketplace. A strong, highly visible hand was needed, one that would be seen to be injecting money directly into the economy, into the pockets of consumers and business owners. But who would provide this hand? Individual entrepreneurs were understandably obsessed with their own financial survival and were unlikely to be able to rise above their fears. What was needed, then, was government, with its ability to draw on the collective resources of the community and to operate in the collective interest. So, when the narrow self-interest of nervous individuals prevented them from pumping money into a failing economy, the broader perspective of government was essential. There were times when the steady bureaucratic hand was preferable to the more exotic invisible one.

Classical economics, by failing to see the inherent weakness in capitalism, failed also to see this solution. Instead, the classical school offered up a mixture of remedies that only made things worse. It emphasized cutting wages, encouraging lower expectations, teaching the merits of denial and doing without. It considered suffering and self-restraint essential. The similarity to Christianity was striking: both suggested that redemption would come from virtuous living and virtuous living alone. As *Bankers' Magazine* had warned, it was vital that Britons not stray from the rightful path of "economy and hard work."

Keynes regarded the piousness and self-denial of classical economics with the same contempt as he regarded religious dogma; both were confining and limiting, imprisoning people in a world of false faith. The dogma of classical economics was particularly lethal during a depression, when what people most needed was to overcome their fears and their natural tendency towards caution. It was not puritanical living that was needed, but exuberant living, the unleashing of the "animal spirits" that lurked inside the human personality. Keynes particularly bristled at the notion that human society thrives on abstinence, on learning to do with less, on shrinking expectations. The importance attached to "saving" over "consuming" in classical economics struck him as fundamentally wrong-headed. The "saver" is the hero in classical economics, but in Keynesian economics, the "saver" is portrayed as a hoarder and miser, a killer of hopes and dreams. As long as people simply hoard their money, nothing will get built, needs will remain unsatisfied, people will remain idle. It is the consumer, the doer, the entrepreneur who makes the economy go around. As Keynes put it: "It has been usual to think of the accumulated wealth of the world as having been painfully built up out of the voluntary abstinence of individuals from the immediate enjoyment of consumption which we call thrift. But it should be obvious that mere abstinence is not enough by itself to build cities or drain fens. . . . It is enterprise which builds the world's possessions."

In the Keynesian view, it is essential to get the world expanding, not shrinking, to harness the life force of human activity towards the goal of satisfying human needs. Keynes is at his best unleashing his fury against the abstinence imposed by the authorities in some misguided attempt to restore government balance sheets, while ignoring the more basic problem of putting people back to work. In a wonderful, rarely quoted commentary, Keynes attacks these death-mongering purveyors of gloom:

Negation, restriction, inactivity—these are the government's watchwords. Under their leadership we have been forced to button up our waistcoats and compress our lungs. Fears and doubts and hypochondriac precautions are keeping us muffled up indoors. But we are not tottering to our graves. We are healthy children. We need the breath of life. There is nothing to be afraid of. On the contrary. The future holds in store for us far more wealth and economic freedom and possibilities of personal life than the past has ever offered.

There is no reason why we should not feel ourselves free to be bold, to be open, to experiment, to take action, to try the possibilities of things. And over against us, standing in the path, there is nothing but a few old gentlemen tightly buttoned-up in their frock coats, who only need to be treated with a little friendly disrespect and bowled over like ninepins.

But how does an economy recapture boldness when it is short of funds? How would all this exuberant living be paid for? Government spending might offer immediate relief, but wouldn't it have to be paid for in the future, as the country was left with inflation and mounting debt? The classical position was clear: there was no such thing as a free lunch, just as there was no easy way into heaven. Sacrifice and good living were the only answers, in economics as in spiritual matters.

But here Keynes had another insight. The answer to the apparently baffling question of how to pay for the government intervention was staring everyone in the face. The new investment would be paid for not by some cache of gold found on a pirate ship but from the idle resources themselves—the unemployed workers and idle plants, mills and factories. By putting them back to work, productive capacity would be created, which was the source of wealth. "When we have unemployed men and unemployed plant and more savings than we are using at home, it is utterly imbecile to say that we cannot afford these things," wrote Keynes. "For it is with the unemployed men and the unemployed plant, and with nothing else, that these things are done."

The assumption that things were unaffordable was based on the notion that not doing them was costless. "[T]he Treasury will reject something on the ground that it will cost money regardless of what they could hope to save on the 'dole' or from increased revenue," Keynes noted. In other words, the increased tax revenue collected from a revitalized economy and the decreased spending on public relief ultimately become the source of the funds to pay for the revitalization. Furthermore, there was a kind of loaves-and-fishes effect from government injecting money into a depressed economy: the benefits multiplied. First there was the direct benefit, as the government money employed someone. Then that person would turn around and spend his or her payment on something, which would cause someone else to be employed. "[I]magine that initial sum of money passing from hand to hand, perhaps twenty times in the course of a year, in exchange for the production of goods and services, which would have gone otherwise without a buyer. Each recipient in turn can become a purchaser and create fresh employment," Keynes wrote enthusiastically in a letter to his mother.

This "multiplier effect," which was similar to the pump-priming idea of Lauchlin Currie, would become key to the Keynesian system. It showed how an injection of seed money from government could have a ripple effect far beyond its initial value, bringing a revived private sector back into play. This suggested that once the initial government spending had succeeded in encouraging the private sector to spend, the government could cut back its spending without cutting off the flow of private sector funds.

And all this could be accomplished without setting off inflation, according to Keynes. It was a basic tenet of classical thinking that pumping extra money into the economy would simply set off inflation, leaving no one further ahead in the long run. Keynes agreed that that was true—under conditions of full employment. But he argued that when so many resources were idle, there was little prospect of inflation; the extra money circulating mostly had the effect of creating more employment—exactly what one would want it to do. So, according to Keynes, one of the key concerns of classical economics— that government deficits would set off inflation—did not apply during a recession, when there was substantial idle capacity to absorb the extra money pumped into the economy. Thus Keynes had deftly turned the classical theory on its head: not only was a large outlay of government funds affordable in a recession, but the outlay would actually pay for itself, without setting off inflation! In some circumstances, there was a free lunch after all.

With the publication of his *General Theory of Employment, Interest and Money* in 1936, Keynes had thrown down a gauntlet to the established order. In hundreds of pages of mostly technical argument, Keynes took aim at the underpinnings of classical economic thought with a sharpness and logic that the orthodox school found more and more difficult to brush aside. Although there was still plenty of resistance, increasingly Keynes was becoming an international superstar

whose influence was spreading throughout the academic
making world. In the United States, the impressiv
Keynesian assault on classical thinking was breathing new ...
the flagging spirits of New Deal reformers. At Harvard, long a bastion of classical economics, a new crop of young economists was
transforming the university into a hotbed of Keynesian activism.
That new crop included many who would go on to be senior policy
advisers and prominent commentators in the post-war years—John
Kenneth Galbraith, Paul Samuelson, James Tobin, Robert Solow.
Galbraith recalls that while classical economics continued to be
taught in Harvard classes by day, "in the evening and almost every
evening from 1936 onwards almost everyone in the Harvard community discussed Keynes."

The ideas were even reaching a popular audience. There was an
enormous popular appeal in the way Keynes put the problem of
unemployment front and centre, whereas the classical school treated
it as a mere byproduct of achieving good economic fundamentals, a
reward for good clean living. Implicitly Keynes seemed to be turning
the equation around, demanding that the economy serve the interests
of the people, rather than demanding that the people fit into some
economist's conception of how an economy should function.

This deeply radical notion meshed with Keynes's desire to replace
dogma with a world governed by human rationality. For Keynes, the
ultimate goal remained a variation of G.E. Moore's aspiration of
attainment of "good states of mind." But he increasingly came to
believe there could be no good states of mind in a society that was in
a state of collapse. Thus, society had to be restored, and a key part of
this restoration involved overcoming the enormous social ill of mass
unemployment. Achieving this was a prerequisite for moving on to
meet the higher goal—a more rational, decent, enlightened human
society. One of Keynes's biographers, Robert Skidelsky, notes, "Today
the main object of business activity is to make a quick profit, the
quicker the better. The main object of contemporary statecraft is
to make societies even richer. To what end, and with what effect on

individual and social virtue, we no longer ask, and scarcely dare think about. Keynes was the last great economist to hold economics in some sort of relation with the 'good life.'"

Keynes's search for a new moral order had led him to mount a compelling attack on the élite's cherished economic theory and replace it with a scheme that would address one of the deepest grievances of the common people. Although he was born into a privileged world and lived all his life among the élite, Keynes had produced a vision of a world where the human intellect would be harnessed to make the economy responsive to popular needs and desires.

What Keynes essentially did was overturn the notion of human powerlessness, the notion that we are mere numbers in a supply-and-demand equation whose fate—whether we have jobs or not, whether we can afford to feed ourselves or not—is determined by some remote natural law over which we have no control. Keynes showed that through government, we can exert enormous control over our economy and therefore over our lives.

There was another way in which Keynes's breakthrough was deeply radical. To the extent that governments were democratic—and in the western world they were elected by popular suffrage—a strong role for government offered the possibility not just of human control over the economy but of *popular* human control over the economy. If economic conditions could be managed by government, and government was elected by the people, then the economy could be managed in the interests of the majority, not in the interests of the élite. For all the rhetoric about democracy, this hadn't really happened. Up until the Second World War, most governments still primarily served the interests of the élite. What Keynes was proposing was a truly revolutionary prospect. Never before in the known history of the world had such a thing happened. Never before had the people come so close to holding the reins of power.

The political obstacles ahead were still immense, but the groundwork had been solidly laid. Keynes had taken the arguments far beyond the mere impetuous desire for corrective action that had inspired the thinking of Marriner Eccles. He had provided some extremely powerful theoretical back-up that pushed the classical school onto the defensive.

The outbreak of the Second World War in 1939 finally put in place Keynes's call for massive human mobilization. Although this hideous war was hardly what Keynes had had in mind as a solution to the unemployment problem, the impressive British war effort eloquently proved his point: putting the nation back to work was largely a question of political will.

Years of intense public debate had taken their toll on Keynes. Although only in his fifties, he was increasingly frail from the after-effects of pleurisy and coronary thrombosis, which he had suffered in the 1930s. Yet, despite his condition, Keynes felt his work was not yet complete. What had started out as a quest for a new moral order had led him to topple the economic orthodoxy of two centuries and reconstruct in its place an economic system aimed at human betterment. A weakened but still determined Keynes now set his sights on nothing less than redesigning the entire international financial system, to make the world safe for human betterment.

CHAPTER SEVEN

Tea with Mr. Skinner

Arrayed against the Keynesian ideas in a stout phalanx were all the practical men. When not able to grasp an idea, practical men take refuge in the innate superiority of common sense. Common sense is another term for what has always been believed.

—John Kenneth Galbraith

FOR A YOUNG ECONOMIST fascinated with international finance, there was probably no more exciting place to be than locked in a room for endless hours of discussion with the world's leading economist. Indeed, Louis Rasminsky could hardly believe his luck. He had been selected to be the junior member of the three-man Canadian delegation that went to London in 1942 to meet with John Maynard Keynes to discuss the great economist's ideas for reconstructing the international financial system. In six long meetings over two and a half weeks, Keynes essentially ran a seminar for the Canadian delegation, as well as for similar delegations from Australia, New Zealand, South Africa and India.

As Keynes unveiled for the first time his scheme for a new system of facilitating world trade, the intimidated delegates listened largely in silence—except for the Canadian delegation, whose members were well versed in issues of international finance. The senior members of the Canadian team, Hume Wrong and W.A. Mackintosh, distinguished economists from the federal government in Ottawa, made significant contributions to the discussions. But all involved were particularly impressed by the highly articulate contribution of Rasminsky who, at the age of thirty-four, turned large parts of the discussion into a memorable Keynes–Rasminsky dialogue.

In the following few years, Rasminsky was to become a key force in helping Britain and the United States work out a post-war agreement on a new system for international trade and finance. As Keynes said in tribute, "Mr. Rasminsky . . . rendered most trojan service as chairman of the most important technical committee and his tremendous assistance in that connection brought results which satisfied all concerned." This major role in international economic statesmanship did not come as a particular surprise to those who knew Rasminsky. From his early years in Toronto, Rasminsky had shown considerable bravado, as well as intellectual brilliance. He always went straight for what he wanted. At the age of twenty-two, after studying at the University of Toronto and the London School of Economics, he had precociously applied for a much-sought-after job with the League of Nations in Geneva. Upon his acceptance by the League, he wired his girlfriend in Toronto: "Have accepted job League of Nations at 13,700 Swiss francs. Will you marry me?" Her reply, which included "What is the exchange rate on Swiss francs?," was positive.

That Keynes managed to fit in time to redesign the world economy, let alone carry on a dialogue with Rasminsky and others, was a testament to his extraordinary abilities. Not only was he weak from failing health, but he was also running much of the British war financing effort as an unpaid adviser to the Chancellor of the Exchequer. Keynes had worked in the Treasury department before and during the First World War, but this time he brought with him the stature of being Britain's most respected economist. And he was treated as such. Although he didn't have so much as an office in the Treasury building, he operated as a free-wheeling, one-man power centre, formulating key economic policies and generally shaping the way the government behaved on a wide range of issues. Keynes was in his element, handling enormously complicated subjects, churning out analyses and devising solutions, managing to steer his way through the bureaucracy, dealing directly with top departmental officials, as well as cabinet ministers and even Prime Minister Winston Churchill. One civil servant, Arthur Salter, recalled, "He was the strangest civil servant Whitehall has ever seen, less the civil servant and more the master of those he served."

The focus of Keynes's interest throughout the war, however, was the shaping of a new international financial system. He was determined that the world not return after the war to the disastrous system that had so badly stifled growth and human endeavour in the pre-war years. His goal was to create a new system that would give governments the power to manage their economies to create full employment and provide adequate social programs. This was what the public clearly wanted and there was no reason, once the restraining dogma of classical economics was shed, that it couldn't be accomplished through rational human management. The importance Keynes attached to full employment was widely shared both inside and outside Britain in the aftermath of the Depression. At one stage in the international negotiations, the Australians even proposed that as a condition of membership in the post-war trading system, each country be *required* to maintain full employment.

Resurrecting the gold standard, with its deflationary effects, was clearly out of the question. But Keynes was also well aware of what had been good about the gold standard—its stable exchange rates, which allowed for a rational system of world trade. In discussions with the Americans in the final years of the war, Keynes pushed for a system that would replicate the stability of the gold standard, while eliminating its destructive deflationary aspects. He outlined his ideas in what became known as the British plan, which included an ambitious scheme for an international bank with its own currency. But the Americans were unwilling to give up ground to such a powerful international institution, and so proposed their own plan. Rasminsky then produced a Canadian plan, which reconciled some of the diverging positions of the two plans. In July 1944, after a couple of years of intense discussions, Keynes and lead U.S. negotiator Harry Dexter

White, with considerable input from Rasminsky, reached agreement on a new world system at a conference in Bretton Woods, New Hampshire. Under the new system, exchange rates were to be fixed, providing the desired stability, but governments were to be free of the deflationary requirements of the gold standard, creating an opportunity for them to focus on growth and employment.

To achieve this best-of-both-worlds solution, the Bretton Woods accords had introduced a new element that had not been present in the gold standard era—controls on the movement of capital. Under the gold standard, as it had operated before the First World War, capital had been free to move wherever its owners chose to move it. In practice, however, capital moved to where the central banks determined it should move, to meet the needs of the international trading system. Capital-holders co-operated like this, because they trusted governments and central banks to operate in ways that protected the value of capital, no matter what the cost to the domestic economy. When this firm dedication on the part of governments and central banks softened under the pressures of democracy, capital-holders could no longer be relied on to move their money in ways that helped countries manage their trade deficits.

On the contrary, capital movements had become a major problem in the inter-war years, creating instability and undermining the independence of governments. When a left-wing government in France proposed higher taxes on the rich in the mid-twenties, the wealthy responded by moving their assets out of the country. The government quickly abandoned its plan. Britain also faced capital fleeing out of the country in 1931 when its central bank seemed unable to impose sufficient deflation to maintain the required value of the British pound under the gold standard. It was this capital flight that finally forced Britain to abandon the gold standard in September 1931—to Sidney Webb's surprise.

As Keynes worked on his plan for the post-war world, he became convinced that countries had to have control over the movement of capital. This wasn't such a wild idea. In fact, controls on the flow of capital in and out of a country were a familiar government tool that, prior to the 1930s, had been primarily used for brief periods to avert a crisis or to deny a hostile foreign power access to the country's capital markets. In the 1930s, however, as governments experimented with more radical policies, they introduced more comprehensive controls and the flow of capital slowed considerably. During the Second World War, as in the First World War, capital controls were a common feature. But war and Depression were special circumstances. Now Keynes was insisting that controls should be maintained in future peacetime. "[C]ontrol of capital movements, both inward and outward, should be a permanent feature of the post-war system," he wrote.

Keynes was explicit about the reason for controls: to prevent the rich from using their power over capital to control the nation's agenda. "Surely in the post-war years there is hardly a country in which we ought not to expect keen political discussions affecting the position of the wealthier classes and the treatment of private property. If so, there will be a number of people constantly taking fright because they think that the degree of leftism in one country looks for the time being likely to be greater than somewhere else." Thus, Keynes concluded, if governments were to have the independence they needed to operate in the broad public interest—instead of simply in the interest of the privileged few—they had to be able to limit the power of the rich to send the economy into a tailspin by moving their capital out of the country.

If this sounded like radical talk coming from someone with the authority to speak for the British government, it wasn't too extreme for the Americans. Keynes found considerable sympathy for his sentiments among certain senior officials of the Roosevelt administration, beyond, of course, Marriner Eccles. It was remarkable just how activist and anti-establishment some segments of the administration were. A.F.W. Plumptre, a Canadian official who worked with U.S. Treasury officials in Washington during the war, referred years later to the "near-revolution" that the Depression had caused in American politics. Plumptre described the left-wing New Dealers he dealt with as being "anti-establishment with a passion and a zeal and often a venom which is difficult even to recall in retrospect."

The Treasury department, under Henry Morgenthau, had indeed become a hotbed of New Deal activism. Morgenthau went so far as to say that the purpose of the Bretton Woods accords was to "drive the usurious moneylenders from the temple of international finance." This made perfect sense to Harry Dexter White, the sharp-tongued, left-leaning economist within the department whom Morgenthau had selected to oversee the quick departure of the moneylenders. White was perhaps even more explicit than Keynes about the need to design a post-war system that would prevent the rich from blocking the democratic wishes of the people. He argued that "the property rights of the 5 or 10 per cent of persons in foreign countries who have enough wealth or income to keep or invest some of it abroad" should not be permitted to "operate against what the government deemed to be the interests of any country."

But there were other parts of the Roosevelt administration that were sharply hostile to such radicalism. And the issue of capital controls—probably more than any other—highlighted the divide between the left-leaning interventionists in the Treasury and Commerce departments, and the more conservative types concentrated in the State department. Also pushing to keep the administration from driving the moneylenders from the temple were the moneylenders themselves—notably, the members of the New York banking community. Many important bankers had been so resistant to Roosevelt's New Deal that they had simply distanced themselves from the administration. Others, such as Winthrop Aldrich of the Chase National Bank, had initially been supportive. That early support had been largely due to Roosevelt's willingness to curb the power and influence of Chase National's competitor, the Morgan financial empire. Once that was achieved in Marriner Eccles's reforms to the Federal Reserve System, these once-sympathetic bankers lost their enthusiasm for other sorts of financial reforms. Certainly, capital controls were out of the question.

These Wall Street bankers represented a formidable force opposed to the implementation of capital controls. Since the end of the First World War, their international dominance had grown immensely, with New York replacing London as the world's leading banking centre. The New York bankers had particularly benefited from the huge flow of speculative capital leaving Europe during the inter-war years. The last thing they wanted was a set of restrictive new rules cutting off this lucrative flow of funds. With their dominant position in world banking, they had the most to gain from the establishment of an international system based on freely moving capital.

Besides, the bankers liked the free movement of capital for the same reason that Keynes and White disliked it: it limited the power of democratic governments. The financial élite, which had lost much of its control over government economic policies during the Depression and war years, saw freely moving capital as the best hope of restoring some of its lost power and influence. The electorate could elect interventionist governments, but the financial community still had an ace up its sleeve as long as capital was allowed to leave when it wanted to, limiting the ability of governments to put in place costly, potentially inflationary policies. It was the next best thing to the gold standard, which seemed impossible to resurrect at this point. Free-flowing capital could act as a disciplinary tool for wayward governments. Robert Warren, of the investment house Case, Pomeroy and Company, argued that freely moving capital could punish the currencies of governments that behaved irresponsibly. "These currencies are distrusted by reason of government deficits either financed by present inflation or threatened with the imminence of inflation." Or, as Winthrop Aldrich put it, free capital movements were necessary to "check domestic inflationary pressures"—pressures created when knaves demanded luxuries like full employment and social programs.

It all came back to the bankers' desire to have the important decisions made by the private marketplace, where they continued to dominate, rather than by government, where they had to share power with the electorate. This dislike of government extending its control was also reflected in the initial resistance of the bankers to the establishment of the International Monetary Fund.

The IMF, which was part of the Bretton Woods agreement, was designed to serve as an international body to facilitate monetary cooperation between nations—a function that had in the past been carried out by central banks. It's not surprising, then, that the IMF was regarded with suspicion by bankers. To them, it was an unproven body—to be controlled by democratically elected governments—that was usurping powers once held by central banks. (Of course, fears that the IMF would become an instrument of the will of the people proved unfounded. In its fifty years of operation, the IMF has forced countless nations around the world to adopt austerity and deflationary policies that would delight the sternest banker.)

The effectiveness of the New York bankers in blocking capital controls was blunted by the ambivalent feelings of their traditional allies, the London bankers. On one hand, the London bankers shared the philosophical orientation of the New York bankers, and believed in the desirability of capital markets imposing discipline on potentially extravagant democratic governments. Similarly, they sided with the New York bankers in opposing the IMF, preferring to see the financial world run by bankers. Certainly, the financial worlds of London and New York had long made common cause together, as in the 1920s, when Montagu Norman and Benjamin Strong had spearheaded a joint campaign to resurrect the gold standard.

But the interests of the two groups of bankers began to diverge after Britain abandoned the gold standard in 1931. A number of Britain's former colonies and close trading associates opted to go off gold too, and link their currencies instead to Britain's sterling currency. These countries, which became known as the "sterling area," formed a little protective trading area, complete with exchange controls. In this exclusive little trading club, London retained its financial dominance—something it keenly sought to protect. If London's financial community were to support the New York bankers in opposing capital controls, the sterling area would presumably have to give up its protective exchange controls and London would lose its dominance in this little trading empire. In a surprising rearrangement of political alliances, the London bankers, along with the Bank of England, ended up siding with Keynes and White in favour of capital controls.

Keynes and White also found allies among some powerful U.S. industrialists, particularly in the important capital-intensive sectors. These industrialists, who were more dependent for their profits on economic growth and consumer markets than were the bankers, had lost confidence in the traditional recipe of balanced budgets and austerity. Having witnessed the failures of classical economics to lift the economy out of the Depression, they were open to more interventionist Keynesian methods. In 1942, some of these influential industrialists came together to create the Committee for Economic Development, which was supportive of the new direction and even advocated capital controls as a way to protect the autonomy of governments—a distinctly Keynesian theme.

In addition to providing more scope for government autonomy, there was another key reason for capital controls that was important to Keynes and White, as well as to the industrialists: they helped facilitate international trade. The free movement of capital caused currencies to fluctuate, rising in value when capital flowed in and falling when it flowed out. The difficulty of maintaining stable exchange rates in the absence of some kind of control mechanism had been amply demonstrated in the speculative binges of the 1920s. The U.S. Commerce department noted in 1943 that without capital controls, world trade would be less stable and this would mean fewer sales of American goods and services.

The showdown between the New York bankers and the Keynes–White alliance over capital controls ran right through the two major international conferences setting up the post-war system, first in Atlantic City and then in Bretton Woods. The difficulty faced by Harry Dexter White—and by those trying to negotiate with him—was that his delegation included strong representation from bankers and pro-banker officials. This banking faction kept up the pressure inside the U.S. delegation throughout the negotiations.

Still, by this point, the New York bankers were quite isolated, since they lacked the support of even the London bankers to provide an equivalent pressure on the British delegation. And, while Keynes and White disagreed over many aspects of the post-war system, they both felt strongly on this issue, thus bringing the full weight of the two most powerful governments to bear on the side of capital controls. Given the degree of support for capital controls, it is an indication of the influence of the New York bankers that they were still able to win some important concessions.

One controversial issue had been the question of whether capital controls should be "co-operative." In other words, should a country not only have the right to impose controls on capital moving in and out of its own borders, but also be able to seek the co-operation of other countries in tracking down such wayward capital, when the capital ended up in bank accounts or investments in these other countries? This was important because the rich would have a much harder time evading controls and moving their money out of a country if other countries assisted the first country in retrieving the money and sending it back to where it belonged. Keynes and White had highlighted this problem early in their discussions. Keynes had strongly pushed for co-operative controls in his draft proposals; White wanted to go further and make the co-operation compulsory.

For the New York bankers, the notion of co-operative capital controls was particularly outrageous. It was bad enough that the rich might have trouble moving their funds out of countries abroad; it was scandalous to think that the U.S. government would become a police force trying to track down these funds and extract them from the control of the New York bankers, who were simply providing a necessary safe-keeping service for the beleaguered financial élite of Europe.

The fierce Wall Street opposition pushed the irascible White to moderate his position. His 1943 draft withdrew the stipulation that countries would be obliged to actually hand over deposits and investments that had unlawfully escaped some other nation's controls. Instead, nations on the receiving end would simply be required to report information about the wayward funds—and only if requested by the IMF. By April 1944, when Britain and the United States issued a joint statement, even this wishy-washy requirement about co-operation was further toned down. The notion that countries would co-operate in the enforcement of capital controls was essentially dead; the bankers had prevailed, creating an opening in the agreement that would later become important in the dismantling of the Bretton Woods system. The bankers' victory was underscored at a Bretton Woods press conference, when a stony-faced White—a longtime and fervent champion of the importance of co-operative controls—simply commented that "the United States does not wish to have them."

The overall impact of the final Bretton Woods accords, however, was to endorse the strongly held commitment of both Keynes and White that nations should have the right to control the movement of capital. The bankers had won some of the skirmishes, but the reformers for now had won the battle. Crucially, the post-war world was to have a mechanism for reining in the power of capital over democratic governments—something that had never clearly existed before in peacetime. A frail and exhausted Keynes appreciated how deeply radical the new international plan was: "Not merely as a feature of the transition, but as a permanent arrangement, the plan accords to every member Government the explicit right to control all capital movements. What used to be heresy is now endorsed as orthodox."

Keynes savoured the victory. Within two years, he was dead.

A VISITING DIGNITARY could scarcely consider his visit to New York complete without "lunch at the Chase." The Chase National Bank represented the pinnacle of Wall Street power in the 1940s. Its chairman, Winthrop Aldrich, presided over a massive $5-billion empire that was the leading financier of big business in the United States and had extensive dealings overseas. Aldrich himself was a patrician by birth and marriage, a leader in the banking community who was active in a number of key banking and government committees, had close contacts with top government officials and politicians and moved in the wealthiest of circles. On his trips abroad, he had had private audiences with, among others, the Pope, the prime ministers of Greece and Portugal, Spanish dictator Francisco Franco and British prime minister Winston Churchill, whom he knew as a friend as well as a political leader.

So the lavish dining room at the Chase head office on Wall Street, where foreign dignitaries were invited for a return visit, was well prepared to deal with the most sophisticated of guests. It was strangely unprepared, however, to deal with a visit by the Chief of the Currency Administration of the People's Commissariat of Finance for the Union of Soviet Socialist Republics.

To the members of the Soviet delegation, the invitation to "lunch at the Chase" was like entering another world. Indeed, the whole experience of coming to America for the Bretton Woods conference had been strange and unfamiliar, and the chief Soviet delegate, Mr. I. Zlobin, carefully recorded his impressions of the curious alien culture. The delegation had visited Harry Dexter White at his "two-storey" home outside Washington, with Zlobin noting, "Generally speaking, America is a two-storey, and not a one-storey country, as it has sometimes been described." In an attempt to get a closer understanding of the American bankers' opposition to the Bretton Woods accords, the delegation wanted to see Aldrich, who invited them to join him for lunch. Receiving them in a small, simply furnished office on the thirty-fourth floor of the Chase National Building rather than the bank's intimidating formal dining room, Aldrich provided the Soviets with "an ordinary, simple lunch," noted Zlobin, commenting on this quaint custom: "It is common practice in America to conduct business talks over lunch."

Over lunch, Aldrich was happy to tell the Soviets of his distaste for the deal reached at Bretton Woods. It centred on his disapproval of assigning such an active role to government in international financial policy. "Aldrich preferred to dispose of his own capital himself," noted Zlobin. The bank chairman made no attempt to hide his view that his own country's Bretton Woods delegation had been inadequate, referring to Harry Dexter White as a "pale version of Keynes." Aldrich considered both White and Morgenthau, in their keenness to impose government regulation on the free movement of capital, to be representatives of a "different world."

This was true. Certainly the world Aldrich lived in was very different from the one occupied by Morgenthau and White, or, for that matter, most of the key figures in the FDR administration, the American public or those in the Soviet delegation. Indeed, it would be hard to live in a much more rarefied world than the one Aldrich inhabited. Born into an old, distinguished New England family, the son of a wealthy Republican senator, Winthrop Aldrich had grown up in a stately home, surrounded by spacious grounds, in the élite College Hill neighbourhood of Providence, Rhode Island. Like his eight brothers and sisters, Winthrop was educated at home by two English governesses. The Aldrich family enjoyed summers at its spectacular waterfront estate near Warwick Neck, Rhode Island, where guests included the president of the United States. With a half-mile of waterfront and extensive boating facilities, young Winthrop developed a lifelong interest in yachting. In every way, his life was one of privilege, wealth and opportunity—and became more so after his sister Abby married John D. Rockefeller Jr., heir to the largest American fortune of the time.

After graduating with high marks from Harvard Law School and practising as a junior partner in a New York firm, Winthrop Aldrich was invited to join the firm Murray, Prentice, Howland, which for years had been chief counsel to the Rockefeller interests. At his new firm, Aldrich impressed his brother-in-law when he spearheaded a successful Rockefeller proxy fight for control of Standard Oil. He also did a good job representing the Equitable Trust Company, a Rockefeller bank. After ten years of handling the bank's affairs, including two complex mergers with other financial institutions, Aldrich had learned a great deal about banking as well as about the Rockefeller empire. In 1933, he became chairman of the product of these mergers, the newly created Chase National Bank, which quickly became the largest and most important on Wall Street.

In the meantime, Aldrich himself had married well, to Harriet Alexander, the daughter of a wealthy and prominent New York family whose social connections were as impressive as the Rockefeller financial connections. The Aldriches eventually had five children and lived a high-society life of exclusive clubs and social events, travelling and spending time at their two summer homes—one for formal entertaining and one for the informal use of the family. Among the financial and social élite, it was hard to be much more well placed than Winthrop Aldrich.

But for all the influence and financial power of Aldrich and his banking friends, they were unable to dissuade Washington from supporting the Bretton Woods deal and its endorsement of more government control over international capital. Indeed, the bankers found themselves pushed to the margins of political power. Few outside the tiny world of banking were keen to restore the 1920s era of private financial power—the era when Montagu Norman and Benjamin Strong could, between themselves, come up with a solution to a major international financial crisis. The widespread financial chaos of the early 1930s had left the public cynical and distrustful of such private banking power, and governments paid less heed to banking interests than they had in the past. As a result, the international banking community had become a much weaker force throughout the Depression and war years. One thing that had kept it together and kept its spirits buoyed was the Bank for International Settlements (BIS), which came to function almost as a club for disgruntled bankers.

Established in Basel, Switzerland, in 1931, the BIS was officially set up by central banks to handle the ongoing debt payments left over from the First World War. More important, it became a meeting place for central bankers and their colleagues in private banks to come together to exchange ideas, develop friendships and reinforce each other's commitment to traditional sound money policies in an era that was more focused on full employment. The idea for such an organization had been proposed earlier by key figures like Norman and Strong, who had become concerned that their own meetings seemed to attract too much interest from the press—which probably wasn't helped by Norman's habit of travelling under the name "Mr. Skinner." With a proper clubhouse where they could meet regularly, central bankers would have less need to travel incognito for fear of setting off a fluctuation in exchange rates or a round of currency speculation.

The BIS clubhouse itself was an unmarked location above a pricey chocolate shop near the Basel train station. Besides being a haven for central bankers longing for a return to the good old days of the gold standard, it also apparently became a safe spot for storing Nazi war booty, looted from the treasuries of invaded countries. Indeed, Montagu Norman and other prominent BIS figures were accused of being Nazi sympathizers. Some, like Vincenzo Azzolini, former governor of the Bank of Italy and one of the original members of the BIS board, ended up in serious legal trouble immediately after the war.

Azzolini had attracted the attention of Italian police over his wartime decision to enlist a senior BIS official to transport by private car large amounts of the Bank of Italy's gold stock to Switzerland, where it was to be watched over by the BIS. The rest of the gold was hidden in Milan. After being sentenced to thirty years in jail, Azzolini sent an English translation of his trial to the BIS, in the hope that it might someday be useful to the person who would "write about the tragic lives of the men who belonged to the board and staff of the BIS." There was much celebrating at the BIS Christmas party in December 1946 at the surprise news that Azzolini had just been released from jail.

While BIS members were much moved by Azzolini's plight, such wartime activities aroused little sympathy among officials in Allied governments. Indeed, the allegation of Nazi collaboration was cited as grounds for a resolution, passed at the Bretton Woods conference, that the BIS be liquidated "at the earliest possible moment." The resolution was introduced by the Norwegian delegation, but had the strong support of Harry Dexter White and Henry Morgenthau. They were keen to destroy this last symbol of the power of the once-dominant international banking community, whose members were the key opponents of the Bretton Woods plan. In the end, the BIS escaped its fate only because the sudden death of Roosevelt in the spring of 1945 brought a new administration to power. John W. Snyder, a St. Louis investment banker who became Treasury secretary in the Truman administration, turned out to be much more sympathetic to the BIS and its aims.

Having survived its near-extinction, the BIS went on to play a significant role in co-ordinating banker opposition to the new regime of government-managed international finance. One of the central figures to emerge was Per Jacobsson, a Swedish-born economist who served as the chief economic adviser of the BIS from its early days, and later headed the IMF. Jacobsson was a tireless, even fanatical champion of sound money policies, expounding often on the subject in his extensive public speaking and writing, as well as in the annual BIS reports. Jacobsson's home, just a short walk from the BIS, became a well-frequented social spot for the BIS crowd, particularly the shy, secretive "Mr. Skinner," who regularly enjoyed tea alone with Per Jacobsson's wife. While Mrs. Jacobsson was privately entertaining the governor of the Bank of England, her husband was always busy championing the cause of sound money by, for instance, co-ordinating the efforts of the BIS and the monetary committee of the International Chamber of Commerce (ICC).

While local chambers of commerce were often simple organizations of small businessmen, best known for wearing brightly coloured ties and promoting local hardware stores, the international chamber was a highly sophisticated pressure group representing multinational corporations and powerful banking and financial interests. Its monetary committee, for instance, included the vice-chairman of the National City Bank of New York and the vice-president of the Chase

National Bank (Aldrich's bank) as well as a number of private European bankers. It's not surprising, then, that the monetary committee was delighted to arrange to publish Jacobsson's writing in the chamber's brochures, thereby making his ideas available to hundreds of thousands of businessmen and bankers around the world. In this way, the BIS and the private banking world worked together to fight the Keynesian ideas that had become so dominant and now even formed the basis of the new international financial system.

Central to the bankers' critique was the notion that government had been given too much power. Jacobsson argued that this created a "too-managed economy." In fact, what he and the others sought wasn't less management, but less management *by government*, and more management by the banking community. Jacobsson made a distinction between "direct control," by which he meant government control (a bad thing), and "financial control," by which he meant control by powerful financial interests (a good thing). Actually, Jacobsson and the bankers didn't even object to government intervention, as long as it was intervention along the lines that they desired—such as measures to protect the value of a national currency. Jacobsson often quoted the nineteenth-century English economic writer Walter Bagehot, who wrote, "Money will not manage itself." The bankers believed there was a necessary role for government in managing the national currency—that is, protecting its value against erosion from inflation or against a decline in its value vis-à-vis other currencies. Beyond this management task, however, government should not venture; all other economic decision making should be left to the private sector.

Of course, the bankers were keen to put a public-spirited spin on their position. And this is where Jacobsson, with his flair for language and marketing, was particularly useful. He presented the bankers' cause as a struggle for cultural and spiritual freedom. In a sweeping analysis, he argued that the highest cultural achievements in human history could be linked to stable currencies. He even suggested that stable currency values had created a climate that made possible such modern institutions as Parliament, trade unions, clubs, sports, the

Salvation Army and the Boy Scouts. His biographer notes that Jacobsson believed the restoration of sound monetary relations among nations was the prerequisite "for freedom of trade, and, maybe, for freedom also in a more spiritual sense."

Outside banking and business circles, this kind of argument had little resonance. When Aldrich attacked the Bretton Woods accords in a speech to the Executives' Club of Chicago in September 1944, Democratic senator Joseph Guffey pointed to Aldrich as an example of the selfishness of international bankers and warned that Aldrich would probably be Treasury secretary if the Republicans won the next election. In a heated speech to the Senate, Guffey insisted that Aldrich was urging "that we scrap the Bretton Woods proposals and abandon Government regulation of our money system and return it to the hands of the private bankers who led us into the orgy of speculation in the twenties and then were helpless to stem the disastrous depression of the early thirties."

The re-election of the Democrats under Harry Truman in 1946 seemed to suggest continuing public support for the government interventionism of the FDR years. But the Truman administration quickly showed itself to be more pro-market in its orientation. One clear sign of that was Truman's appointment of Aldrich to head an important new presidential advisory committee on finance and foreign trade. The selection was all the more surprising, given Aldrich's strong ties to the Republican party, including the fact that his father had been a Republican senator. In appointing Aldrich and a handful of other prominent bankers to the advisory committee, as well as appointing the investment banker John Snyder as Treasury secretary, Truman was signalling that he planned to listen more to the financial community on key economic and financial issues than his Democratic predecessor had.

This new orientation had huge implications. The U.S. government had been, along with the British government, the principal instigator and designer of the Bretton Woods accords. But now, under Truman, the government was moving away from supporting the controls on capital mobility called for at Bretton Woods. Meanwhile, European governments were increasingly coming to appreciate the need for these kinds of controls. The European economies, unlike the American one, were devastated by the war, and their political situations were unstable. Their situations were made even more fragile by the vigorous demands of the electorate for full employment, modernization and industrialization, which were seen as the key elements in the post-war era. Unable to hold on to power without providing some hope on these fronts, European governments quickly found themselves piling up new debts on top of their massive war debts.

As the European rich responded by moving their assets to more stable environments outside their own countries, most European nations imposed controls on such capital flight. Some went further in agreeing to co-operate among themselves to enforce controls at both ends. These were the "co-operative controls" that Keynes and White had fought for but failed to achieve in the Bretton Woods accords. While these co-operative controls worked well in Europe, there was one major problem—most of the money was being moved to the United States, where there was little interest in helping European governments stem the exodus of capital.

The New York bankers hadn't softened their position on co-operative controls. With their new influence in the Truman administration, they were more determined than ever to do away with any kind of control over the free movement of capital. And so the fervent requests of European governments, particularly the French, for U.S. co-operation in stopping illegal capital flight out of Europe were coolly rebuffed by the Truman administration. Two years after the war, some $4.3 billion in assets had managed to dodge European controls and had ended up in the U.S. banking system. This was over and above the $800 million of European assets that had made it to the United States during the war years. The New York bankers had some simple advice to offer struggling European governments: the best way to keep capital at home was to make it feel welcome by imposing the kind of anti-inflationary policies capital-holders like.

As it turned out, the United States came up with another solution: massive U.S. foreign aid. The Marshall Plan, as it was called, was to channel billions of U.S. government dollars into European countries to help rebuild their shattered economies in the late 1940s and early 1950s. The plan was effective in reconstructing Europe, which had been drained of much of its capital. The huge flow of U.S. aid into Europe helped compensate for the huge flow of domestic capital out of Europe. But this raised an interesting question: why should U.S. taxpayers, rather than European capital-holders, be shouldering the costs of rebuilding Europe? This question sparked some feisty debates in the U.S. Congress where critics—Senator Henry Cabot Lodge was one—questioned whether the cost of the Marshall Plan couldn't be reduced substantially if Washington would co-operate with repeated French requests for help in keeping French capital at home. The American Veterans Committee added its voice: "[T]he American tax-payer should not be obliged to provide necessary funds for the pro-gram while well-to-do Europeans continue to hold on to their private hidden investments in the United States."

It certainly seemed like a compelling case. The idea that the United States should help repatriate European capital won considerable sup-port from some senior government officials, including Federal Reserve chairman Marriner Eccles. It was hard to imagine that the rights of rich Europeans to protect their capital would evoke much sympathy or concern among U.S. taxpayers. Still, rich Europeans had staunch defenders among the New York bankers, who convinced Trea-sury secretary Snyder that U.S. co-operation with capital controls would damage New York's position as the world's financial centre. In the end, Washington would agree only to help European governments locate funds that had been smuggled to the United States during the war. The much larger flow that had come in since then, and that was expected to continue to arrive in the future, would not be controlled.

With massive Marshall Plan aid on the table by this point, the Euro-pean countries were not inclined to push the issue. In fact, the Mar-shall Plan provided a solution to a thorny problem. It provided for the reconstruction of Europe, a rebuilding that was necessary to develop a strong post-war world economy centred on the United States. Another benefit was that with massive U.S. aid available under the plan, European governments stopped pushing the United States to co-operate in repatriating European capital. This meant that U.S. banking interests got to hold on to the billions of dollars' worth of European financial assets stored in their banks. Not surprisingly, Winthrop Aldrich gave his unqualified support to the plan.

Essentially, the U.S. public was paying for the bail-out of capital-deficient Europe, thereby allowing U.S. bankers to profit from handling the missing capital. Ordinary Americans probably also benefited from the deal, since the revived European economies provided an important market for U.S. exports. But the question of why U.S. tax-payers—rather than rich Europeans—ended up footing the bill for European reconstruction remained unanswered. Mostly, it happened because the U.S. public had little idea what was going on.

Still, capital controls were proving an enormous annoyance to financial interests. The post-war international financial system, according to one analyst, was like "a mini-golf course, with some hole or other always accessible, but others shut off and a variety of shifting obstacles to be negotiated." It was precisely to escape the unpredictable terrain of this mini-golf course that the international financial community gravitated towards what soon became a booming financial market beyond the reach of capital controls.

That market, which became known as the Euromarket, was a kind of disembodied international financial system that operated outside the jurisdiction of any government. It was located in London and operated out of the major London financial houses, with the full approval of the British government—but it was exempted from British financial controls. Under this strange arrangement, the London financial houses conducted their usual domestic business, subject to British financial regulation. But they were also now permitted to handle foreign accounts, primarily in American dollars, which were free of regulation. The Euromarket was essentially an "offshore" haven, operating right on British soil. From the late 1950s on, international capital, particularly from the United States, flowed to the Euromarket to take advantage of the most liberal financial market the world had seen since the 1920s.

What is striking is how much the British and U.S. governments encouraged the developing Euromarket, even though it offered private financial interests an opportunity to evade their own regulations. In the case of Britain, it solved a tricky domestic problem. In the late 1950s, Britain finally took steps to remove remaining wartime controls on its currency so that pounds would be freely exchangeable with other currencies. But this triggered a wave of capital flight out of Britain. The British government responded by raising interest rates and cutting spending, causing considerable hardship. When London tried to impose another round of austerity measures soon after, domestic opposition became intense. In response, the government—even though it was Conservative—imposed new restrictions on capital mobility. This way, it would be able to prevent an outflow of capital from triggering a balance of payments crisis that would force it to cut government spending further, thereby jeopardizing its popular support.

However, the British government was also anxious to help the financial community achieve its goal of restoring London's status as the world's leading financial centre. Thus, the government was very supportive when the financial community came up with the idea of the Euromarket as a way to get around the new restrictions preventing British pounds from leaving the country. This way, the British government could maintain its controls on British capital leaving the country, but still allow the country's financial community to handle a lucrative business in foreign U.S.-dollar accounts. So the British government and the Bank of England gave their approval, allowing this "Eurodollar" market to function free of all the normal financial regulations. In 1962, the Bank of England even gave its blessing to the extension of the activities of the Euromarket into the selling of bonds, which became known as Eurobonds.

The British government was trying to achieve something that was in many ways similar to what the U.S. government had achieved with the Marshall Plan: a solution that would allow it to simultaneously placate the interests of the people and the interests of the financial community. By placing restrictions on the flight of capital out of Britain, the government was able to preserve popular social programs. At the same time, it allowed London financial houses to flourish, handling their foreign accounts outside the reach of Britain's restrictive regulations.

The U.S. government also found that the Euromarket created an opportunity for it to once again appease popular interests while satisfying financial interests. When the American dollar came under speculative attack in the early 1960s, the Kennedy administration was faced with the same problem of capital flight that Britain encountered in the late 1950s. Washington was reluctant to respond by making cuts in its domestic—or military—spending. Instead, it came up with a form of capital controls. Rather than impose direct controls on capital leaving the country, the Kennedy administration designed a tax, called the Interest Equalization Tax, to discourage outflows of U.S. capital. But, like the British government, the U.S. administration wanted to allow its financial community to continue to carry on foreign business without the interference of controls. So the U.S. government, with the full support of the Treasury department and the Federal Reserve Board, actively supported the decision of the New York banks to move their foreign business to the Euromarket.

For both the British and the U.S. governments, then, the Euromarket was almost a political safety valve. By offering the financial community access to this unregulated market, London and Washington were able to placate this powerful interest group without being forced to abandon government commitments to maintain popular social and economic policies.

Thus, the growth of the Euromarket—which increasingly undermined the Bretton Woods system—was a development that had the full support and encouragement of the two key post-war powers. Political scientist Eric Helleiner argues that if the United States and

Britain had instead taken steps to shut down the Euromarket, they likely could have snuffed it out. "If co-operative controls had been introduced 'at both ends' and imposed on Euromarket activity, the freedom of private financial operators to act at the international level would have been severely constrained." This is a crucial point, because it throws into question the popular assumption that it was technological and market forces that eventually made it impossible for governments to stand up to the power of international capital. Helleiner reasons that this emphasis on these apparently uncontrollable forces is misplaced; the crucial decisions to increase the power of financial markets were made by governments, partly to satisfy the demands of powerful financial interests. Helleiner concludes, "[S]tates have played a much more central role in the re-emergence of global finance."

Interestingly, outside the United States and Britain, there was strong support in the other direction—for strengthening restrictions on capital. This sentiment became stronger as the burgeoning Euromarket created a huge flow of speculative capital between currencies, posing serious problems for the stable exchange rate system that was a key feature of the Bretton Woods system. The Belgian Finance minister Willy De Clerq expressed the displeasure of many European officials: "Is it reasonable that such speculative movements should influence the flow of international trade, and hence the jobs of millions of persons throughout the world? We are convinced that it is not."

The Europeans and the Japanese were keen to take action to limit the speculative flows of capital. Their lobbying revived the long-standing debate over whether countries should be obliged to co-operate with capital controls. In negotiations with the United States in 1972, the Europeans, led by the French, once again pressed the Americans to co-operate in controlling capital and raised the possibility of using the IMF to act as a co-ordinating body for capital controls. The French also suggested that the Euromarket be subjected to some kind of co-ordinated international control. This echoed a proposal made by Guido Carli, the governor of the Italian central bank, that the Euromarket be regulated—a move strongly opposed by the Bank of

England. The most that could be agreed on was that central banks would limit the amount of their own funds that they placed in the Euromarket. In fact, this reveals the extent of official complicity in the Euromarket; even government-owned central banks were using it to handle funds held in their institutions.

In the end, the repeated requests of the Europeans and Japanese for stronger controls on capital movements failed to move U.S. and British officials. By March 1973, with huge capital flows causing turmoil in the fixed exchange rate system, the Bretton Woods regime was essentially dead, almost thirty years after its implementation. Along with it seemed to go the last vestiges of the Keynesian dream of giving the public some kind of democratic control over international capital.

THE COLLAPSE OF Bretton Woods liberated capital, finally restoring the free, unhindered capital movements that had prevailed in the late nineteenth and early twentieth centuries. Brought to an end was the radical thirty-year experiment in which the rights of the population as a whole were given a higher priority than the rights of capitalholders. Those thirty years were arguably the best years "ordinary people" have ever seen. But that experiment has now been effectively withdrawn, removed from the realm of public choice, declared offlimits by politicians, experts, business people, the media. It is no longer considered possible for governments to respond to popular demands for full employment and well-funded social programs. We now live in a world in which the powerlessness of governments in the face of financial markets is such a widely held belief that it has entered the realm of cliché.

In the next chapter, we will examine just how much truth there is to the cliché. But here it is important to emphasize a crucial point—that the thirty-year experiment in putting the rights of the public before the rights of capital did not collapse because of the forces of technology or globalization. Rather, the experiment collapsed because governments withdrew their support for it, under considerable pressure from the financial community. Since the experiment was first established by the United States and Britain at the end of the war, the financial community had resisted it and eventually succeeded in convincing those two governments to reject it as well. Even the U.S. decision to allow the BIS to continue to function—thereby providing a rallying point and organizing centre for bankers keen on dismantling controls—helped contribute to the demise of the unique experiment.

Indeed, the role of government in that demise went beyond simply withdrawing support. By the '60s, Britain and the United States were actively encouraging the development of the Euromarket, thereby helping to create a gaping hole in the Bretton Woods system of controlling capital flows. Essentially, the two most powerful nations created a haven for international capital to avoid regulation. So, while there's no question that innovative technology helped the Euromarket to flourish, the market existed in the first place because governments had decided to allow it. If they had wanted to, Britain and the United States could have undoubtedly made it much more difficult, if not impossible, for the Euromarket to operate. Imagine if they had also taken steps to inform the public about what was at stake, thereby managing to generate public support to preserve the Bretton Woods system, which ultimately favoured the public's interest. With coordinated effort among governments and an educated and supportive public, Britain and the United States could almost certainly have nipped the Euromarket in the bud.

The subsequent establishment of the more wide open, liberal international financial regime, in which capital supposedly stalks the earth all powerful and unchallenged, seems to have been somewhat precarious in its early stages. If it had faced serious opposition from government—particularly governments acting collectively against it—the story of international finance might well have turned out differently.

One of the first tests of the power of the newly liberated financial markets came in Britain in 1976. In a scenario that was to become familiar in the liberal financial era that followed Bretton Woods, Britain's Labour government faced the disturbing prospect of a show-down with international financial speculators.

It is necessary to back up for a moment and point out that finan-cial speculation became much more of a problem in the post–Bretton Woods liberal financial era, when currencies no longer had fixed rates of exchange. With "floating" exchange rates, investors had more opportunity to engage in speculation over currency values. If investors —or perhaps "speculators" is a more accurate term—bought British pounds, and then the pound rose in value, the speculators would make a profit on cashing in their pounds. Conversely, if the pound dropped in value after they'd bought them, the speculators would lose money. The point is that with constant movement in the value of currencies due to floating exchange rates, the opportunity for cur-rency speculation was endless.

Such speculation created a problem for governments, since the actions of speculators influenced the value of each nation's currency. If speculators bought a large number of pounds, the value of the pound would rise. If they sold a large number of pounds, the pound's value would drop. Some analysts—including Milton Friedman—argued that there was nothing wrong with this, since speculators tended to buy the currencies of countries with sound money policies, and sell the currencies of countries that engaged in harmful, infla-tionary policies. In other words, the market would reward good behaviour and punish bad.

This notion raised the old question of good and bad—*for whom?* Anti-inflationary measures, for instance, might benefit the financial community but be harmful to people more concerned about remain-ing employed. Furthermore, there was another problem. The actions of speculators weren't always logical or rational. Often, rumours would set off a rush to buy a currency or sell one, and the trend would be reinforced by a herd-like mentality as others rushed to get in on what seemed like a hot idea. Or sometimes speculators would dump a currency because they didn't like certain things the government was doing—perhaps for ideological reasons—even though the country's economic fundamentals were sound.

This is more or less what happened in Britain in 1976. Britain's balance of payments situation was improving and its inflation was decreasing—two indicators that are considered signs of good economic fundamentals. Normally this situation would cause speculators to buy more British pounds, anticipating that the pound would rise, allowing them to make a profit. Instead, however, speculators started selling pounds, making bets that the pound would drop in value. The reasons for this sell-off were unclear, but it may have had something to do with speculators' general dislike of the Labour government's continuing support for Keynesian-style policies, despite the rise of more market-oriented ideas in Britain and the United States.

As the speculators' actions drove down the value of the British pound, the Labour government propped it up by buying pounds with funds borrowed from the BIS and a number of western nations. Several months later, the pound's value was still badly sagging, so Britain tried to borrow more foreign money. This time, however, something curious happened—the United States and West Germany stipulated that they would extend further credit only if Britain imposed an austerity package, designed by the IMF, of spending cuts and monetary targets.

The requirement was an interesting departure. In the past, industrial countries had generally been able to obtain foreign loans from one another just by asking, without strings being attached. Now, two important powers were insisting that Britain's Labour government follow the trend towards more pro-market policies if it wanted to be saved from the speculators. In effect, the United States and West Germany were siding with the speculators. Rather than trying to help another government face down the power of financial markets, Washington and Bonn were helping establish the power of financial markets to dictate policy to governments.

The Labour government in Britain was confronted with a difficult choice: accept the IMF austerity package and effectively end the welfare state, or ignore the ultimatum and impose a new round of exchange controls to prevent a further flight of money out of the country. A faction of British cabinet ministers, led by Tony Benn, pushed for full exchange controls, which would mean strict controls on the exchange of all British money into foreign currencies. This policy would be very disruptive, since it would have an impact not just on the movement of financial capital, but also on all Britain's international trade in goods and services—something the government did not want to interfere with. In the end, the Labour government decided to sacrifice Keynesianism and the welfare state, and accept the IMF package.

But was that really the only choice? Had the Labour government really exhausted all the possible sources of financing? In fact, there was some evidence that German chancellor Helmut Schmidt was prepared to come through with a loan if Britain really needed it. Furthermore, a more clear-cut commitment by the British government to resisting the IMF austerity package would have also created more certainty in international circles over Britain's position, thereby discouraging potential creditors from trying to push a wavering government off its course. Instead, reports circulated of high-level officials within the British Treasury and the Bank of England openly supporting the austerity measures proposed by the IMF, essentially sabotaging the bargaining power of their own government.

But if Britain had no alternative—a debatable point—it had been helped into that position by the failure of other governments to come to its aid and to act jointly to curb the power of financial markets. Crucially, the most important government—the U.S.—was actively siding with the financial markets. Statements made later by key U.S. officials who were involved in the saga reveal that the United States was very worried that Britain might opt for exchange controls—and thereby risk throwing into jeopardy the new liberal financial regime.

In other words, senior U.S. officials were not interested in helping Britain in its showdown with the markets. On the contrary, they were anxious to ensure that Britain's actions didn't weaken the new international financial regime, which was considered somewhat fragile.

According to William P. Rodgers, who had been U.S. secretary of state at the time, "[W]e were concerned about Tony Benn precipitating a policy decision by Britain to turn its back on the IMF. I think, if that had happened, *the whole system would have come apart. . . .* So we tended to see it in cosmic terms [italics added]." In a similarly cataclysmic vein, Brent Scowcroft, the former U.S. national security adviser, later recalled that he had "spent more time on this matter during those weeks than anything else. It was considered by us to be *the greatest single threat to the Western world* [italics added]."

Really? It's unlikely Scowcroft feared that the world would blow up if Britain imposed exchange controls. Rather, what he apparently feared was that the use of exchange controls by a major country would have delivered a serious—perhaps lethal—blow to the new liberal international financial order, with its free-moving, unconstrained capital. To the small group of senior advisers in the U.S. administration, this potential blow to the rights of capital apparently amounted to "the greatest single threat to the Western world."

It's hard to imagine that most of the people in the western world would have agreed. But Scowcroft's comment is a good indication of how much things had changed since the days when the United States and Britain had collaborated to create the Bretton Woods accords. If there was any lingering notion that the interests of the public should take precedence over the interests of capital, it was clearly a sentiment that was no longer shared among those running the most powerful country in the world.

IN THE PEACEFUL hills of Fitzwilliam, New Hampshire, Harry Dexter White died in 1948 in a state of extreme agitation. It was only four years after he had been a prominent figure on the national stage, receiving daily press attention for his leading role in setting up the Bretton Woods system. Not long after, he had developed heart problems, but that didn't stop him from serving as the first U.S. director of the IMF. Whatever serenity he continued to enjoy, however, was shattered forever in early 1948 when he was publicly accused of being a secret informant in an alleged wartime Soviet spy ring.

White vehemently denied the accusation, describing it as the "most fantastic thing I ever heard." Appearing before Joseph McCarthy's committee on un-American activities, White vigorously rejected the accusation that he had used his high-ranking position within the Treasury department to help Communist agents get access to secret information. But the committee members, enjoying a wave of publicity for their apparent patriotic, investigative zeal, were unmoved by his denials and seemed to become more suspicious because of his difficulty in coping with the stress of his appearance before them. Privately, White pleaded with the committee chairman for more rest periods, explaining that his heart condition made it difficult for him to deal with the strain of the aggressive questioning. But his request only seemed to provoke the chairman, who responded with snide remarks about White's condition.

Within a week of his testimony, White suffered a heart attack and was ordered by his doctor to rest at his farm in Fitzwilliam. Two days later, a devastated Harry Dexter White, having been transformed in less than three weeks from a respected public figure and a key architect of the post-war world into a suspect in a Soviet spy ring, suffered another heart attack and died miserably at the age of fifty-six.

Over the next few years, the McCarthyites also went after other Keynesian economists—including former FDR economic adviser Lauchlin Currie and prominent academic Lawrence Klein—whose main offence against the United States appears to have been an interest in making the economic system more responsive to the demands of the public. To some of the zealots in the U.S. Congress at the time, such ideas were considered dangerously left-wing, even a threat to capitalism.

The irony in this is that in some ways, what Keynes and the New Deal reformers did was save capitalism by figuring out how to make it work in a way that provided real benefits to large numbers of people.

The utter failure of classical economics and the gold standard to provide sufficient employment and liveable wages for millions of people in the 1930s led to a deep level of dissatisfaction. While difficult—even unbearable—conditions for working people were hardly new, what was new was that the people now had the right to vote. So they had to be, at some level at least, consulted. An implicit pact was struck: capital got labour to accept capitalism, and labour got a better deal under capitalism. The fruits of capitalism were to be shared more equitably.

The following three decades saw dynamic economic expansion, a huge growth in international trade and increased equality throughout the advanced world. Despite the enormous overhang of debt most western nations faced at the end of the Second World War, governments pumped money directly into their economies, greatly increasing the scope of government to provide services and programs, and to regulate just about every area of commerce and public life. Programs for returning veterans led to programs to help young families, and then to programs to help the elderly. Interest rates were deliberately kept low to keep the economy capable of growing. And, to a large extent, it worked: growth rates soared, unemployment was kept low and social programs delivered health, education and financial security. A prosperous new middle class emerged—well fed, well educated and with boundless hope for the future—only one generation after many of their parents had grown up in crushing poverty with a sense of hopelessness.

It has become commonplace to look back now and assume that all this was unaffordable, a free lunch that the current generation paid for later in large deficits. In fact, there's little evidence to support this proposition. Yes, the deficits were real, but they were more a product of the breakdown of the Keynesian deal than a product of the deal itself. In Canada, for instance, all through the early post-war decades, even as we built up social programs and enlarged the scope of government, we were well able to pay our way. We generally didn't have much in the way of deficits from the mid-forties to the mid-seventies;

indeed, we often had surpluses. We came out of the Second World War with a colossal overhang of debt—much bigger relatively than the debt we have today. Yet, with strong economic growth, we reduced that debt to a manageable size, so that it represented a much smaller proportion of our economy. By the early 1970s, both our deficits and our debt were well under control; we were definitely living within our means, and living much better than we ever had before.

All that changed dramatically in the next decades. An inflationary surge that was magnified by the oil crisis in the mid-seventies led to a questioning of the Keynesian system. And it is true that Keynes, who did his key work in the deflationary 1930s, hadn't anticipated the inflation problem that emerged in the 1970s. But it is also true that central banks responded with an extreme about-face, returning sharply to the classical approach that they had never really given up believing in. Their willingness to use very high interest rates to clobber inflation greatly compounded the problem, by driving up unemployment and thus enlarging the deficit. Real short-term interest rates that had averaged about 1 percent in the post-war years of the Keynesian compromise shot up to an average of about 5 percent in the 1980s and 1990s. This had the utterly predictable effect of slowing down the economy and throwing large numbers of people out of work. Unemployment, which had remained low in the post-war boom, doubled in the following decades. Equally predictably, the deficit rose as a result: high interest rates meant higher financing charges for government and, with so many people out of work, tax revenues sharply declined and government spending rose.

So was it really that Keynes's system didn't work, that his vision of full employment and a fairer distribution of resources was simply unattainable? Or was it that with the first sign of problems, members of the financial élite were quick to try to recapture some of the ground they had been obliged to cede to the common people at the end of the war? Certainly, the enthusiasm with which they repudiated Keynes and his dream of human betterment was striking, as they scrambled to turn back the clock to the once-discredited classical economics of austerity, reduced expectations and less equality.

In some ways, the McCarthyite attempt to tarnish Keynesian economists as subversive traitors was the first shot across the bow for the more subtle attack to come: the élite's attempts to destroy the vision of economic empowerment that Keynes had laid out, producing for the first time in history a system in which the needs and desires of ordinary people had to be taken into account. This feeling of empowerment, above all, had to go. What was needed was a return to a knave-proof world.

CHAPTER EIGHT

Defying the
Cult of Impotence

~

We regard those people as leaders who have been able to break out
of the existing cast of thought and blaze new trails. That those in
power were unable to do so shows that they were poor leaders, not
that the task was impossible.   —Peter Temin

~

WHEN IT COMES TIME for the big moral battles in life, one can
only hope that the side one is cheering for will be ably represented. So
it was with some regret that those opposed to the dominance of international capital watched as their cause was taken up on the world
stage by Dr. Mahathir Mohamad, prime minister of Malaysia. As the
once-booming tiger cubs of Southeast Asia were taken down in a vir-
ulent bout of financial turbulence in the summer and fall of 1997,
Mahathir lashed out at what he considered the perpetrators of the
problem. Although he made some valid points about the role played
by currency traders in the financial turmoil, he unfortunately went
further. In a pitch aimed at his largely Muslim population, Mahathir
argued that what was going on was part of a Jewish agenda. There was
also the problem that Mahathir is a dictator.

If all this wasn't bad enough, Mahathir's opponent in the big moral
battle was George Soros, who wasn't nearly bad enough. To be sure,
Soros's credentials as a speculator-provocateur are unquestioned; he's
the notorious currency trader who made a billion dollars in a day

speculating against the British pound, much to the detriment of the British treasury. But in early 1997, Soros had written a surprisingly thoughtful piece in *The Atlantic Monthly* on the threat that such unbridled capitalism poses to the world. Soros argued that the spread of the market ethos into all areas of modern life was replacing shared values that hold society together.

The response from the market camp was swift and angry. *The Economist* condemned Soros for failing to see that markets represented freedom. *The Globe and Mail*'s business columnist Terence Corcoran dismissed Soros as a "crackpot." Rick Salutin observed in his media column that the *Globe* had reprinted *The Economist*'s fairly lengthy attack on Soros without ever giving *Globe* readers a chance to read Soros's original thoughts on the dangers of modern capitalism. Salutin commented, "What really bugs [Soros's] critics is he made all that money from this system but without treating it like a religion."

So it was clearly a strange pair of adversaries who mounted the world stage for a match in Hong Kong at the annual meeting of the IMF and the World Bank in late September 1997. None of this was in the original script. When the Hong Kong event had been in the planning stages, Southeast Asia was booming. Holding the annual meeting of these two major international bodies in the area was expected to help showcase capitalism's bright spot in the developing world. But by the time the drab international banking crowd started arriving in Hong Kong, the economies of Malaysia, Indonesia, Thailand and the Philippines were on the ropes, their citizens having lost tens of billions of dollars' worth of purchasing power in the previous couple of months. Nerves were understandably frayed; Southeast Asia wasn't in the mood for a celebration of capitalism.

Still, Mahathir stunned the gathering in the giant hall on Saturday night when he let loose a tirade against currency traders, whom he described as "unnecessary, unproductive and immoral." The outspoken prime minister struck a responsive chord with many Southeast Asians when he suggested that currency speculation should be regulated or even outlawed. "Currency traders have become rich—very,

very rich—through making other people poor. They are billionaires who really do not need any more money." Mahathir heightened the drama of his attack by singling out one such billionaire, Soros, whom he described as a "rogue speculator" and an "unscrupulous profiteer."

The next night, as word spread that Soros was going to respond, the media chased him through the sprawling convention centre, knocking over potted plants and bankers who were themselves hustling towards the hall for the second instalment of the great debate on world capitalism. And Soros did not disappoint the media, calling Mahathir's attack "vile." The world's richest currency trader went on to label Mahathir a "loose cannon" and a "menace to his own country" who is "using me as a scapegoat to cover up his own failure." The staid bankers, pushed to the limit of excitement by Soros's emotional defence of himself and, implicitly, of capitalism, cheered wildly and called out "Bravo!" All was apparently forgiven for the piece in *The Atlantic Monthly*.

Behind the fireworks, which were front-page news around the world, some crucial events were going on. Among them was a battle within the IMF over capital controls. At issue was the question of whether nations should retain the right to impose such controls or whether they should be effectively outlawed. It should be noted that while capital controls have fallen into disuse in the western world in recent decades, they have not disappeared in the Third World. Although the economies of Southeast Asia have increasingly opened their markets to foreign capital, and largely benefited from the huge inflow, they have also retained some controls. Unlike the west, Southeast Asia has been more cautious in its embrace of full-fledged capitalism. Malaysia, Indonesia and Thailand—like Chile and Colombia —have imposed various measures to try to regulate the flow of capital in and out of their borders.

These measures have been an annoyance to rich western nations, which have tried to get international bodies to endorse the principle of free capital mobility. This principle was endorsed by the OECD in 1989, with the establishment of a doctrine called the Capital Movements

Code. (The MAI treaty, currently being negotiated at the OECD, will simply strengthen the capital mobility principle already established in the Capital Movements Code.)

Although the United States considered it important to have bodies like the OECD endorse the principle, this wasn't really enough to secure the rights of capital to full international mobility. After all, the OECD had only twenty-nine member-nations and these were mostly the rich western ones that already subscribed to free capital mobility anyway. So the leading western nations set their sights on a bigger goal—getting the principle enshrined in law at the IMF, the most powerful international body, which ultimately plays banker to the entire world.

This brought the proponents of full capital mobility into a battle with the last vestiges of Keynesianism—the defence of which had now shifted to the Third World. Ironically, the IMF was originally designed to play a role in protecting the Keynesian system. As we've seen, the IMF was a creation of the Bretton Woods accords, and the original articles establishing it reflected the thinking of Keynes and Harry Dexter White. Crucially, Article Six specified that nations had the right to impose controls over capital movements—a right that Keynes and White considered necessary for nations in managing their domestic economies.

By the 1990s, this article was viewed with disdain by the rich western nations. Led by the United States, they pushed to get rid of this offending part of the IMF creed. In April 1997, an internal committee recommended amending the IMF's articles in a way that would effectively lead to the end of capital controls. Nations wanting IMF loans— and no nation seeks an IMF loan unless it is truly desperate—would have to ensure free capital mobility.

The Third World countries balked and voiced their opposition strongly at the Hong Kong meeting five months later. Not that they were opposed to free-moving capital. For the most part, they welcomed it, although they didn't want to be overwhelmed by it. They also welcomed further liberalization of laws governing capital movements, but they wanted to be able to control the pace of such liberalization and to retain the right to intervene in capital markets when they felt it necessary. Above all, they were opposed to attempts to make their willingness to accept full capital mobility a condition of future access to IMF loans.

But the odds were stacked against them, partly because of the way the IMF is structured. Although almost all countries belong, rich western nations dominate the IMF, much more so than they dominate other international bodies. Rich nations, for instance, hold only 17 percent of the votes in organizations like the United Nations and 24 percent in the World Trade Organization. But they hold a solid 61 percent majority in the IMF. This explains why rich western nations have sought to increase the power and scope of the IMF in supervising the international economy. It also explains why Third World countries, now the bastions of what's left of Keynesianism, are unlikely to be able to hold back the tide of even greater capital mobility in the future—without at least some help from sympathizers in the west.

IN THE CAFÉ-RESTAURANT of the Radisson Hotel in Ottawa, Pierre Fortin is picking away at a pale mixed salad. He is in Ottawa because he has been invited to make a brief comment at the Bank of Canada's weekend conference on price stability. Bank of Canada conferences are even more rigid and orthodox in their economic tastes than C.D. Howe conferences, like a Catholic celebration of high mass compared with a potluck supper in a United Church basement. But when it comes to debate on monetary policy in Canada, Fortin, as we've seen, is a key player, an annoying gadfly whose careful analysis makes his dissenting views hard to simply brush aside. So the Bank of Canada, like the C.D. Howe Institute, seems to feel obliged to at least give him a brief chance to speak, which he will have at the weekend conference. He arrived a day early, under the impression that there was a conference dinner being held the night before at the Bank of Canada, but it turned out to be only a cocktail party. Hence he and I had more time to spend together, doing what any two sensible adults do on a Friday night in Ottawa—we discussed monetary policy.

We have been having a wide-ranging discussion on all manner of interesting things when I finally pop the important question: do we as a country have any freedom in our economic policies, given the power of international markets? Fortin spears a slippery tomato and, without missing a beat, answers, "We have full freedom." It's easy to see why this guy isn't given a lot of speaking time at Bank of Canada conferences.

Fortin goes on to explain that, yes, international markets are powerful. But, he argues, we can have the kind of employment-creating economic policies we want—even if they are not exactly what the financial community wants—provided that we accept the consequences of a fluctuating dollar (that is, a rise or fall in our exchange rate). The problem, Fortin insists, is that members of the international financial community don't want a lower dollar. After all, they've spent billions of dollars buying Canadian government bonds, which are denominated in Canadian dollars. If the dollar drops in value, those bonds are suddenly worth less, in terms of other currencies. The Bay Street commentators whom we turn to for analysis of financial matters are usually people who have been involved in selling those bonds. The last thing they want is for those bonds to lose their value.

"It's a question of the bond salesmen defending the interests of those they've sold bonds to," says Fortin.

Of course, the Bay Street commentators never point out this conflict of interest. That might discredit everything they have to say on the subject. Instead, they simply imply that we're powerless as a country to defy the wishes of international markets.

Fortin's point is that flexible exchange rates—the regime that has prevailed since the collapse of the Bretton Woods system in 1973—shouldn't mean an end to governments having control over their economic policies. Indeed, when flexible—or "floating"—exchange rates first became the norm in the early 1970s, there was a widespread belief among economists that flexible exchange rates would actually increase the policy autonomy of governments. Such a system, it was argued, would remove the pressure on a government to impose anti-inflationary austerity measures in order to maintain the value of its currency. A government would be free to put in place expansionary policies and simply allow the value of its currency to decline, if necessary, relative to other currencies—something that hadn't been possible when currency values were fixed. Thus, under floating exchange rates, governments and their electorates would have a choice of pro-growth expansionary policies or policies that protect the external value of their currencies, with the first choice benefiting the population at large and the second primarily benefiting bond-holders.

So, the new liberal international financial system did not have to spell the end to the power of governments. True, the new system had abandoned the major tool Bretton Woods had handed government—control over the flow of capital. But at the same time, it had handed government a new tool—control over the value of its currency. While both tools were rough instruments that had to be handled carefully, they both did give governments a fair amount of clout in dealing with financial markets. In principle, at least, governments should still be able to maintain significant control over their economic policies under the current international financial regime.

There is an economic theory that explains this rather well. Called the Mundell–Fleming thesis, after the two economists who formulated it, the theory highlights the fact that the key to international financial relations between countries is the need for a mechanism for adjustment. This goes back to the discussion in Chapter 6 over what can be done when one country buys more products from another country than it sells to that country. How is the bill to be settled between the nations? Essentially, there must be an adjustment. Something must give.

In the days of the gold standard, currency values were rigidly fixed, so the adjustment had to take place elsewhere—and it took the form of imposing deflation on the population. Under Bretton Woods, capital mobility was sacrificed. Under the new liberal financial system, in which capital has full freedom of mobility, it is the stability of exchange rates that must be sacrificed. The Mundell–Fleming thesis notes that in international finance, a nation has a choice of three key items on the menu: stable exchange rates, capital mobility and policy autonomy for government. Essentially, democratic nations have a choice of any two of these, but not all three. (One must be sacrificed to allow for adjustment.) So, if a government wants to maintain its policy autonomy, it must choose to sacrifice either stable exchange rates or capital mobility. If it is willing to sacrifice exchange rate stability, it can have policy autonomy, even when capital is fully mobile.

What this means is that Canada can have the autonomy to pursue policies aimed at full employment and well-funded social programs. Ottawa has implied that it is powerless to enact such policies, since fully mobile capital will flee. But, as Fortin suggests, this failure of government to deliver on these policies is not because of any real powerlessness. Rather, it springs from an unwillingness on the part of government to allow the national currency to drop in value when necessary—for fear of angering the influential financial constituency. Thus, what we have now is not real impotence but a self-imposed variety.

IT WASN'T ALWAYS THIS WAY.

As we've seen, in the days before the First World War, ordinary people really were powerless to do much to determine their economic fate. The gold standard meant that adjustments in international finance had to be made through deflationary policies that imposed austerity on the working population. Without the full development of democracy and democratic rights, the general public was unable to use government to fight for its goals. The power of financial capital, backed up by the gold standard with its system of full capital mobility, went mostly unchallenged.

The rise of popular democracy after the First World War changed this scenario dramatically. A more assertive population, with more extensive democratic rights, emerged as a force to be reckoned with. Using their collective voting and union power, ordinary citizens were able to push government to champion their interests or, at least, to moderate its support for financial capital. The result was that governments were reluctant to impose the old-style deflationary remedies required by the gold standard. The failure of governments to impose these sorts of policies left the international financial system in chaos, with no reliable means of ensuring that capital move as needed to make necessary balance-of-payments adjustments between nations. As a result, there was massive capital flight out of nations that put in place policies favoured by electorates but disliked by financial capital. When the New York stock market crashed in 1929, the instability in the international financial system pushed what should have been a fairly isolated development into a massive worldwide Depression throughout the 1930s.

Out of the experience of the Depression and the Second World War emerged a radically different approach. Under the influence of John Maynard Keynes and others, the top priority of government was to be full employment and the betterment of living conditions for the population at large. These goals were to take precedence over the rights of financial capital. This priority given to the economic rights of the general population was to be protected through a new international financial system, worked out at Bretton Woods, which placed limits on the mobility of capital. As it turned out, the early post-war years produced enormous economic gains for both the general public and for financial capital, creating an era with relatively little friction between the two.

By the early 1970s, the Bretton Woods system was breaking down, as the post-war boom started to fade and the Arab oil embargo helped fuel inflation. With deteriorating economic conditions, there was a smaller economic pie to divide and hence a renewed struggle between the general public and the financial élite over who would get what portion of the dwindling pie. The financial élite has proved more effective at asserting its claim, and has largely succeeded in restoring the kind of privileged economic position it enjoyed before the First World War. This has been no small feat, because a major change has occurred since those earlier times: the rise of democracy. It was one thing to impose the financial élite's recipe of austerity measures on an unhappy public in the days when voting power rested heavily with the élite. It is quite another to do so in an era when an unhappy population has access to full voting rights. The task has been made easier, however, by the emergence of the widespread belief that governments are powerless—because of technology and globalization—to do anything other than what financial markets dictate.

Essentially, then, the financial élite has managed to restore the dominant position it enjoyed when sound money policies were enforced by the requirements of the gold standard, even though the current international financial regime does not require the enforcement of these policies. The public really was powerless under the gold standard; now it only *believes* it is powerless.

By the way, I'm not suggesting here that this is part of some grand conspiracy, that senior members of the financial community sat down and figured out how to promote the notion that government is powerless. Rather, it seems, the notion arose fairly naturally, from many quarters, including from commentaries by academic, government and media observers, on both the right and the left. Partly it was deduced from the evidence all around us: governments *have* retreated from imposing many of the regulations that they imposed in the past, particularly in the area of financial regulation. So it wasn't a huge leap from there to conclude that this was happening owing to forces beyond government control. Indeed, that seems to be the logical conclusion. Since this notion has become deeply ingrained in our way of thinking, repeated constantly in the media, it has barely been necessary for financial players or politicians to do much more than to occasionally reinforce the point by making references to "the power of global markets" or "the harsh realities of the global age" or even just to invoke that magical word "globalization."

This theory of government powerlessness found a theoretical back-up, as we saw earlier, in the arguments put forward eloquently and forcefully by Milton Friedman. Of course, Friedman's point wasn't to argue that governments were powerless. On the contrary, he argued that there was a major role for government to play in keeping a lid on inflation. But when it came to the crucial question of whether government could use its power—through its central bank and through its fiscal policy—to create full employment, Friedman answered with a resounding no. Governments had no choice but to accept "the natural rate of unemployment," which he said was necessary to keep inflation in check. (Governments wanting to reduce unemployment had to do so by taking away social supports, increasing the desperation level of workers and therefore their willingness to work.) Friedman provided a sophisticated new theoretical justification for the old positions traditionally championed by the financial community—policies aimed at keeping inflation and the power of labour under control. Friedman's formula, then, gave a new twist to the notion of government powerlessness; it argued that governments have the power to deliver what financial markets want, but they are powerless to deliver what the general public wants.

Is this really the case? Has the policy autonomy of governments actually been limited in this way? Interestingly, Pierre Fortin's point that the current financial system gives governments policy autonomy through the mechanism of flexible exchange rates is generally ignored or rejected. At the time of Ottawa's crucial 1995 budget, Fortin argued that Canada had more policy autonomy than was widely believed. Canada could avoid the deep spending cuts, Fortin insisted, if it was willing to let the dollar drop. In articles and public statements, including to the Commons Finance Committee, Fortin noted that what the Canadian economy desperately needed was lower interest rates, to stimulate growth and employment, which would also raise tax revenues for deficit reduction. But lower interest rates would have meant the Canadian dollar was less valuable to hold, so the Bank of Canada would have had to be willing to let the dollar drop—a strategy Bay Street opposed.

Fortin argued that contrary to claims that Canada would be unable to sell its bonds at the lower interest rate, investors would still buy the bonds because they would anticipate that the Canadian dollar would later return to its higher value. This would allow them to collect an attractive capital gain, which would compensate for the lower rate of interest. Although this line of argument was in fact perfectly consistent with established economic theory, Fortin's advice was so contrary to the howling calls for spending cuts coming from Bay Street that he was simply ignored.

And, as we saw earlier, Fortin's view was also of little interest to Martin's key advisers, who were firmly of the opinion that spending cuts were the only answer. Peter Nicholson, one of those top advisers, had vigorously pushed the view that it all came down to simple arithmetic—given the size of the deficit and the rate of interest, the deficit problem would soon soar into the stratosphere. "That was the heart of the issue that ultimately convinced Martin," he said in a recent interview. Nicholson maintained that this view was based on pure arithmetic and was free of ideology or assumptions. But he conceded on further questioning that in fact his theory contained a "smuggled-in assumption"—namely that interest rates had to remain the same. Fortin's whole point, however, was that the Bank of Canada could lower interest rates, thereby completely changing the arithmetic. Nicholson agreed that Fortin's point is a legitimate one that can be debated, but one that was "never seriously entertained" in the internal discussions that led up to the budget.

This is not meant to dismiss all concerns about using the exchange rate to achieve policy autonomy. There are legitimate fears that investors, seeing a central bank allow the nation's currency to drop in value, by even a little bit, will overreact and flee from the currency. This is known as "overshooting," and it is a real problem, given the often herd-like behaviour of financial speculators. But this is part of the overall problem of the excessive volatility of the market, which measures like the Tobin tax are specifically designed to address. The Tobin tax would seem to provide an appropriate solution to the overshooting problem, by slowing down the impulse to move money quickly in and out of a currency. And the Tobin tax is merely one of the ideas that has been proposed to deal with this sort of problem. Yet the financial community and government policy makers are actively hostile to even considering these sorts of proposals.

Indeed, the zeal with which the established voices reject any proposal to regulate the free flow of capital is revealing. The implication is always that the ideas proposed are so impractical as to be unworthy of consideration. *The Economist,* for instance, once commented that the idea for a Tobin-style tax "pops up as frequently as reported sightings of the Loch Ness monster," the suggestion being that anyone who supports the tax probably also reports seeing the Loch Ness monster. The line also implies that the tax has received the kind of excessive public attention and scrutiny that was devoted to, say, the circumstances surrounding Princess Diana's death—a particularly bizarre suggestion in view of the fact that few people outside policy circles have even heard of the Tobin tax. (Most Canadians, on hearing of it, assume that it's a tax on fish imposed by Newfoundland premier Brian Tobin.) *The Economist* was certainly quick to dismiss the idea for the tax, noting that "most economists reckon that in practice it would not work. . . . The main problem is that it would be unenforceable." This argument about its alleged unenforceability, which is the standard one used to dismiss the tax, seems to pop up as frequently as the Loch Ness monster.

But is there any validity to such a glib dismissal? A little-publicized deal reached at BIS headquarters in Basel in 1987 suggests otherwise.

THE POTENTIAL FOR CHAOS in the international financial system following the breakdown of Bretton Woods had not gone unnoticed. But on August 12, 1982, the issue was brought dramatically to world attention, when the Mexican government announced that it lacked the money to meet the interest payments on its debts. This Mexican crisis—not to be confused with the 1994 peso crisis discussed earlier—was the direct result of the U.S. Federal Reserve's decision to push interest rates punishingly high, driving up the cost of meeting interest payments on the mountain of debt that Mexico had accumulated over the previous decade. Since many other Latin American countries had acquired similar debts, there was a sudden fear in Washington and other world capitals that the international financial system could be about to collapse, possibly bringing much of the world economy down with it. Even though this dire scenario didn't happen, there were clearly still serious problems for many of the world's major banks, which faced losing billions of dollars in bad loans.

Federal Reserve Board chairman Paul Volcker, who had largely brought on the crisis by raising interest rates, was concerned about the potential fall-out. Volcker and Donald Regan, Treasury secretary in the Reagan administration, worked out a strategy in the summer and fall of 1982 for trying to bring some order to world finance and banking. What was needed, they decided, was a stronger supervisory role for the IMF. But this would require more money for the IMF, and when the Reagan administration went to Congress to seek an additional $8.4 billion in its IMF funding, Congress balked. To Congressional politicans, the proposal smacked of bailing out the big banks—something they were reluctant to be seen to be doing. They told the administration that they would support the increased funding only if it were coupled with a new package of stringent banking regulations, such as requiring banks to increase their capital-to-asset ratio, to ensure that U.S. taxpayers wouldn't face future requests for bank bail-outs.

The banks, however, were resistant to the idea of the more stringent regulations, which were aimed at making the banks more financially sound and therefore less at risk of failing. The banks complained that being subjected to such regulations would hurt their ability to compete for foreign business with banks in other countries where restrictions did not apply. This argument had a lot of impact in political circles and presented Congress with a classic dilemma. Congressional politicians felt the need to be seen to be protecting the interests of the U.S. public by making American banks financially sound, but they were reluctant to take measures that would make U.S. banks less internationally competitive. There was an obvious solution: convince other countries to adopt similar regulations. The task was handed to Paul Volcker.

Volcker was a giant among central bankers, both physically and politically. At an imposing 6 foot, 7 inches tall, Volcker was a dominant presence. Of course, the head of the U.S. central bank is always a huge political figure, but in Volcker's case, there was an added dimension: he had led the charge that had finally brought inflation under control in western countries in the early 1980s—a feat that commanded a kind of awe among central bankers. But for all his prestige and political clout, Volcker was unable to bring the central bankers onside when he made his pitch for standardized international regulations at a BIS gathering in Basel.

That might have been the end of it, had it not been for the near failure of one of the largest U.S. banks, the Continental Illinois, in 1984. The faltering bank required an infusion of $6 billion from the Federal Reserve System, pushing the issue of more stringent banking regulations back to the political forefront. Once again, the banks protested that they would lose their international competitiveness, and once again Volcker was dispatched to try to win foreign support. This time, however, he tried a different strategy. Rather than attempting to win over a large contingent of central bankers, he focused on winning over just one. Flying to London, Volcker met with the governor of the Bank of England, Robin Leigh-Pemberton. By January 1987, they had signed a deal, bringing the same stringent banking regulations into effect in the world's two largest financial centres. The U.S. banks continued to resist, however, saying they would still be at a disadvantage in competing with European and Japanese banks. So Volcker, now with the added clout of having the Bank of England in his camp, turned his attention to Japan.

Together the two central banks made their pitch to Tokyo, making it clear that Japanese financial firms would be denied access to the British and American markets if they did not co-operate. Tokyo was sufficiently concerned about losing access to these key markets that it quickly knuckled under and signed on. Pressure was also put on other central banks at BIS-organized conferences, and they soon fell into line as well. By the end of 1987, the ten leading central banks had signed an agreement in Basel to adopt the same stringent banking regulations. As Ethan Kapstein, director of studies at the Council on Foreign Relations in Washington, notes, "The Basel Accord represented the most far-reaching international agreement among banking supervisors ever achieved."

The point of all this is not to extol the virtues of international banking regulations. Rather, it is to show that such far-reaching regulations have been put in place without full international support—in fact, with a great deal of initial international resistance. This is relevant to the repeated argument that the Tobin tax would be unenforceable unless every country in the world agreed to participate. Without this sort of worldwide co-operation, it is alleged, the Tobin tax would be unenforceable, because banks and investment houses would simply move their operations to countries where the tax was not applied.

This same argument could have been made to dismiss the feasibility of the Basel Accord. Banks were clearly anxious to avoid the more stringent regulations, and could presumably have moved their head offices to one of the tax haven countries that have not signed on to the accord. Yet there has been no big exodus of banks to these countries. The truth is that there are many factors a financial institution takes into consideration in a decision over where to locate, and a more stringent set of financial regulations is only one of them. While banks complained about the new regulations, and fought to prevent them from being put in place, in the end they accepted the rules once they became a *fait accompli*. It's likely that it would be the same with the Tobin tax, although there would be much huff and bluster denying this until the tax became a reality.

Perhaps the larger point illustrated by the story of the Basel Accord is that there *are* financial regulations in place. Contrary to the persistent myth that the financial world is an ungoverned arena where twenty-two-year-olds in brightly coloured suspenders make all the decisions, in fact there is already considerable regulation, much of it by less flashy banker types inside the IMF, the BIS and central banks around the world.

This regulation is extensive, although almost completely out of the public eye. It began in 1974 with the establishment of a group called the Basel Committee, which was made up of central bankers from the major industrialized countries who had been in regular contact through the BIS. The committee's purpose was to provide some kind of scrutiny and supervision of the international financial system following the collapse of the Bretton Woods regulatory regime. The committee drew up a document, called the Basel Concordat, which set out a number of regulations and established the important principle that no international bank would be permitted to escape supervision. Under the Concordat, countries were required to carry out the supervision of their own banks, with the Basel Committee proposing certain "minimum standards." By the mid-eighties, it was difficult for countries to escape the Basel regulations; the Concordat had been amended in a way that made it possible for the BIS to deny banks permission to operate in countries that had not signed it. Under this kind of pressure, a total of eighty-five countries had signed on by 1983.

It was this sort of regulation, according to Kapstein, that prevented the more recent 1994 Mexican peso crisis from spinning out of control and leading to a world financial crisis, as some predicted at the time. Contrary to expectations, the Mexican crisis and other financial shocks in recent years—such as the speculation scandals that brought down the venerable Barings Bank in England and the Daiwa Bank's New York office—have not rocked the financial system, or had long-term effects on interest rates. Kapstein notes, "Over the past twenty years the leading economic powers have created a regulatory structure that has permitted the financial markets to continue toward globalization without the threat of systemic collapse."

So it is not accurate to see the demise of the Bretton Woods regime as the end of international financial regulation. Rather, the Bretton Woods regulatory regime has been replaced by a new regulatory regime. This regime, which Helleiner calls the "BIS regime," has generally imposed regulations favoured by the conservative banking types who dominate the BIS and international banking. These regulations are aimed at providing a sound footing for international finance—*but in the context of an international system based on the free mobility of capital.* As Helleiner astutely puts it, "Whereas the Bretton Woods financial order represented an 'anti-market' type of regulation, the regulations of the BIS regime [are] a 'pro-market' type of regulation designed to prevent financial crises."

These new regulations are also backed up by the commitment of the major industrial countries to support this international financial order—with a great deal of cash if necessary. In the 1994 Mexican crisis, the United States and other leading western nations put together, virtually overnight, a $50-billion bail-out package. Some critics have argued that this bail-out package wasn't even necessary, that there was no real risk of widespread bank failure, partly because of the more stringent bank regulations imposed by the Basel Accord and also because much of the investing had been done by individuals rather than banks. If so, the bail-out amounts to an unnecessary taxpayer subsidy of speculators, who were protected from substantial losses.

Even if one assumes that the bail-out was necessary to prevent a wider financial crisis, it is important to see that it also had the effect of propping up the existing BIS regime. As we saw, the Mexican crisis was to a large extent the product of the uncontrolled flow of capital, which zoomed into Mexico to make quick profits and zoomed out when it appeared that the good times were about to end. By injecting $50 billion into the situation, the western nations possibly prevented the financial system from experiencing a world crisis that would have dramatized just how dangerous this unrestricted flow of capital can be. By avoiding such a crisis, the western nations avoided scrutiny of the existing financial order. The lesson commonly drawn from the

Mexican experience seems to have been that the power of international capital is awesome and countries better behave themselves.

But here's another way to look at the situation: if we are able to regulate and prop up (with enormous funds) a world financial order based on protecting the rights of capital, why aren't we able to do the same for a different sort of world financial order—one that would be based instead on protecting the rights of the public?

Imagine, for instance, if the major western countries applied the same kind of financial pressure that they applied to Japan and other nations to get them to support the Basel Accord, but instead used that pressure to push nations to accept the Tobin tax. The resistance to the tax might well fall apart quickly under this sort of pressure, especially since governments would soon come to see certain advantages in being able to keep some of the revenue from the tax.

Or, for that matter, consider what might happen if the major western countries were to stick together in the face of pressure from international financial markets. What if, for instance, they had come forward with funds in 1976 to help Britain hold on to its economic independence in the face of speculative market pressures? If Britain had had access to a $50-billion package of loans to help it through its difficulties, rather than the active disapproval of the major western governments, the outcome would almost surely have been different. And if joint government action along these lines had succeeded back then in standing up to the markets—with the result that the speculators would have suffered considerable losses—speculators might have been less keen to get into future showdowns, knowing how high the stakes could be. Even today, when the resources of speculators are collectively bigger than those of central banks, a united effort by governments would likely deter much speculation. If it were known that governments would stick together to defend one another's economic independence—rather than leaving each government to face a private showdown with the forces of free-wheeling capital—capital would likely stalk the world with a great deal less swagger. Imagine.

Ultimately, governments have the power to change their political orientation—from supporting the free movement of capital to supporting the economic independence of government. And this would undoubtedly make a huge difference in the power balance between markets and governments. But there is still the nagging question: do governments also have the *technical* means of monitoring and controlling capital flows? In other words, is it technologically possible to regulate the flow of capital in this age of computerization?

The financial community insists that it is not. They point to the speed with which computers can move funds instantly around a worldwide market that operates twenty-four hours a day. Impressive stuff indeed. But what is usually left out of the discussion is that this computer technology is a two-way street. The same technology that allows capital to be moved so quickly also allows for this movement to be traced. It hardly needs to be said that one of the most significant ways that the computer has changed society is its potential for tracking and recording information of all kinds. It is scarcely possible to keep any aspect of modern life from surveillance by the state, now that governments keep such extensive computerized records of citizens, corporations, vehicles, livestock, the natural environment. Governments even co-operate with one another to gather information, sharing computer records for purposes such as tracking down criminals. International surveillance of the activities of organized crime, particularly in drug smuggling and money laundering, is increasingly sophisticated, with governments sharing their extensive computer data to track down suspects and build criminal cases against them.

Why couldn't the advanced technology that has made capital so nimble be used to keep tabs on it as well? The UN conference of experts that examined the feasibility of the Tobin tax concluded that the tax was technically feasible and deserved further study by governments—a recommendation that has not been acted on. For that matter, Rodney Schmidt has become more convinced of the feasibility of the tax since he wrote his two papers on the subject for the Finance department.

In a more recent paper, Schmidt maintains that "the same advances in communications and payments processing technology that lie behind the massive volume of foreign exchange transactions and scale of international capital flows make the Tobin tax feasible." He notes that banks have an electronic record of all currency transactions. These records are ultimately available to central banks through their regulatory powers. This means that central banks could force financial institutions, both onshore and offshore, to collect a Tobin-style tax on each currency transaction. Schmidt realized that this point—which cuts to the heart of the issue of the feasibility of the tax—would be of no interest to his superiors in the Finance department, who remained resolutely opposed to the tax. So he prepared this paper on his own.

Furthermore, other tracking mechanisms exist. All international financial transactions are carried through three U.S.-based clearing systems—Fedwire, CHIPS and SWIFT—which are distinct from systems carrying other electronic information. Fedwire, which is operated by the U.S. Federal Reserve System, processed an estimated $200 trillion worth of transactions in 1990, while CHIPS, the major wholesaler operating between international banks, handled an estimated $222 trillion. These highly centralized systems, which are fully integrated, compatible and subject to the same industry standards, could conceivably be used to monitor the movement of capital.

The first steps towards this kind of monitoring have already been taken. On July 30, 1992, western governments pressed SWIFT to transmit a message to all its member banks—some 2,400 institutions in almost sixty countries—requesting that they identify all their customers who were using the system. This could be the first step to creating a kind of "closed-circuit system," in which access would be granted only to those willing to accept certain terms—such as paying a transaction tax. As one analyst notes, "If the world community adopts a closed-circuit system, it will be essential to enter that system in order to take part in the western financial system."

This threat of restricting access to the financial system has already been used by the U.S. government in an area that is a top priority for Washington—drug control. The Kerry Amendment to the 1988

Anti-Drug Abuse Act empowered Washington to deny access to the U.S. financial system, including its clearing systems, to governments that refused to co-operate with U.S. demands that they sign anti-money-laundering agreements. Washington regarded these agreements as essential to its efforts to prevent drug lords from laundering their ill-gotten gains, estimated to be worth $100 billion a year. Foreign governments, faced with the threat of losing access to the U.S. financial system, quickly signed the the anti-money-laundering agreements.

As a result of these agreements, as well as the Basel Committee's requirements, national governments and central banks already monitor their domestic financial institutions to a considerable extent. This monitoring could be extended to include requiring banks and investment houses to collect a Tobin-style tax or to make reserve deposits with central banks. Co-operation might not even be a problem once it became clear that the major countries were onside. Governments around the world quickly co-operated with the Basel Accord once it was obvious that the major powers were serious about enforcing it.

While the task of monitoring billions of dollars in daily capital flows seems daunting, is it any more daunting than other kinds of international regulations that governments have undertaken with vigour? It is hard to imagine an area much more difficult to regulate, for instance, than the protection of "intellectual property"—that is, the exclusive ownership rights to ideas, inventions or artistic works. Protecting these rights is an area of concern not just to musicians, artists, writers and filmmakers but also to the multi-billion-dollar industries that sell their work, and to corporations anxious to protect patent rights to everything from pharmaceutical drugs to gas barbecues. The difficulty in regulating this area can be seen in the warning notice that comes on at the beginning of every commercial video, advising that copying for commercial purposes is against international law. Yet in an age when millions of people around the world have access to the technology that allows for the quick and easy reproduction of such videos, the task of regulating and controlling intellectual property rights is clearly immense.

Still, the difficulty of the task has never deterred the U.S. government from pursuing this goal with great determination and ingenuity. Under pressure from its domestic film and drug industries, the U.S. government has relentlessly pushed for strong international regulations to protect intellectual property. Such regulations were a key battleground in the negotiation of the Canada–U.S. Free Trade Agreement, with the United States insisting on strong language to protect intellectual property. Ottawa gave in to this pressure, even though it effectively meant an end to Canada's popular generic drug program, which allowed for the sale of cheaper generic versions of patented, brand-name drugs. The United States has been similarly aggressive in pushing for strong intellectual property protections in other international trade agreements, including in current negotiations for the MAI.

It is conceivable that enforcing the international protection of intellectual property is actually a more difficult task than collecting a Tobin tax would be. In the case of intellectual property, the monitoring involves potentially anyone in the world who might try to steal an idea or copy a movie, whereas the Tobin tax would involve surveillance only of financial institutions, which are already well monitored for other purposes. But what is striking is the intensity of the effort devoted—at the most senior levels of government—to the cause of patrolling the intellectual property marketplace. Equally striking are the bullying tactics the United States is prepared to adopt to get nations onside in its anti-money-laundering campaign.

By comparison, there is virtually no effort at any level of government devoted to exploring the possibility of developing a means for controlling international capital flows. The very mention of the Tobin tax seems to provoke irritation on the part of government officials. What explains these different reactions? Is it really that governments have the power to enforce laws that protect intellectual property and control the laundering of drug money but are powerless to control capital flows? Or could the difference be that governments *want* to control intellectual property and stop money laundering, because powerful interests demand these policies, but governments *don't want* to control capital flows, because powerful interests demand free capital mobility. Could it be, in other words, that governments are practising a form of selective impotence?

~

WHENEVER AN ISSUE touches on the big questions of international finance, the desire to call in Paul Volcker seems overwhelming. And so it was that Volcker was summoned to the task of overseeing the prestigious international commission that looked into the state of world finance in the post–Bretton Woods era. Known as the Bretton Woods Commission and timed so its report would be released in 1994 for the fiftieth anniversary of the signing of the Bretton Woods accords, the commission delivered a surprisingly negative report card on the liberal financial regime that has been in place since the collapse of the accords in 1973: "Since the early 1970s, the long-term growth in the major industrial countries has been cut in half, from about 5 percent a year to about 2.5 percent a year. Although many factors contributed to this decline in different countries at different times, low growth has been an international problem, and the loss of exchange rate discipline has played a part."

This analysis, linking the current international financial regime with the growth slowdown of the past two decades, is not what we normally expect from the financial community. Yet the commission included the most senior bankers and economists in global finance, and its sponsors were some of the world's most powerful financial institutions, including banks that have profited enormously from the currency markets in the past two decades. Had these key players finally seen the devastation they had wrought and sought to turn themselves in, or at least to hand over their tools of destruction? Not exactly.

It turned out that while the commissioners were quite forthcoming in identifying the problems in the current financial regime, the solutions they recommended were very specific and—can this possibly be surprising?—very self-serving. Essentially, the senior bankers who sat on the commission proposed more international supervision of the financial system to enforce the kinds of policies that they have long been advocating. Under their recommendations, governments would agree to fixing their exchange rates (within a certain band) and then be required to maintain these exchange rates by imposing the familiar menu of restrictive domestic policies. This government discipline would be enforced by the ultimate discipline of the IMF. As U.S. writer William Greider explains, "The IMF would be authorized to discipline governments in the advanced economies, more or less as it already does with the poorer developing nations."

So what Volcker and his commission recommended amounted to a strengthening of the BIS regime: policies favoured by the international financial community would not only become compulsory throughout the world, but the IMF would be given the power to discipline governments that failed to enforce these polices. Is this not turning every notion of democracy on its head? We are being told that we should put in place regulations that curb the power of democratic governments to serve popular interests so that the interests of financial capital can be protected.

One interesting aspect of the Bretton Woods Commission is the strong support, at the most senior levels of government and private finance, for more regulation of the world financial system—a case strengthened by the financial turbulence in Southeast Asia in the fall of 1997. The fact that this blue-ribbon commission came to an agreement on the need for more international regulation means that more international regulation is almost surely on the way. Perhaps the only issue is: what kind of regulation will it be, and whose interests will it serve—those of the general public or those of financial capital? But given the virtual exclusion of the public from debate over such issues, to even pose the question may seem quaint.

～

THE CLOSEST THE WORLD ever came to having this issue publicly debated was perhaps the Halifax Summit of June 1995. Of course, the debate never happened, nor did it even come close to happening. But it could have happened. In the wake of the Mexican peso crisis six months earlier, it was the perfect time for one of the G-7 nations to raise the question of whether there was any feasible means of controlling capital flows. Canada, as host, had considerable influence over the agenda, and Paul Martin had an interest in the Tobin tax. But senior Canadian officials dismiss the notion that the subject of the Tobin tax or controlling capital flows could have ever been raised at the summit. They denounce the tax as unfeasible and also point out that Martin had tried privately to sound out other Finance ministers and found them mostly unsupportive. In diplomatic terms, this apparently put the issue right off the agenda, since no political leader wants to be seen pushing an idea that has no support. Undoubtedly this is the way things are viewed in the diplomatic and political world. It would have taken real courage then for Martin to break out of this strait-jacket, to defy the expectations of the political, diplomatic and financial establishment by suggesting an idea simply because it was in the public interest.

Instead, Martin and Chrétien, along with the world leaders gathered in Halifax, took the safe route and followed in the direction advised a year earlier by Volcker's Bretton Woods Commission. Thus they endorsed the notion that the IMF should act as a semi-disciplinary body, applying pressure to wayward governments (in the developed as well as in the developing world) to ensure that they adopt investor-friendly policies. The summit stopped short of endorsing the Volcker commission's call for the IMF to be given actual disciplinary powers. Instead, the summit recommended that the IMF's authority be beefed up in a milder way: that the IMF be called on to deliver more critical rebukes to governments that don't practise sound economic and financial policies. The thrust of the summit's position, however, was to further endorse the notion that there should be international mechanisms in place to bring democratic governments to heel, whether by pressure or by force, whenever they strayed from the pre-scribed path. This is exactly the opposite of the Tobin tax's attempt to free governments from the constraints imposed by international financial capital.

In the end, the Halifax Summit passed without attracting much public attention. Certainly few ordinary citizens had any notion that the issues being discussed dealt with the question of how much power democratic governments would be allowed to have in the global economy. *The Economist*, however, recognized the importance of the issue and decided to highlight it in a special thirty-eight-page cover story several months later. The article is a remarkable piece of journalism, worthy of close examination, because it sets out extremely clearly the thinking that shapes economic and financial policy throughout the developed world. For that matter, to call it journalism is a bit misleading. While the arguments are presented in a very readable fashion—indeed, the magazine notes that multiple copies of the article can be obtained at a discount price for classroom use—it was compiled with the active involvement of the most ortho-dox of economists. A special notice at the end of the piece states, "Of the many people who have helped with this survey, the staff of the BIS, the IMF and the OECD are due special thanks." In many ways, this extensive cover story is a very articulate summary of the position long advocated by the BIS, carefully reproduced in a journalistic man-ner for the consumption of regular *Economist* readers as well as stu-dents unfamiliar with the subject.

It might come as a suprise, then, to learn that its cover title is: "The myth of the powerless state." A cover drawing shows a host of tiny male currency traders, positioned in front of computer terminals, wearing the obligatory suspenders. In the drawing, these little men are struggling vainly, using nothing more than a flimsy rope, to tie down an enormous arm and clenched fist that hovers above them, appar-ently representing the power of government. One might easily con-clude that the article was an attempt to debunk the myth of the powerless state and show that governments actually have considerable power in relation to financial markets.

This is not at all what the article is about. The gist of the piece is that the myth is largely true: governments have lost a lot of power to financial markets, but this is a good thing! *The Economist* explains, "The appropriate attitude to the global capital market is neither blind devotion nor white-knuckled fear, but healthy respect. . . . [M]ost, if not all, of the changes that financial markets have forced on governments in recent years have been in the right direction. . . . [F]ears about governments being left powerless to defend their countries' economic interests have been overdone. On the whole, markets take power away from governments that do the wrong things."

According to *The Economist* and the BIS, it is appropriate and desirable for financial markets to have power over governments, to play the role of "disciplinarian," forcing governments to impose the kinds of sound policies favoured by the markets. The world leaders therefore did the right thing at the Halifax Summit, agreeing that governments should provide more economic information in the interests of making the global capital market "cleverer" and therefore better able to perform "its disciplinary role." After all, *The Economist* notes, "Markets cannot be expected to be wise disciplinarians unless they have good information."

The Economist never explains who authorized global markets to perform this task of disciplining democratically elected governments. The magazine simply asserts that governments need discipline. "The markets are not perfect, but the alternative is worse," says *The Economist*, in a stunning distortion of the sentiment Winston Churchill once expressed about democracy. It now seems that markets—not democracy—are the imperfect but best solution we can hope for. The alternative, in this case, is the apparently antiquated notion that government should respond to the wishes of the people who elected it. This could lead to the possibility that government would "succumb to the temptation of a pre-election spending spree," by providing funding for, say, health care and education. So, the magazine advises, governments must commit themselves firmly to sound monetary and fiscal policies and to a system "which punishes them if they renege on their pledges."

In a truly contorted piece of logic, *The Economist* argues that states are not in fact powerless because they have the power to do what markets want. It points out, for instance, that if governments want to help their economies, they can use their power to make their tax systems more favourable to capital and to remove labour market regulations. (This echoes Milton Friedman's argument that the only way governments can lower unemployment is to take away labour market supports, thereby making the worker more desperate.) *The Economist* goes one step further into its own bizarre world of political philosophy with the argument that the best way for governments to enhance their power is to give more of it away! "Thus, paradoxically, governments' best defence against the increased clout of financial markets is to forsake even more discretionary power. By tying their own hands and so removing themselves from temptation, policy-makers will retain more influence over their economies." Strange, isn't it, that the most powerful individuals and institutions throughout history managed to hold on to their power without twigging on to this little secret.

One of the most astonishing aspects of the article is how it deals with the tricky question of whose interests are served by this *Economist*–BIS vision of how the world should operate. The clear suggestion in the article is that sound money management, as favoured by financial markets, is in the best interests of all of us. But the article does address, if only briefly and at the very end, "the widespread worry that the markets give a vote only to those with money." Some readers might have thought that this was a sufficiently large worry that it should have been addressed before the last column of a thirty-eight-page article. Nonetheless, there it finally is.

But no sooner does it appear than it is quickly whisked aside, like a bothersome mosquito on a hot summer night. *The Economist*–BIS analysts assure us that it is not true that financial markets represent only those with money. "[F]inancial markets do not just represent the rich; most people have some savings, whether in a small savings account, a mutual fund or their future pension. . . . Indeed, in some ways, capital markets driven by the decisions of millions of investors and borrowers are highly 'democratic.'" While it may be true that many people have small savings, it is grossly misleading to imply that this makes the markets "democratic." The ownership of capital is highly concentrated—and this has the effect of concentrating power, too.

Oddly, *The Economist* can't seem to bring itself to admit directly that the ownership of capital is highly concentrated. Yet even a pro-business publication like *Business Week* acknowledges the gross inequality in the distribution of wealth when it, for instance, noted that "juicy market returns do little for the average person. Instead they fatten the wallets of the top quarter of households, which own 82 percent of all stock." Where would we be without *Business Week* to inject a little balance into the debate?

But the real issue here is not the inequality in the distribution of wealth, which is obvious, even if *The Economist*–BIS feel uncomfortable admitting it. The real issue is: whose interests are served by shifting power from democratic governments to financial markets, as advised by *The Economist*–BIS team?

Actually, the article vaguely alludes to this key issue when it notes that central banks face a difficult task when they must choose between "two contradictory missions . . . full employment and price stability" since "these goals often conflict." Exactly. The clash between the interests of the public and the interests of financial markets usually comes down to this battleground: will we have full employment or will we have price stability? This is a clash that governments and central banks have considerable power to mediate, through their fiscal and monetary policies. The *Economist*–BIS support for sound financial policies simply echoes the view of financial markets—and the rich people who are the major holders of financial assets—that inflation control is more important than full employment. For most citizens, however, full employment is more important, and their only power to achieve this goal rests in their democratic right to vote. In advocating that markets be given disciplinary power to override the wishes of voters, *The Economist*–BIS team is pushing for the ultimate negation of democracy, for a system structured so that the interests of the financial élite take precedence over the interests of the rest of society.

Perhaps the most alarming aspect of the article is that it has been made widely available for classroom use.

IN EARLY SEPTEMBER 1997, the temptation to see meaning in the public grief over the death of Princess Diana proved almost irresistible for most pundits. *Globe and Mail* columnist Michael Valpy weighed in with a piece called "Diana and the decline of deference." Valpy argued that the ultimate lesson to be drawn from the enormous public reaction to Diana's death was "that the decline of deference in Western society is real. . . . It is a rejection of authority and tradition. It is the loss of faith in conventional leadership, whether it be political, corporate or in religious and educational institutions. It is an erosion of collective action. It celebrates autonomy."

Valpy was expressing a familiar theme of current commentary: the apparent public disaffection for the institutions that hold power in our society, particularly government. Valpy, being a monarchist and a clever pundit, added the twist of seeing evidence of this disaffection in the public's pique against the Royal Family for not displaying sufficient grief over the loss of Diana. It's possible that there's a simpler explanation: people felt Prince Charles had been immensely unfair to Diana with his infidelity, and the Royal Family had compounded this unfairness by siding with him and punishing her. The public thus felt strongly that someone they really liked had been mistreated in life and inadequately honoured in death. This explanation suggests that the outpouring of emotion had everything to do with people's feelings about this hugely dramatized public soap opera, and little to do with attitudes about government or collective action. (There was no public criticism of British prime minister Tony Blair or his government.)

The notion that people have lost faith in the institution of government is widely held, but is it really true? It is true that there's considerable disaffection with specific governments and what they've been doing. But some observers have gone on to suggest that this is part of a general disaffection with the role of government itself and the notion of collective action, and that the public now wants a society more oriented towards individualism and self-reliance. In this view, governments should limit themselves to safeguarding the private rights of individuals, mostly by staying out of the way. The notion that there is a common good—a collective interest that transcends the private interests of individuals—is seen as outdated. Governments that seek to advance and protect the common good are only offering false hope, because they are no longer able to deliver what the public wants: they can't afford generous social programs and they are powerless to reduce unemployment. In the age of globalization, so the theory goes, there's not too much we can or should expect from government.

Given the prevalence of this notion, it's interesting to recall how different the thinking was only a short time ago. In the 1940s, 1950s and 1960s, government was generally seen as able and public-spirited. Its employees were referred to as "public servants"; they were seen as serving the public interest. This derived from the fact that after the war, government began taking on a larger role in providing for the public good. While the élite in Canada had always enjoyed access to health care, education and financial security, these items came to be regarded, in the post-war years, as important elements in the lives of all citizens. Ensuring they were available to all citizens came to be regarded as a common good, and one that government played a crucial role in delivering. It's not surprising that people involved in implementing programs to advance this common good were seen as "public servants." Today, the term is rarely heard. Government employees are now commonly called "bureaucrats"—a term that was used with derision during the Cold War to refer to Soviet officials. The cynicism towards government that this language conveys reflects how government has changed, not how the public has changed. Polls show that Canadians still value a strong role for government, in providing social programs and in fighting unemployment. But governments, claiming impotence, have abdicated any responsibility for delivering what the public wants.

Yet, as we've seen, governments are not really powerless. Rather, they have succumbed to pressure from the financial élite, which has insisted that its interests be given precedence. No wonder people are disaffected with governments. It's not that governments are powerless, it's that they have ceased to use their power to defend the public interest.

IN A SUNNY CORNER of a narrow little bistro in downtown Toronto, Doug Peters is having a glass of wine with lunch. It's one of the perks of no longer being a cabinet minister; you can enjoy your lunch. Since his decision not to run again in the June 1997 election, Peters has been having a lot of lunches at this charming gourmet restaurant near his condo. They know him well here. He doesn't even have to ask for the discreet little bowl of red sauce. The ketchup just appears on the table, next to his steak.

If he's bitter over the way he was ignored in government, he hides it well. But he is willing to criticize the direction of the government that he was a part of. He repeats what he often said to Paul Martin: "We don't have an economic policy; we have a deficit policy." And he's quick to attack the Bank of Canada's interest rate hikes in the summer and early fall of 1997. "There's not one iota of evidence of inflation."

For the most part, Doug Peters seems content in his retirement. After all, he hasn't done badly for someone who flunked out of university twice and went on to collect scholarships, academic honours and a Ph.D. from an Ivy League university. Then he became chief economist and vice-president of one of Canada's biggest banks, and a member of the federal cabinet. Altogether, it's not a bad cv.

Still, after his long career as a mild-mannered but tough-minded iconoclast, there are grounds for disappointment. Peters wasn't able to push the Chrétien government from its deficit-obsessed course. He repeatedly argued that fighting the deficit should take a back seat to fighting unemployment. After a while, the key people stopped listening, and Peters decided to retire. The loss is Canada's more than his.

In a different way, Rodney Schmidt could also be seen as a casualty of Ottawa's rigidity. After Schmidt produced his second, unauthorized paper, which favoured the Tobin tax, it became clear to him that his superiors were not pleased. "In Finance, everybody is very tightly controlled by their immediate superior," he said. "To advance, you have to be a kind of lackey to your superior." Certainly, Schmidt could see that the Finance department was not the place for someone anxious to open up new avenues of discussion on economic policies, particularly controversial ones. So he left the department in the fall of 1997. But it's unlikely to be steak-and-ketchup lunches for Rodney Schmidt. In what surely is one of the more dramatic transitions for someone leaving the Finance department, Schmidt has joined an international aid agency and will be based in Hanoi. And the department will no longer have to put up with bothersome arguments about the need for a tax to give democratic governments more control over international financial markets.

～

SOME FINAL THOUGHTS on impotence?

One striking thing about impotence is how *un*fashionable it is, except when applied to democracy. One of the most prominent themes running through the popular business literature of the past decade—in books, magazines and seminars—is the theme of empowerment, the notion that anything is possible, with the right attitudes and efforts. No positive-thinking book seems too simple-minded to find an audience, from Norman Vincent Peale to almost any book on *Business Week*'s best-seller list.

Anthony Robbins turned himself into a mega-millionaire with *Unlimited Power*, which was all about unleashing the power within oneself. Robbins managed to convince people in business audiences all over North America to actually take off their shoes and walk briskly over hot coals to prove to themselves they were capable of doing it. And if one can conquer hot coals, surely beating international sales records or downsizing thousands of employees are piddling problems to worry about. Indeed, this hot-coal walk became a regular feature of Robbins's power-unleashing seminars, even after press reports provided the scientific explanation that a strange reaction of the skin on the sole of the foot allows humans to survive unharmed a very brief exposure to extreme heat.

The point is that a sense of empowerment—even machismo—is a central theme in today's business and financial world. Impotence is nowhere to be found. If someone were to advance impotence as an excuse, it would be greeted with disdain, if not disbelief. Imagine a business leader standing up in front of the company's shareholders and telling them it just wasn't possible to increase market share. Or imagine the governor of the Bank of Canada explaining in a speech to the National Club in Toronto that although he would like to control inflation, he really can't, due to globalization and technology. So, he might continue, there is no point in establishing inflation targets and taking steps to meet those targets; we can only *hope* that inflation will stay low. Such a governor would not likely still be governor by the end of the day.

Yet somehow this enormous sense of empowerment, this belief in the endless possibilities of human initiative and creativity, disappears when we enter the domain of democracy. Somehow, the notion that we can collectively achieve great things, indeed, that we can achieve even *basic* things that were regularly achieved centuries ago—like providing work, shelter and food for everyone in the community—these things are now considered beyond our reach! So while a culture of machismo guarantees the delivery of the market agenda—in which Gordon Thiessen must prove himself and Paul Martin vows to meet his targets

"come hell or high water"—all that testosterone disappears wh
comes to fighting unemployment or delivering social programs.

It's worth recalling John Maynard Keynes's wonderful suggestion,
quoted in an earlier chapter, for how to deal with the élite: "Under
their leadership we have been forced to button up our waistcoats and
compress our lungs. . . . There is no reason why we should not feel
ourselves free to be bold, to be open, to experiment, to take action, to
try the possibilities of things. And over against us, standing in the
path, there is nothing but a few old gentlemen tightly buttoned-up in
their frock coats, who only need to be treated with a little friendly disrespect and bowled over like ninepins."

The first group who must be treated with a little friendly disrespect
are those—in our central bank, in our Finance department, in meetings of the C.D. Howe Institute—who have accepted the use of the
NAIRU as an instrument of public policy. The NAIRU has provided the
intellectual underpinning for the notion that government is powerless
to use its key levers to attack the problem of unemployment. The
NAIRU must be seen for the sham that it is—a brilliant theory that has
nothing to do with the laws of natural science and everything to do
with the ideological preferences of those who have enthusiastically
endorsed it. James Galbraith put it succinctly when he noted that only
by getting rid of the NAIRU can we redirect public policy towards rec-
onciling a reasonable degree of inflation control with a maximum
amount of employment growth. "To abandon the NAIRU as a construct in policy discussion," writes Galbraith, "is essentially to abandon the pretext of the impossibility of this task."

To an alarming extent, we have become convinced that we are collectively powerless in the face of international financial markets. And,
with the widespread acceptance of this view, the rich have proceeded
to create a world in which the rights of capital have been given precedence over and protection against interference from the electorate. In
spite of democracy, they have largely succeeded in creating a knave-
proof world.

Another group needing to be treated with a little friendly disrepect are the supporters of the MAI as well as those pushing to amend the IMF's article on capital mobility. Both these efforts are aimed at strengthening the rights of capital-holders to move their capital free of democratic constraint. Thus, the intent is to remove the possibility of democratic control, much as the gold standard succeeded in doing in its day. If the MAI comes into force and the IMF article is amended, the impotence of democratic governments will not only be a reality but one enshrined in international law.

The only hope is the only one we've ever had—democracy. No matter how tarnished, how distorted by consumerism and the TV culture, how remote it sometimes seems, democracy is an enormously powerful tool, as Keynes's generation discovered. It's our only mechanism for saying to those in power: we've had enough impotence, thank you. Now if you'd just line up, we'd like to bowl you over like ninepins.

Imagine.

CHAPTER ONE: *Introduction to the Cult*

p. 2 *It goes without saying* . . . William Dudley, "Budget Blues: Belgium, Canada, Italy and Sweden," *Goldman Sachs International* (Sept. 16, 1994).

p. 6 *One school of thought* . . . Editorial, "Ignoring the debt leaves us vulnerable in the future," *Financial Post* (June 27, 1997).

p. 6 *Other prominent participants* . . . Editorial, "The deficit is dead, now slay taxes," *Globe and Mail* (May 5, 1997). See also Editorial, "Shed unwanted debt, painlessly," *Globe and Mail* (May 20, 1997). Jeff Rubin, "What will federal budget balances look like over the next mandate?" *Monthly Indicators*, CIBC Wood Gundy, Economics (May 7, 1997). John Geddes, "Relief is just a mandate away," *Financial Post* (March 22, 1997).

p. 7 *In the mid-1980s* . . . *Budget Plan* (Ottawa: Department of Finance, March 6, 1996), Chart 1.4, p. 12.

p. 7 *Depending on the formula the government uses* . . . John McCallum, "Fiscal Dividend," Royal Bank of Canada (Sept. 30, 1997).

p. 7 *As Martin has noted* . . . *Budget Plan* (Ottawa: Department of Finance, Feb. 27, 1995), p. 9.

p. 7 *Asked about this* . . . Some, of course, argue that it was high social spending that caused the deficit. For a rebuttal of this, see my *Shooting the Hippo: Death by Deficit and Other Canadian Myths* (Toronto: Viking, 1995).

p. 8 *There's little evidence* . . . Edward Greenspon and Hugh Winsor, "Spending increase favoured, polls finds; Jobs, health care given priority over deficit-cutting or tax reduction," *Globe and Mail* (Jan. 23, 1997), p. A1. In the fall of 1997, an Angus Reid poll, done in conjunction with *The Globe and Mail*, seemed to contradict the Environics finding, suggesting that debt reduction and taxes were the top fiscal goals of Canadians (Scott Feschuk, "Cutting debt, taxes top Canadians' list," *Globe and Mail*, Nov. 1, 1997). However, the nature of the questions asked in the

Angus Reid poll might explain the result. Canadians were asked about their support for "spending more on government programs," which sounded like initiating new spending, something that worries many Canadians concerned about deficit problems in the future. When asked instead about *restoring* government programs, support seemed to be much stronger. As the *Globe* noted, "A solid majority—71 percent—said Ottawa should restore provincial funding that was cut as part of the deficit fighting campaign rather than embark on the creation of new drug-insurance or home-care programs, both of which have been cited as Liberal goals for the current mandate." Furthermore, the Angus Reid poll found that "55 percent also contended that the federal government caused too much pain across the country by cutting too deeply in its bid to eliminate the budget shortfall." Another poll that same month by Ekos Research Associates, done for the federal Human Resources Department, reinforced the Environics results, showing strong public support for spending the fiscal dividend on child poverty, unemployment and health care above debt reduction or cutting taxes. (Edward Greenspon, "Ottawa advised to stress welfare of children," *Globe and Mail*, Nov. 10, 1997.) The *Globe* story quoted Ekos president Frank Graves criticizing the Angus Reid poll for failing to distinguish between different types of spending.

p. 9 *"Today, we're in a position . . ."* Paul Martin, "Pamela Wallin," CBC Newsworld (Oct. 23, 1997).

p. 11 *An expert is holding forth* . . . Dr. Ian Angell, interviewed on "Sunday Morning," CBC Radio (Dec. 1, 1996).

p. 15 *Fortunately, however, Lars Osberg* . . . Lars Osberg, "The pyramiding costs of excess unemployment," unpublished paper, Department of Economics, Dalhousie University, Halifax, 1996.

p. 16 *A recent analysis* . . . Stuart Kirkland Wier, "Insight from Geometry and Physics into the Construction of Egyptian Old Kingdom Pyramids," *Cambridge Archaeological Journal* (Vol. 6, 1996), pp. 150–63.

p. 19 *Axworthy, then minister* . . . Edward Greenspon and Anthony Wilson-Smith, *Double Vision: The Inside Story of the Liberals in Power* (Toronto: Doubleday Canada, 1996).

p. 22 *In their session* . . . Sarah Schmidt, "Much ado about the MAI," *The Varsity* (Nov. 11, 1997).

p. 23 Toronto Star *columnist* . . . Richard Gwyn, "Investment deal a threat to our economic nationalism," *Toronto Star* (Nov. 23, 1997). See also "Oh, MAI!" *Left Business Observer* (#79, Sept. 29, 1997).

p. 24 *Typical of this school* . . . Walter Wriston, *The Twilight of Sovereignty* (New York: MacMillan, 1992), p. 61.

p. 24 *Wriston attributes this* . . . *Ibid.*, p. 59.

p. 24 *Or as new-age guru* . . . Jeremy Rifkin, *The End of Work: The decline of the global labor force and the dawn of the post-market era* (New York: G.P. Putnam's Sons, 1995), p. xv.

p. 24 *This is acknowledged by even enthusiastic advocates* . . . "Back to the Future," *The Economist* (Oct. 7, 1995). See also, Paul Hirst and Grahame Thompson, *Globalization in Question: The International Economy and Possibilities for Governance* (Cambridge, U.K.: Polity Press, 1996), pp. 26–31.

p. 25 *At the turn of the century* . . . For an interesting discussion of the speed difference between telegraph and computer technology, see Gerard Wyrsch, "Treasury Regulation of International Wire Transfer and Money Laundering: A Case for a Permanent Moratorium," *Denver Journal of International Law and Policy* (Vol. 20, No. 3, Spring 1992), pp. 515–35. See also *op. cit., Globalization in Question*, p. 9, and Alan S. Blinder and Richard E. Quandt, "The Computer and the Economy," *The Atlantic Monthly*, Dec. 1997.

p. 26 *Eric Helleiner* . . . Eric Helleiner, "Sovereignty, Territoriality and the Globalization of Finance," in D. Smith, D. Solinger and S. Topic (eds.), *The State Still Matters* (forthcoming).

p. 28 *While banks and stockholders* . . . Pierre Fortin, "The Great Canadian Slump," *The Canadian Journal of Economics* (Vol. 29, No. 4, Nov. 1996). See also Andrew Sharpe, *Perspectives on Federal Fiscal Policy in the 1990s and Beyond* (Ottawa: Centre for the Study of Living Standards, Sept. 22, 1997).

CHAPTER TWO: *Milton Friedman and the Pursuit of Powerlessness*

p. 31 *The call was from the Royal Swedish Academy* . . . Peter Passell, "Two Theorists of Real-Life Problems Get Nobel," *New York Times* (Oct. 9, 1996).

p. 32 *Particularly, he was incensed* . . . William Vickrey, "Today's Task for Economists," *Challenge* (March–April 1993), p. 10. This article is an adaptation of Vickrey's presidential address to the annual meeting of the American Economic Association, Jan. 6, 1993.

p. 32 *He came to view* . . . William Vickrey, "Fifteen Fatal Fallacies of Financial Fundamentalism: A Disquisition on the Demand Side of Economics," unpublished essay (Oct. 5, 1996), p. 22.

p. 32 *Vickrey dismissed the notion* . . . Vickrey, *op. cit.*, "Today's Task for Economists," p. 10.

p. 35 *About forty-five minutes later* . . . Janny Scott, "After 3 Days in the Spotlight, Nobel Prize Winner Is Dead," *New York Times* (Oct. 12, 1996).

p. 36 *If Vickrey's presidential address* . . . Milton Friedman, "The Role of Monetary Policy," *The American Economic Review* (Vol. LVIII, No. 1, March 1968), p. 1. (This is Milton Friedman's presidential address that he delivered at the annual meeting of the American Economic Association, Dec. 29, 1967.)

p. 37 *A recent headline* . . . Dean Foust, "Can the Economy Stand a Million More Jobs?" *Business Week* (Nov. 27, 1995).

p. 38 *He introduced the concept* . . . For a good discussion of Friedman's reworking of the Phillips curve, see Robert Eisner, *The Misunderstood Economy: What Counts and How to Count It* (Boston: Harvard Business School Press, 1994), pp. 169–94. For a more technical, but still readable account of the evolution of NAIRU theory, see Marco A. Espinosa-Vega and Steven Russell, "History and Theory of the NAIRU: A Critical Review," *Federal Reserve Bank of Atlanta Economic Review* (second quarter, 1997), pp. 4–25.

p. 41 *The late British economist* . . . Cited in Robert Eisner, *op. cit., The Misunderstood Economy*, p. 184.

p. 44 *James Galbraith, an economist* . . . James K. Galbraith, "Time to Ditch the NAIRU," *Journal of Economic Perspectives* (Vol. 11, No. 1, Winter 1997), pp. 93–108.

p. 46 *It followed, then* . . . While NAIRU theory seems to rely most heavily on removing social supports as a means to reduce unemployment, it also allows for programs aimed at improving the efficiency of the labour market, such as those that offer skills training and/or assist job searchers in finding jobs. The important point I wish to emphasize here is that NAIRU theory specifically rules out the use of the powerful levers of macroeconomic policy, namely monetary and fiscal policy.

p. 51 *Lars Osberg, from Dalhousie* . . . M.A. Setterfield, D.V. Gordon and L. Osberg, "Searching for a Will o' the Wisp: An Empirical Study of the NAIRU in Canada," *European Economic Review* (Vol. 36, No. 1, January 1992).

p. 51 *Shelley Phipps, another Dalhousie economist* . . . Shelley Phipps, "Does Unemployment Insurance Increase Unemployment?" in Brian K. Maclean and Lars Osberg (eds.), *The Unemployment Crisis* (Montreal and Kingston: McGill-Queen's University Press, 1996), pp. 129–50.

p. 51 *But perhaps the most intriguing* . . . Pierre Fortin, "The Unbearable Light-ness of Zero-Inflation Optimism," *Canadian Business Economics* (Spring 1993).

p. 53 *This phenomenon, which was dubbed* . . . Olivier J. Blanchard and Lawrence H. Summers, "Hysteresis and the European Unemployment Problem," in S. Fischer (ed.), NBER *Macroeconomics Annual 1986* (Cam-bridge, Mass.: MIT Press, 1986), pp. 15–78.

p. 55 *In one of its surveys of Canada* . . . OECD *Economic Surveys 1995–1996 Canada*, p. 157.

p. 57 *Consider two recent Canadian studies* . . . The Canadian studies are dis-cussed in *ibid.*, pp. 158–59. Note Table A1.

p. 57 *The* NAIRU *has also proved elusive* . . . Galbraith, *op. cit.*, "Time to Ditch the* NAIRU," pp. 100–101.

p. 57 *Some economists have gone off* . . . See for instance Robert J. Gordon, "The Time-Varying NAIRU and its Implications for Economic Policy," *Journal of Economic Perspectives* (Vol. 11, No. 1, Winter 1997), pp. 11–32.

p. 58 *A number of other prominent* . . . Robert Eisner, *op. cit.*, *The Misunder-stood Economy*, pp. 169–94.

p. 58 *U.S. economist Franco Modigliani* . . . Cited in *ibid.*, p. 184.

p. 58 *Furthermore, in recent years* . . . See for instance David M. Gordon, "The Un-Natural Rate of Unemployment: an econometric critique of the NAIRU hypothesis," *The American Economic Review* (Vol. 78, No. 2, May 1988).

p. 58 *James Galbraith notes* . . . Galbraith, *op. cit.*, "Time to Ditch the NAIRU," p. 102.

p. 60 *The aging members* . . . Elizabeth Folberth, "Trying to Keep Alive Nobel Laureate's Ideas," *New York Times* (Jan. 19, 1997).

CHAPTER THREE: *The Suit Goes to Ottawa*

p. 64 *This suggestion was made* . . . "Pamela Wallin Live," CBC-TV Newsworld (May 8, 1997).

p. 64 *Campbell had received strong backing* . . . Sandro Contenta, "Campbell says she'll cut debt, not just deficit," *Toronto Star* (April 5, 1993).

p. 72 *Weintraub accused Milton Friedman* . . . Sidney Weintraub, "Incomes Policy for Full Employment Without Inflation," Economic Council of Canada, Discussion Paper No. 54, March 1976. (This paper was prepared by Weintraub during a stay in Ottawa in 1976.)

p. 80 *Peters told the committee* . . . Doug Peters, "An Alternative Monetary

Policy for Canada," paper presented to the Standing Committee on Finance of the House of Commons, May 15, 1989.

p. 83 *Relying on calculations . . . Agenda: Jobs and Growth: A New Framework for Economic Policy* (Ottawa: Department of Finance, Oct. 1994), p. 20. The 8 percent estimate is cited from David E. Rose, *The NAIRU in Canada: concepts, determinants and estimates* (Ottawa: Bank of Canada, Technical Report No. 50, Dec. 1988).

p. 85 *To the extent that they diverted . . . Op. cit., Agenda: Jobs and Growth*, p. 21.

p. 88 *At the meeting in the* Globe's *. . .* From taped recording of *Globe* meeting with Paul Martin, March 1, 1994.

p. 91 *It argues that the rise in Canadian unemployment . . . Op. cit., Agenda: Jobs and Growth*, pp. 19–20. See also footnote 3 on p. 20.

p. 91 *Hence the Purple Book . . . Ibid.*, footnote 3, p. 20.

p. 91 *Realizing that they are straying . . . Ibid.*, p. 21.

p. 92 *A whiff of this sort . . .* "Top finance official challenges costs of high unemployment," *Toronto Star* (Jan. 28, 1997).

p. 93 *In his reply, Martin sounded almost like Patty Hearst . . .* Paul Martin letter to Robert White, Feb. 15, 1996.

p. 94 *Asked recently about the NAIRU . . .* Author interview with Paul Martin, Nov. 12, 1997.

p. 94 *Within a few days of Martin's reckless comment . . .* Shawn McCarthy, "Memo contradicts Finance Minister," *Globe and Mail* (Sept. 18, 1997).

p. 95 *Asked if there was a difference of opinion . . .* Author interview with Paul Martin.

p. 95 *"Yes, I do," . . .* Author interview with Paul Martin.

p. 96 *The Goldman Sachs report . . . Op. cit.,* "Budget Blues: Belgium, Canada, Italy and Sweden."

p. 99 Double Vision *treats the cutbacks . . . Op. cit., Double Vision,* p. 278.

CHAPTER FOUR: *Gordon Thiessen and the Machismo Thing*

p. 103 *Many of them had contributed . . .* Richard G. Lipsey (ed.), *Zero Inflation: The Goal of Price Stability* (Toronto: C.D. Howe Institute, Policy Study 8, March 1990).

p. 103 *The tone at the conference . . .* The conference was held on Oct. 19, 1996, at the C.D. Howe Institute in Toronto. Howitt's paper, "Low Inflation and the Canadian Economy," along with other papers and comments from the conference were reprinted in John Grant, Peter Howitt and Pierre L. Siklos (eds.), *Where We Go from Here: Inflation Targets in*

Canada's Monetary Policy Regime (Toronto: C.D. Howe Institute, Policy Study No. 29, March 1997).

p. 104 *It was only four months since* . . . Pierre Fortin, "Presidential Address: The Great Canadian Slump," *Canadian Journal of Economics* (Vol. XXIX, No. 4, Nov. 1996), pp. 761–87.

p. 105 *To their horror* . . . Paul Krugman, "Stable prices and fast growth: just say no," *The Economist* (Aug. 31, 1996), pp. 19–22.

p. 107 *Howitt turned to a study* . . . Robert J. Barro, "Inflation and Economic Growth," NBER *Working Paper 5326* (Cambridge, Mass.: National Bureau of Economic Research).

p. 108 *Howitt's weak case* . . . Pierre Fortin, "A Comment," in *op. cit., Where We Go from Here*, pp. 76–88.

p. 109 *A recent* IMF *study looked at eighty-seven countries* . . . Michael Sarel, "Nonlinear Effects of Inflation on Economic Growth," IMF *Staff Papers* (Washington: International Monetary Fund, Vol. 43, No. 1, March 1996).

p. 109 *A recent study done* . . . Steve Ambler and Emanuela Cardia, "Testing the Link Between Inflation and Growth," paper presented at Bank of Canada conference, May 3–4, 1997.

p. 110 *In his comment, Crow* . . . John W. Crow, "A Comment," in *op. cit., Where We Go from Here*, pp. 68–75.

p. 111 *The final word* . . . Michael Parkin, "Monetary Policy and the Future of Inflation Control in Canada: An Overview of the Issues," in *op. cit., Where We Go from Here*, pp. 246–76.

p. 112 *When Alan Greenspan was appointed* . . . For an account of Greenspan's desire to show his independence and his toughness on inflation, see Dean Foust, "Alan Greenspan's Brave New World," *Business Week* (July 14, 1997), p. 47.

p. 112 *The move caught markets* . . . *Ibid.*, p. 47.

p. 113 *If there was another drum* . . . For an account of Greenspan's connection to Ayn Rand, see Michael Lewis, "Alan Greenspan: Playing God at the Fed," *Worth* (May 1995).

p. 115 *As* Canadian Banker . . . Alan Freeman, "Inside the Bank of Canada," *Canadian Banker* (Jan./Feb. 1995), p. 17.

p. 119 *In a speech in Boston* . . . Gordon Thiessen, "The recent economic record in Canada and the challenges ahead for monetary policy," Notes for remarks to the New England–Canadian Business Council, Boston, Sept. 16, 1997.

p. 119 *As U.S. unemployment dropped close* . . . See *op. cit.*, "Alan Greenspan's Brave New World."

p. 120 *A study done by Michael Wolfson . . .* Michael C. Wolfson and Brian B. Murphy, "Income Inequality in Canada and the U.S.—Trends and Comparisons," Statistics Canada working paper; forthcoming in *Monthly Labour Review* (Washington: U.S. Bureau of Labor Statistics, Spring 1998).

p. 121 *One interesting measure of this . . .* Jane Coutts, "Medicare gives poor a better chance; cancer survival rates worse in U.S.," *Globe and Mail* (Aug. 1, 1997), p. A1.

p. 123 *But a two-year study by the Ottawa-based . . .* The findings of the research project carried out by the Centre for the Study of Living Standards are summarized in W. Craig Riddell and Andrew Sharpe, "The Canada–U.S. Unemployment Rate Gap: An Introduction and Overview," *Canadian Public Policy* (Special Issue on the Canada–U.S. Unemployment Rate Gap, to be published Feb. 1998).

p. 123 *This conclusion was in keeping . . . Op. cit.,* Fortin, "Presidential Address: The Great Canadian Slump."

p. 124 *If Paul Martin is aware . . . The Economic and Fiscal Update* (Ottawa: Department of Finance, Oct. 15, 1997).

p. 125 *For that matter, if we were to use . . .* Andrew Sharpe, "Perspectives on Federal Fiscal Policy in the 1990s and Beyond," Centre for the Study of Living Standards, Sept. 22, 1997. For a good summary of these findings, see Bruce Little, "Amazing Facts: Why Canada is 13th of 13 in the GDP race," *Globe and Mail* (Sept. 22, 1997).

p. 126 *As Doug Peters . . .* Doug Peters, Testimony before House of Commons Finance Committee, May 31, 1993, p. 64:6.

p. 126 *In fact, this "growth scenario" . . .* Jim Stanford, *Over the Rainbow: The Balanced Budget, How We Got It, and How to Hang onto It* (Ottawa: Canadian Centre for Policy Alternatives, Oct. 1997). Table 1, p. 4. I have adjusted Stanford's numbers to exclude the increased cost of carrying a larger debt burden, since I am trying to focus exclusively on the question of which factors contributed to deficit *reduction*, and by what amount.

p. 126 *Stanford, who is co-chair . . . Ibid.,* p. 2.

p. 127 *They insist that the lower interest rates . . .* In fact, it is important to make the distinction between nominal interest rates and *real* interest rates. Nominal rates are the ones commonly cited in the media. But they are ultimately less important than the inflation-adjusted *real* interest rates. For instance, with an inflation rate of 1.5 percent and a nominal interest rate of 7 percent, the real interest rate is 5.5 percent; this represents the real return that investors receive on their money. Despite the low nominal interest rates of the past couple of years, which have received great attention, real interest rates have remained high compared with earlier decades. That's because inflation has been so low in the 1990s. For a good discussion of the persistence of high real interest rates in the 1990s, see Howard Gleckman, "The Bond Markets Need a Reality Check," *Business Week* (Sept. 1, 1997), p. 30.

p. 127 *He said in Vancouver . . . Op. cit., The Economic and Fiscal Update,* p. 1.

p. 127 *Thus,* Globe and Mail *business reporter . . .* Angela Barnes, "Reality check: market watchers underestimated TSE's rise," *Globe and Mail* (Nov. 29, 1996), p. B12.

p. 128 *But, in an article published . . .* Jim Stanford, "Is There a Risk Premium in Canadian Interest Rates?" *Canadian Business Economics* (Vol. 5, No. 4, Summer 1997), pp. 43–60.

p. 128 *The case for the latter . . .* For a comprehensive look at how high interest rates contribute to the build-up of deficits and debt, see Lars Osberg and Pierre Fortin (eds.), *Unnecessary Debts* (Toronto: James Lorimer & Company, 1996). For a more popular account, see my *Shooting the Hippo: Death by Deficit and Other Canadian Myths* (Toronto: Viking, 1995).

p. 128 *Thiessen himself suggested . . .* Ann Gibbon and Marian Stinson, "Dollar set to climb, Thiessen says," *Globe and Mail* (Oct. 8, 1997), p. B1.

p. 129 *Thus,* The Globe and Mail *is anxious . . .* Editorial, "Unemployment, not poverty, is the issue," *Globe and Mail* (Nov. 15, 1997).

p. 129 *Stanford considered two scenarios . . .* Stanford, *op. cit., Over the Rainbow,* pp. 13–14.

p. 130 *In Vancouver, there was . . .* Andrew Willis and Susanne Craig, "Brokers flush with success," *Globe and Mail* (Oct. 6, 1997), p. B1.

p. 131 *When critics repeatedly . . .* John Partridge, "Bank of Montreal joins billion-dollar club, Globe and Mail," *Globe and Mail* (Nov. 27, 1996), p. B1.

p. 131 *In the United States . . .* Steven A. Holmes, "Income Disparity Between Poorest and Richest Rises," *New York Times* (June 20, 1996).

p. 131 *A Republican congressman . . .* "96 percent in poverty," *Left Business Observer* (#70, Nov. 4, 1995).

p. 131 *Ominously, the same sort of . . .* Susanne Craig, "Millionaires' club triples to 22,000," *Globe and Mail* (Nov. 11, 1997).

p. 131 *Statistics Canada data showed . . .* Unpublished data from the Survey of

Consumer Finances, Statistics Canada, cited in csls *News* (Ottawa: The Centre for the Study of Living Standards, No. 1, January 1996), p. 2.

p. 132 *The result, according to a study . . .* Edward N. Wolff, "The Distributional Effects of the 1969–75 Inflation on Holdings of Household Wealth in the United States," *The Review of Income and Wealth* (Series 25, No. 1, March 1979).

p. 133 *Sadettin Erksoy, an economist . . .* Sadettin Erksoy, "The Effects of Higher Unemployment on the Distribution of Income in Canada: 1981–1987," *Canadian Public Policy* (Vol. xx, No. 3, 1994), pp. 318–28.

p. 134 *Dutch statistician Jan Pen . . .* See my *Behind Closed Doors: How the Rich Won Control of Canada's Tax System . . . and Ended Up Richer* (Toronto: Viking, 1987), pp. 35–40.

p. 136 *The Fed still collects the data . . .* "Wealth in America," *Left Business Observer* (No. 72, April 3, 1997).

p. 136 *Too bad that almost no one . . .* Gene Koretz, "Where Wealth Surged in the 1990s," *Business Week* (Aug. 25, 1997).

p. 136 *Another U.S. study . . .* Cited in Aaron Bernstein, "Sharing Prosperity," *Business Week* (Sept. 1, 1997), p. 67.

p. 137 *A 1996 national survey of Canadian households . . .* Jonathan Chevreau, "Funds held by 40% of households, survey finds," *Financial Post* (Sept. 26, 1996).

CHAPTER FIVE: *How Rodney Schmidt Tried to Save the World*

p. 143 *Furthermore, Lawrence Summers . . .* Lawrence Summers and Victoria Summers, "When Financial Markets Work Too Well: A Case for a Securities Transaction Tax," in Daniel Siegel (ed.), *Innovation and Technology in the Markets: A Reordering of the World's Capital Market Systems* (Chicago: Probus Publishing Co.), pp. 151–81.

p. 143 *The House of Commons committee . . . Report of the House of Commons Standing Committee on Foreign Affairs and International Trade on the Issues of International Financial Institutions Reforms for the Agenda of the June 1995 G-7 Halifax Summit* (Ottawa: House of Commons, May 1995), pp. 56–57.

p. 143 *And Lloyd Axworthy . . .* Lloyd Axworthy, "Notes for an Address by the Honourable Lloyd Axworthy, Minister of Human Resources Development, to the World Summit for Social Development," Copenhagen, Denmark, March 9, 1995, p. 4.

p. 143 *"I raised the issue . . ."* Transcript of talk by Finance Minister Paul Martin to the North–South Institute Board of Directors and Staff, Ottawa, Nov. 21, 1996.

p. 144 *So he wasn't surprised* . . . Rodney Schmidt, "Taxing International Short-Term Capital Flows," Aug. 17, 1994, internal Finance department document obtained under Access to Information legislation.

p. 144 *For Canadians lying on sun-drenched Mexican* . . . For a good overview of the Mexican peso crisis, see Paul Krugman, "Emerging Market Blues," pp. 28–44, and Moises Naim, "Sobering Growth Realities," pp. 45–61, in *Foreign Affairs* (Vol. 74, No. 4, July–Aug. 1995). See also William Greider, *One World Ready or Not: The Manic Logic of Global Capitalism* (New York: Simon & Schuster, 1997), pp. 259–84; and Catherine Caufield, *Masters of Illusion: The World Bank and the Poverty of Nations* (New York: Henry Holt and Company, 1996), pp. 126–65.

p. 146 *During the decade of reforms* . . . Caufield, *op. cit*, p. 153.

p. 148 *To head off such major financial repercussions* . . . Barrie McKenna, "IMF thrust into the limelight as Asian economies crumble," *Globe and Mail* (Nov. 24, 1997), p. A6.

p. 149 *The authors of* Double Vision . . . Edward Greenspon and Anthony Wilson-Smith, *op. cit.*, *Double Vision*, p. 235.

p. 151 *The essential idea behind the Tobin tax* . . . Tobin has set out his ideas in James Tobin, "A Proposal for International Monetary Reform," *The Eastern Economic Journal*, (4:3–4, 1978), pp. 153–59, and in James Tobin, "On the Efficiency of the Financial System," *Lloyd's Bank Review*, July 1984, pp. 1–15. See also Alex C. Michalos, *Good Taxes: The Case for Taxing Foreign Currency Exchange and Other Financial Transactions* (Toronto: Dundurn Press, 1997).

p. 157 *From almost nothing, a huge* . . . See *Central Bank Survey of Foreign Exchange and Derivatives Market Activity*, 1995 (Basel: Bank for International Settlements, Monetary and Economic Department, May 1996), pp. 1–3.

p. 157 *Schmidt set all this out* . . . Rodney Schmidt, "Feasibility of the Tobin Tax," Jan. 1995, internal Finance department document obtained under Access to Information legislation.

p. 158 *International currency trading* . . . *Bank of Montreal Annual Report 1995* (Toronto: Bank of Montreal, 178th Annual Report), pp. 33.

p. 161 *Ottawa's position was reflected* . . . Ehsan Choudri and Prakash Sharma, *Capital Controls: Rationale and Implications: For Canadian Trade and Investment Policy* (Ottawa: Department of Foreign Affairs and International Trade, Nov. 1996).

p. 161 *In a paper for a United Nations conference* . . . Guillermo Le Fort and Carlos Budnevich, "Capital-Account Regulations and Macroeconomic Policy: Two Latin American Experiences," in *International Monetary and Financial Issues for the 1990s* (Geneva: United Nations Conference on Trade and Development, Research Papers for the Group of Twenty-Four, Vol. VIII, 1997), pp. 37–58.

p. 165 *That support culminated* . . . Mahbub ul Haq, Inge Kaul and Isabelle Grunberg (eds.), *The Tobin Tax: Coping with Financial Volatility* (New York and Oxford: Oxford University Press, 1996).

p. 166 *If Tobin is too jaded* . . . Rudi Dornbusch, in *op. cit.*, *International Monetary and Financial Issues for the 1990s*, pp. 27–36.

p. 166 *As Keynes noted* . . . John Maynard Keynes, cited in *ibid.*, p. 30.

p. 168 *Maxine Waters, a Democrat* . . . Quoted in Caufield, *op. cit.*, p. 156.

p. 169 IMF *managing director* . . . Address by Michel Camdessus, "Drawing Lessons from the Mexican Crisis: Preventing and Resolving Financial Crises—the Role of the IMF," 25th Washington Conference of the Council of the Americas, Washington, D.C., May 22, 1995.

CHAPTER SIX: *How John Maynard Keynes (Briefly) Did Save the World*

p. 173 *"Nobody told us . . ."* Quoted in Barry Eichengreen and Alec Cairncross, *Sterling in Decline: The Devaluations of 1931, 1947, 1967* (Oxford: Basil Blackwell, 1983), p. 5.

p. 173 *Contrary to what one might think* . . . Karl Polanyi, *The Great Transformation: the political and economic origins of our time* (Boston: Beacon Press, 1944) pp. 163–64.

p. 175 *Indeed, in the days before* . . . *Ibid.*, p. 87.

p. 176 *As William Townsend noted* . . . Quoted in *ibid.*, p. 113.

p. 177 *In an interesting twist* . . . Cited in *ibid.*, p. 117.

p. 177 *The only impediment* . . . Cited in *ibid.*, p. 118.

p. 178 *This failure of the poor* . . . *Ibid.*, p. 123.

p. 178 *In its simplest form* . . . My account of the gold standard and its impact is largely drawn from the following sources: Barry Eichengreen, *Golden Fetters: The Gold Standard and the Great Depression, 1919–1939* (New York and Oxford: Oxford University Press, 1992); Beth A. Simmons, *Who Adjusts?: Domestic Sources of Foreign Economic Policy During the Interwar Years* (Princeton, N.J.: Princeton University Press, 1994); Charles S. Maier, *Recasting Bourgeois Europe: Stabilization in France, Germany and Italy in the Decade after World War I* (Princeton, N.J.:

Princeton University Press, 1975); Peter Temin, *Lessons from the Great Depression* (Cambridge, Mass.: MIT Press, 1989).

p. 180 *Largely derived from the late-eighteenth* . . . Adam Smith did warn, however, that if monopolies were left unchecked, they would restrict competition, thereby distorting market efficiency.

p. 183 *Thus, there was little empathy* . . . Polanyi, *op. cit.*, pp. 172–77.

p. 186 *A committee headed by Lord Cunliffe* . . . Robert Skidelsky, *John Maynard Keynes, Vol. Two: The Economist as Saviour, 1920–1937* (London: Papermac, 1994), p. 187.

p. 189 *At hearings of the Chamberlain committee* . . . *Ibid.*, pp. 189–91.

p. 189 *The anti-democratic power of the gold standard* . . . Geoffrey Ingham, *Capitalism Divided?: The City and Industry in British Social Development* (London: Macmillan, 1984), pp. 182–83.

p. 190 *Economist Edwin Cannan* . . . Quoted in *ibid.*, p. 183.

p. 190 *In the words of Arthur Kiddy* . . . *Ibid.*, p. 276, footnote 33.

p. 190 *According to Norman* . . . *Ibid.*, p. 180.

p. 190 *Ironically, despite the intense fears* . . . In Skidelsky, *op. cit.*, p. 189.

p. 191 *They were particularly keen* . . . *Ibid.*, pp. 191–93.

p. 192 *Ironically, Montagu Norman was slightly disappointed* . . . D.E. Moggridge. *British Monetary Policy 1924–1931: The Norman Conquest of $4.86* (Cambridge: Cambridge University Press, 1972), pp. 57–58.

p. 192 *Particularly important on Norman's agenda* . . . *Ibid.*, pp. 58–60.

p. 194 *As the Depression deepened* . . . Quoted in Skidelsky, *op. cit.*, p. 297.

p. 194 *In the grim winter of 1933* . . . The hearings of the U.S. Senate Finance Committee in February 1933 are described in Sidney Hyman, *Marriner S. Eccles: Private Entrepreneur and Public Servant* (Stanford, Cal.: Graduate School of Business, Stanford University, 1976), pp. 3–8.

p. 196 *As senior Fed official George W. Norris* . . . Quoted in William Greider, *Secrets of the Temple: How the Federal Reserve Runs the Country* (New York: Touchstone, 1987), p. 300.

p. 196 *Towards the end of the Senate committee hearings* . . . Hyman, *op. cit.*, *Marriner S. Eccles*, pp. 5–7.

p. 197 *Almost immediately, Eccles was drawn* . . . Greider, *op. cit.*, *Secrets of the Temple*, pp. 304–21.

p. 199 *When another bank in town failed* . . . *Ibid.*, pp. 304–5.

p. 200 *He was particularly inspired* . . . *Ibid.*, p. 316; see also Skidelsky, *op. cit.*, p. 580.

p. 201 *Desperate to communicate the urgency* . . . James MacGregor Burns, *Roosevelt: The Lion and the Fox* (New York: Harcourt, Brace and Company), pp. 328–29.

p. 203 *For someone who was to tear down* . . . My account of Keynes and his impact is largely drawn from Skidelsky's comprehensive two-volume biography, *John Maynard Keynes,* cited above. See also D.E. Moggridge, *Keynes* (Toronto: University of Toronto Press, 1976); and Dudley Dillard, *The Economics of John Maynard Keynes* (Englewood Cliffs, N.J.: Prentice-Hall, 1948).

p. 207 *As* Bankers' Magazine *had warned* . . . Quoted in Ingham, *op. cit., Capitalism Divided?,* p. 276, footnote 33.

p. 208 *"It has been usual to think . . ."* Quoted in Skidelsky, *op. cit., John Maynard Keynes,* p. 318.

p. 208 *"Negation, restriction, inactivity . . ."* Quoted in *ibid.,* p. 306.

p. 209 *"When we have unemployed men . . ."* Quoted in *ibid.,* p. 298.

p. 209 *"[T]he Treasury will reject something . . ."* Quoted in *ibid.,* p. 354.

p. 209 *"[I]magine that initial sum . . ."* Quoted in *ibid.,* p. 449.

p. 210 *And all this could be accomplished* . . . See Walter S. Salant, "The Spread of Keynesian Doctrines and Practices in the United States," in Peter A. Hall (ed.), *The Political Power of Economic Ideas: Keynesianism across Nations* (Princeton, N.J.: Princeton University Press, 1989), p. 38.

p. 211 *At Harvard, long a bastion* . . . Robert Bryce and Lorie Tarshis, two Canadian economists who had studied under Keynes at Cambridge, played an important role in spreading Keynes's ideas in U.S. academic circles. Bryce arrived at Harvard in 1936 and began the process of converting the economists there to Keynesianism, even before the publication of *The General Theory.* Shortly after this, Tarshis arrived at nearby Tufts University, and helped spark the growing interest in Keynes both at Tufts and Harvard. Bryce later returned to Canada and joined the Finance department, serving as deputy minister in the '60s. Tarshis went on to have a distinguished academic career in the U.S. and Canada.

p. 211 *Galbraith recalls that* . . . Quoted in Skidelsky *op. cit., John Maynard Keynes,* p. 580.

p. 211 *One of Keynes's biographers* . . . *Ibid.,* p. xxiii.

CHAPTER SEVEN: *Tea with Mr. Skinner*

p. 214 *For a young economist* . . . For a good account of Rasminsky's role in the Bretton Woods accords, see J.L. Granatstein, "The Road to Bretton Woods: International Monetary Policy and the Public Servant," *Journal of Canadian Studies* (Vol. 16, Nos. 3 & 4, Fall–Winter 1981), pp. 174–87.

p. 216 *One civil servant, Arthur Salter . . .* Quoted in Moggridge, *op. cit., Keynes*, pp. 127–28.

p. 216 *At one stage in the international negotiations . . .* W.A. Mackintosh, "Canadian Views," in A.L. Keith Acheson, John F. Chant, Martin F.J. Prachowny (eds.), *Bretton Woods Revisited: Evaluations of the International Monetary Fund and the International Bank for Reconstruction and Development* (Toronto: Macmillan, 1972), p. 40.

p. 216 *Rasminsky then produced a Canadian plan . . .* See Granatstein, *op. cit.*, "The Road to Bretton Woods," especially pp. 179–84. The Canadian plan, as tabled in the House of Commons on July 12, 1943, can be found in J. Keith Horsefield (ed.), *The International Monetary Fund 1945–1965: Twenty Years of International Monetary Cooperation* (Washington: International Monetary Fund, Vol. III: Documents, 1969), pp. 103–18.

p. 217 *When a left-wing government in France . . .* See Beth A. Simmons, *op. cit., Who Adjusts?*, pp. 140–73.

p. 218 *Now Keynes was insisting that controls . . .* Quoted in Eric Helleiner, *States and the Reemergence of Global Finance: From Bretton Woods to the 1990s* (Ithaca and London: Cornell University Press, 1994), p. 33. My account of the debate over capital controls and the importance of controls in the post-war system is drawn largely from Helleiner's book, as well as from Louis W. Pauly, *Who Elected the Bankers?: Surveillance and Control in the World Economy* (Ithaca and London: Cornell University Press, 1997).

p. 218 *"Surely in the post-war years . . ."* Quoted in *ibid.*, p. 35.

p. 218 *A.F.W. Plumptre, a Canadian official . . .* A.F.W. Plumptre, "Canadian Views," in *op. cit., Bretton Woods Revisited*, pp. 41–42.

p. 219 *Morgenthau went so far . . .* Quoted in Eric Helleiner, *op. cit., States and the Reemergence of Global Finance*, p. 4.

p. 219 *White was perhaps even more explicit . . .* Quoted in *ibid.*, pp. 34–35.

p. 220 *Free-flowing capital could act . . .* Robert Warren and Winthrop Aldrich, quoted in *ibid.*, p. 40.

p. 222 *Keynes and White also found allies . . .* See Robert M. Collins, "Positive Business Responses to the New Deal: The Roots of the Committee for Economic Development, 1933–1942," *Business History Review* (Vol. LII, No. 3, Autumn, 1978), pp. 369–91. See also Kim McQuaid, *Big Business and Presidential Power: From Roosevelt to Reagan* (New York: William Morrow, 1982), pp. 11–121.

p. 224 *The bankers' victory was underscored . . .* Quoted in Eric Helleiner, *op. cit., States and the Reemergence of Global Finance*, p. 49.

p. 224 *"Not merely as a feature of the transition . . ."* Quoted in Louis W. Pauly, *op. cit., Who Elected the Bankers?*, p. 94.

p. 224 *A visiting dignitary could scarcely consider* . . . For an insight into the thinking of prominent members of the New York banking community and their opposition to the Bretton Woods accords, see Arthur M. Johnson, *Winthrop W. Aldrich: Lawyer, Banker, Diplomat* (Boston: Graduate School of Business Administration, Harvard University, 1968).

p. 225 *Indeed, the whole experience of coming to America* . . . The visit of the Soviet delegation is recounted in *ibid.*, p. 291–92.

p. 227 *Established in Basel* . . . For the origins of the BIS and its development into a club for frustrated bankers, see Erin E. Jacobsson, *A Life for Sound Money: Per Jacobsson, His Biography* (Oxford: Clarendon Press, 1979).

p. 228 *Indeed, Montagu Norman* . . . See Isabel Vincent, *Hitler's Silent Partners*, (Toronto: Knopf Canada, 1997), p. 106.

p. 228 *Some, like Vincenzo Azzolini* . . . Erin E. Jacobsson, *op. cit.*, *A Life for Sound Money*, p. 190–91.

p. 230 *Jacobsson argued that this created* . . . *Ibid.*, pp. 400–13.

p. 230 *He even suggested that stable currency* . . . *Ibid.*, p. 221.

p. 231 *Outside banking and business circles* . . . Arthur M. Johnson, *op. cit.*, *Winthrop W. Aldrich*, pp. 285–89.

p. 232 *Two years after the war* . . . Eric Helleiner, *op. cit.*, *States and the Reemergence of Global Finance*, p. 55. For a more detailed discussion of the capital flight issue, and a comparison of U.S. attitudes towards capital flight from Europe in the 1940s and from Latin America in the 1980s, see Eric Helleiner, "Handling 'Hot Money': U.S. Policy Toward Latin American Capital Flight in Historical Perspective," *Alternatives* (Vol. 20, 1995), pp. 81–110.

p. 233 *The Marshall Plan, as it was called* . . . Eric Helleiner, *op. cit.*, *States and the Reemergence of Global Finance*, p. 59, including footnote 20.

p. 235 *What is striking is how much the British* . . . *Ibid.*, pp. 81–91.

p. 236 *Political scientist Eric Helleiner* . . . *Ibid.*, p. 121 and p. 81. For a discussion of Canada's failure to co-operate with some key aspects of the Bretton Woods accords, see Michael C. Webb, "Canada and the International Monetary Regime," in A. Claire Cutler and Mark W. Zacher (eds.), *Canadian Foreign Policy and International Economic Regimes* (Vancouver: UBC Press, 1992), pp. 153–85. Webb argues that Canada's actions had little impact on the fate of the Bretton Woods accords and the evolution of the international monetary regime, since Canada was not a major player (p. 160).

p. 237 *The Belgian Finance minister* . . . Quoted in *ibid.*, Eric Helleiner, *op. cit.*, *States and the Reemergence of Global Finance*, p. 101.

p. 237 *The Europeans and the Japanese . . . Ibid.*, pp. 102–11.

p. 239 *One of the first tests . . . Ibid.*, pp. 124–30.

p. 243 *According to William P. Rodgers . . .* Rodgers and Scowcroft quoted in *ibid.*, p. 128.

p. 243 *In the peaceful hills of Fitzwilliam, New Hampshire . . .* "H.D. White, Accused in Spy Inquiry, Dies," *New York Times* (Aug. 18, 1948), p. 1.

CHAPTER EIGHT: *Defying the Cult of Impotence*

p. 248 *As the once-booming tiger cubs . . .* John Stackhouse, "Asian slump fuels firefight; Malaysian PM, currency trader spar over financial crisis," *Globe and Mail* (Sept. 22, 1997), p. A1. See also Seth Mydans, "PM blames Jews for Malaysian money woes," *Globe and Mail* (Oct. 17, 1997), p. A22.

p. 249 *But in early 1997, Soros had written . . .* George Soros, "The Capitalist Threat," *The Atlantic Monthly* (Feb. 1997).

p. 249 The Economist *condemned Soros . . . The Economist*, "Of heresy and hallucinations," reprinted in *The Globe and Mail* (Jan. 25, 1997).

p. 249 The Globe and Mail's *business columnist . . .* Terence Corcoran, "Capitalist Crackpot," *Globe and Mail* (Feb. 4, 1997), p. B2.

p. 249 *Rick Salutin observed . . .* Rick Salutin, "Short-sighted journalists forgo reality for rhetoric," *Globe and Mail* (Feb. 14, 1997), p. C1.

p. 250 *Behind the fireworks . . .* Aziz Ali Mohammed, "Issues Relating to the Treatment of Capital Movements in the IMF," in G.K. Helleiner (ed.), *Capital Account Regimes and the Developing Countries* (forthcoming from Macmillan Press in association with the United Nations Conference on Trade and Development).

p. 250 *This principle was endorsed . . .* Louis Pauly, *op. cit., Who Elected the Bankers?*, p. 37.

p. 251 *By the 1990s, this article . . .* Aziz Ali Mohammed, *op. cit.*, "Issues Relating to the Treatment of Capital Movements in the IMF."

p. 251 *The Third World countries balked . . .* John Stackhouse, "Rich and poor square off over freer capital markets," *Globe and Mail* (Sept. 26, 1997), p. A15.

p. 252 *But the odds were stacked . . .* Ngaire Woods, "Governance in International Organizations: The Case for Reform in the Bretton Woods Institutions," *International Monetary and Financial Issues for the 1990s* (Vol. XI, forthcoming from the United Nations).

p. 254 *There is an economic theory . . .* Robert Mundell, a Canadian-born economist who teaches at Columbia University, has had an enormous impact on the study of international macroeconomics.

p. 258 *Fortin argued that* . . . Fortin notes that when investors make decisions about whether to buy Canadian bonds, they are not concerned about the value of the Canadian dollar per se, but rather about how this value is expected to change over the period they want to hold the bond.

p. 259 *This is not meant to dismiss all concerns* . . . The "overshooting" concept was developed by MIT economist Rudi Dornbusch, a former student of Robert Mundell's. I am indebted to Adam Harmes, a Ph.D. student in global finance at York University, for some insightful remarks on the overshooting problem and how the Tobin tax might address it.

p. 260 The Economist, *for instance* . . . *Op. cit,* "The myth of the powerless state," *The Economist* (Oct. 7, 1995), p. 31.

p. 261 *Federal Reserve Board chairman Paul Volcker* . . . The story of the Basel Accord is recounted in detail in Ethan B. Kapstein, "Governing Global Finance," *The Washington Quarterly* (Vol. 17, 1994), pp. 77–87. See also Ethan B. Kapstein, *Governing the Global Economy: International Finance and the State* (Cambridge, Mass.: Harvard University Press, 1994), pp. 1–29 and pp. 103–28.

p. 264 *Kapstein notes* . . . Ethan B. Kapstein, "Shockproof: The End of the Financial Crisis," *Foreign Affairs* (Vol. 75, No. 1, Jan./Feb. 1996), p. 2.

p. 265 *This regime, which Helleiner calls* . . . Eric Helleiner, *op. cit., States and the Reemergence of Global Finance,* pp. 190–91.

p. 267 *In a more recent paper* . . . Rodney Schmidt, *A Feasible Foreign Exchange Transactions Tax* (Ottawa: North–South Insitute, 1997).

p. 268 *All international financial transactions* . . . Gerard Wyrsch, *op. cit.,* "Treasury Regulation of International Wire Transfer" (*Denver Journal of International Law and Policy,* Vol. 20, No. 3, Spring 1992), pp. 517–21.

p. 268 *As one analyst notes* . . . Stephen Zamora, "Remarks," *Proceedings of the 86th Annual Meeting of the American Society of International Law,* Washington, 1992.

p. 268 *This threat of restricting access* . . . Eric Helleiner, in *op. cit.,* "Sovereignty, Territoriality and the Globalization of Finance."

p. 271 *And so it was that Volcker* . . . See William Greider, *op. cit., One World Ready or Not,* pp. 250–58.

p. 272 *As U.S. writer William Greider explains* . . . *Ibid.,* p. 256.

p. 274 The Economist, *however, recognized the importance* . . . *Op. cit.,* "The myth of the powerless state," *The Economist.*

p. 278 Globe and Mail *columnist Michael Valpy* . . . Michael Valpy, "Diana and the decline of deference," *Globe and Mail* (Sept. 8, 1997).

p. 279 *In this view, governments should limit themselves* . . . I am not attributing this view to Michael Valpy, whom I know to support the notion of a common good.

p. 283 *James Galbraith put it succinctly* . . . James Galbraith, *op. cit.*, "Time to Ditch the NAIRU."

A C K N O W L E D G M E N T S

I AM DEEPLY INDEBTED to many people who helped me in putting together this book. First and foremost, economist Andrew Sharpe was extremely generous with his time, and played a major role in honing the ideas and shaping the themes in the book. I am also extremely grateful for the help of the following experts: Eric Helleiner, Pierre Fortin, Peter Spiro, Charles Flynn, Michael McCracken and Lars Osberg, as well as others who prefer not to be named. Adam Harmes, a Ph.D. student in global finance, provided what amounted to an ongoing tutorial in international financial markets, which helped me greatly. My longtime friend and colleague Tom Walkom provided some valuable insights into the gold standard, during a wonderful afternoon at Toronto Island. And, as always, I am grateful to my mentor, Neil Brooks.

The team at Penguin did their usual amazing work. Many thanks to this extraordinary group of fun and talented people: Cynthia Good, Brad Martin, Kevin Hansen, Scott Sellers, Karen Cossar, Martin Gould and a particular thanks to Jem Bates (for his thoughtful reading of the manuscript), as well as freelance copy editor Wendy Thomas, Alison Reid, my researcher Sarah Ives and my agent, Bruce Westwood. And a special thanks to my editor, David Kilgour. After five books together, I can't imagine doing a book without David, who is not only a joy to work with but also has excellent judgment and a keen sense of how to make a book work.

(I would also like to belatedly thank Nanda Choudhry, who helped me with my last book, without being thanked.)

On a personal note, I'd like to thank my parents, Audrey and Jack McQuaig, for countless things over the years, as well as my many great siblings, particularly my brother Peter. I'd like to mention some special friends: Linda Diebel, Jane Spanton, Jim Laxer, Anne Wordsworth, Gord Evans, Rod Mickleburgh, John Gunn, Carol Wilton and Ken Finkleman. Thanks also to Clayton Ruby and Harriet Sachs for memorable weekends at their cottage. Bhagyavathi Patel is still the most generous person I know. Peter Duffin, who has taken it upon himself to keep me constantly supplied with coffee and chocolates, surely deserves a mention. And I never would have gotten the book done without David Cole and Barbara Nichol, who contributed greatly to what became known as the "Oakville situation." As Stickspeed might say, "Keep you minds on your brains."

Final thanks go to my fantastic six-year-old daughter, Amy. Her little work area in my office has grown since my last book; her delightful crafts now adorn the room. She never ceases to amaze me with her wit, her intelligence and her affection. When I went through a difficult time halfway through the writing of this book, I remember her passing me a note she'd written: "I am lucky to have such a great mommy." I'm the one who is lucky.

L.M.